Transatlantic Counter-terrorism Cooperation

The events of 9/11 brought the subject of international terrorism to the top of the global security agenda. This book focuses on the way that the transatlantic allies have sought to combat international terrorism.

Since the end of the Cold War, Europe and the United States have adapted the security regime that proved so effective in ensuring peace on the continent. Transatlantic counter-terrorism cooperation has required the full range of international instruments: from the use of military force and intelligence sharing to novel forms of working together such as over law enforcement and border security.

Wyn Rees traces the development of transatlantic security relations, focusing on key issues such as:

- The US-led 'War on Terrorism' and whether it has resulted in convergence or divergence in US and European policies towards combating terrorism
- The importance of transatlantic organisations in channelling efforts to deal with the threat
- The pressure for both internal and external security cooperation in transatlantic relations
- The tensions and challenges that emanate from attempting to generate cooperation between unequal state actors

This text will greatly interest students and scholars of international relations, international security, and transatlantic relations.

Wyn Rees is a Professor in the School of Politics and International Relations at the University of Nottingham.

Transatlantic Counter-terrorism Cooperation

The new imperative

Wyn Rees

Routledge
Taylor & Francis Group

LONDON AND NEW YORK

First published 2006
by Routledge
2 Park Square, Milton Park, Abingdon, Oxon OX14 4RN

Simultaneously published in the USA and Canada
by Routledge
270 Madison Ave, New York, NY 10016

Transferred to Digital Printing 2008

*Routledge is an imprint of the Taylor & Francis Group,
an informa business*

© 2006 Wyn Rees

Typeset in Times New Roman by Taylor & Francis Books
Printed and bound in Great Britain by CPI Antony Rowe,
Chippenham, Wiltshire

British Library Cataloguing in Publication Data
A catalogue record for this book is available from the British Library

Library of Congress Cataloging in Publication Data
A catalog record for this book has been requested

ISBN10: 0–415–33138–2   ISBN13: 978–0–415–33138–8 (hbk)
ISBN10: 0–415–33139–0   ISBN13: 978–0–415–33139–5 (pbk)

This book is dedicated to Susan and Marcus.

Contents

Acknowledgements

The author would like to acknowledge the financial assistance of the British Academy in the completion of this project.

The author is indebted to a wide variety of senior officials in the US government, the Council of the European Union, the European Commission and Europol for the interviews they gave for this project. Although they are not named here, the author is grateful for their kindness.

The author would like to thank colleagues who read and commented upon chapters of the manuscript. Particular thanks are due to Richard Aldrich, Dieter Mahncke, Valsamis Mitsilegas, Matthew Rendall, Mark Webber and Neville Wylie. They bear no responsibility for any shortcomings in this book.

Introduction

Background

This book seeks to illuminate a relatively new sphere of transatlantic security cooperation: countering the threat from international terrorism. This cooperation began in the post-Cold War period but it has only gathered momentum since the 11 September 2001 (9/11) attacks on the United States. It has not evolved out of a vacuum, however. Rather, this cooperation has grown out of a relationship that has been rich in security collaboration since the end of the Second World War. Before investigating the emergence of US–European counter-terrorism cooperation it is necessary to place it within the context of a security relationship that has spanned the last fifty years.

The post-war US-European relationship was one of fundamental inequality. The US acted as the guardian of a group of European powers in two ways. First, as the guarantor of the continent's security from the perceived threat of the Soviet Union and its allies. Second, as the protector of the Europeans from themselves; from the fratricidal history of two wars in the twentieth century that had broken the power of the leading continental states. In the words of Joffe, the US played the role of 'Europe's pacifier',[1] mediating relations between Germany and its former adversaries and helping to promote reconciliation between states such as Greece and Turkey. The European states coalesced around the leadership of the US both in terms of deterring Soviet power and smoothing intra-European tensions.

Military security was the bedrock of the relationship. US conventional military forces occupied a central position in the defence of West German soil, on one of the key axis routes of an expected attack by the Warsaw Pact. The strategy of 'Forward Defence' was predicated on American forces situated in Germany and on the dispatch of large-scale reinforcements from across the Atlantic at the outset of hostilities. The underpinning of the conventional defence of the continent came from the US extended nuclear deterrent. Forward-based American nuclear forces and ultimately its strategic nuclear forces linked the fate of the continent to the American homeland. In essence, the US risked the devastation of its own territory in a thermonuclear holocaust in order to guarantee the security of its West European allies.[2]

The security relationship between the transatlantic allies witnessed plenty of disagreements and crises during the Cold War. For the Europeans, there was always a level of uncertainty over whether their ally would really commit suicide on their behalf. Trust was a very hard virtue when the survival of Western countries was at stake. In addition, the Europeans found frequently that Washington conducted a relationship with the Soviet Union in which they were relegated to mere observers. Whether over arms control or in the case of periodic crises, European governments experienced a sense of powerlessness as US officials took decisions, with little consultation, that affected their security.

As for the US, its chief complaint in its defence relationship with Europe was the inadequacy of the burden-sharing arrangements. Immediately after the war, with continental economies in ruins and the US economy operating at near full capacity, it seemed justifiable that America's allies should be heavily reliant for their security. But once European economies had recovered and were prospering, there was much less justification for perpetuating an unequal level of spending. Successive American administrations were critical of European willingness to see the US sustain a higher level of defence expenditure than their own. By the 1970s this US dissatisfaction was expressed in terms of periodic pressure from within the Congress for troop withdrawals and for Europe to deploy new generations of nuclear missiles to repair the credibility of the strategy of 'Flexible Response'.[3]

Security concerns outside of Europe were a perpetual source of transatlantic irritation. A consistent European priority was to keep the US focused on their security and prevent it from turning its attention to other areas of the world. The wars in Korea and Vietnam caused consternation in European capitals that the US was dissipating its energies on peripheral areas. Washington responded that European governments were too parochial and that they were abdicating responsibility for global security by leaving it to the US. This criticism was not relevant to all European countries, as Britain and France prided themselves on their global activism. Nevertheless, America criticised Western Europe for its insular outlook, as demonstrated when Secretary of State Henry Kissinger in 1973 made his notorious remark that the US had global interests whilst Europe had only regional ones.[4]

The organisational expression of the transatlantic security relationship was the North Atlantic Treaty Organization (NATO). It evolved during the Cold War into the principal forum for strategic dialogue between Europe and the United States. The decisive voice within the Atlantic Alliance was that of America: although its highest decision-making body, the North Atlantic Council, operated on the basis of *de jure* equality. Through patient diplomacy the US had to convince others of its point of view and it could not always guarantee to secure what it wanted. But no European country was strong enough to challenge US leadership. President de Gaulle of France rejected the American role within Europe on the grounds that the continent's interests were not being best served; but his country was unable to offer a viable alternative locus of power.[5] France attempted to lure Germany away from its Atlanticist orientation in 1963, but the German Chancellor made it clear that he would not abandon the American embrace.

An attempt was made in 1954 to launch a European Defence Community (EDC) which would have created a European army, defence minister and procurement agency.[6] This would have offered a real alternative to the conduct of European defence through an Atlanticist framework. But the failure to ratify the EDC ensured that defence remained apart from the process of European integration for the next four decades. The US became an enthusiastic promoter of the European Community (EC), regarding it as a way to build the continent's economic and political strength and resist communism.[7] The fact that the EC remained a civilian power meant that America's hegemonic status in security was never put at risk.[8] In fact it was not until the end of the Cold War that a fundamental challenge arose to America's privileged position in European security.

The post-Cold War transatlantic order

The end of the Cold War marked the beginning of a period of flux in transatlantic security relations. Many observers were of the opinion that the US and Europe were at risk of drifting apart due to the fact that the Soviet threat no longer bound them together.[9] The 'transatlantic order' has always rested upon a complex mix of bilateral relationships between Washington and each of the main European capitals, as well as multilateral relationships such as NATO and the US-EC. It was unclear how this patchwork of interactions and cooperation would evolve in the post-Cold War era and which relationships would enjoy primacy. For example, President George Bush Snr and

Secretary of State James Baker promulgated the idea of a 'New Atlanticism' in which Germany would become the favoured partner of the US in Europe.[10] But this position was swiftly reassessed after the limitations on Germany's role in international security were exposed by the first Gulf War. What was evident was that the transatlantic relationship could no longer be taken for granted and that it would require new patterns of cooperation to ensure its continued relevance.

A problem in transatlantic relations that was compounded by the end of the Cold War was the likelihood that US attention would be drawn away from Europe. In the words of Daalder, 'America's and Europe's immediate concerns have increasingly diverged – one focusing globally, the other locally.'[11] The US believed that the foremost security challenges were no longer in Europe.[12] The continent was integrated, free and politically stable. The US saw the threats from nuclear proliferation and rogue states presenting the gravest concerns, and it wanted its allies to contribute more towards addressing them. There were calls for a global partnership that would have the effect of drawing the US and Europe together.[13] Unfortunately, the Europeans as a whole were unwilling to acquiesce in this US-led agenda. They looked to the security concerns of their own backyard: not only did they have former adversaries in Eastern Europe who desperately needed to be stabilised, but they also eyed the countries bordering the Mediterranean with increasing concern.

European preoccupation with the security of their own continent was complemented by pressure for closer political and economic integration. Reaching out to Eastern Europe was an acknowledgement of the need for 'widening', but this was to be complemented by the development of a 'deeper' Europe. Those who foresaw a federal destiny for the European project saw in the end of the Cold War a propitious moment. The result was the Maastricht Treaty and the creation of the European Union (EU). Once it was ratified in November 1993, the Treaty on European Union (TEU) provided a range of new competences including a 'Common Foreign and Security Policy' (CFSP) and 'Justice and Home Affairs' (JHA). The EU was now a fully fledged political actor with powers in the fields of foreign policy and internal security.

These steps forward in European integration raised the prospect of the EU developing as a potential counterweight to the United States. Such rhetoric caused alarm in Washington for a number of reasons. The fear arose of a strategic competitor that not only put at risk America's unipolar status but also threatened to undermine the most important forum for transatlantic strategic interaction – NATO. It also excited concern about a 'fortress Europe' in which a closed caucus of states would prevent America from benefiting fully in the economic affairs of the continent. Without the over-riding security issue to bring transatlantic relations back together there was the possibility of a long and agonising divorce. The idea to build up Europe into a rival power centre to the US found resonance in the French ambition of post-Cold War European unity. France had long held visions of a Europe defined in opposition to America, resistant to the leadership offered by Washington and capable of acting alone on the international stage. France made no secret of its desire to restrict NATO to the residual role of providing collective defence, whilst creating a European defence identity within the EU.[14] President Chirac and various French foreign ministers have argued the need for a multipolar world rather than a unipolar one centred upon America. Germany supported France's efforts to some extent by participating in the creation of European-only structures, such as the Eurocorps, which offered military capabilities separate from NATO.

Yet it would be mistaken to suggest that views of building Europe into a rival of the US enjoyed universal support or had a realistic prospect of success. There was no unity of view on the continent about creating a defence identity in the EU that eclipsed NATO. Countries such as the Netherlands and Denmark were firmly opposed to challenging the primacy of NATO. In addition, Germany was circumspect about any steps that put the Atlantic Alliance at risk. Whilst many of these countries were sympathetic to calls for Europe to be stronger, they believed that this should only be undertaken in ways that were compatible with the US and preserved the unity of the Atlantic Alliance. The United Kingdom put the survival of Atlanticism at the top of its agenda and was unwilling to place it in jeopardy. Without the active participation of the UK, any attempt to construct a meaningful defence identity apart from NATO was doomed to failure.[15]

A further obstacle to realising the most ambitious vision of European rivalry to the US was the harsh reality of limited European political unity and military strength. The European Union failed repeatedly to speak with one voice. Its CFSP remained weak and represented little more than a loose amalgam of the national foreign policies of the fifteen members. Militarily, the majority of European states sought to benefit from a post-Cold War 'peace dividend' and cut back their defence spending. The modest amounts of money that remained suffered from the problem that much of the defence programmes were duplicated.[16] In short, the EU was a long way from being the sort of united and capable security actor that could have offered a challenge to Atlanticism.

Amidst this turbulence in the transatlantic relationship, the military security agenda was also changing. Security issues no longer had the over-riding priority that they enjoyed during the Cold War now that the risk of major inter-state war had receded. There was a growing recognition that the US and Europe would have to adapt their security relationship to new realities. With no immediate challenge to their territories, the transatlantic allies were faced by the prospect of conflicts of choice rather than necessity. The conflict in the Balkans in the early 1990s provided the sharpest evidence of both transatlantic divergences and the need to adapt to new military roles. At first the Europeans tried to manage the wars in Croatia and Bosnia independently, but they found themselves lacking in the political will and military capacity to impose a peace upon the warring factions. Meanwhile, the US was criticising the Europeans from the sidelines, advocating a more interventionist strategy against the Bosnian Serbs. It was not until the summer of 1995 that the US assumed leadership in the crisis and used its military power to impose the Dayton Peace Accord. The experience was a salutary one as it demonstrated that an external conflict could be immensely destructive of the transatlantic relationship, and it highlighted the need for US leadership in crises.

The new security agenda

In parallel with the reordering of the military security agenda, the period since the end of the Cold War has witnessed the emergence of a range of new security issues. These issues have tended to be non-military in nature and have included international crime, the inflow of illegal drugs and immigrants and the rise of cross-border terrorism. These were not new phenomena, they had existed during the Cold War. Yet such problems had not been hitherto the focus of attention in transatlantic relations. They had not been regarded as security issues because of the over-riding importance of the East-West military confrontation. The disintegration of the Soviet Union changed fundamentally the calculus about the threat of military power to the continent. With the down-grading of the military security agenda, 'new threats' received a much higher level of attention.

Transnational organised crime, drug trafficking and international terrorism also figured more prominently as security concerns because of trends that were apparent on both the European and international stage. At the European level there was the economic and political instability in the eastern half of the continent that resulted from the collapse of the majority of the communist regimes. This presented a vacuum that was quickly filled by criminal organisations eager to exploit commercial opportunities and the weakness of law enforcement systems. The western half of the continent was more vulnerable to the penetration of illegal activity due to the plan to establish a Single Market for goods and services by 1992 and the accompanying Schengen agreement aimed at facilitating the free movement of goods and people within that zone.[17] The drawback to these arrangements, however, were that once the common external border of the Community had been breached, there were no internal barriers to criminal organisations, illegal migrants or terrorists moving freely between the territories of neighbouring countries. At the international level, the process of globalisation has made the world more interconnected. Goods, services and people enjoy much more rapid movement and greater speed in communication, but the same is also true for transnational criminal activities.

Attempts to address this new security agenda have been problematic. Unlike traditional military threats, these new security challenges have been more diffuse. Organised criminals and drug traffickers pursue their activities covertly because they want to avoid detection and apprehension. Consequently there is no objective data on the extent of these problems. Concomitantly, states tend to disagree about the most appropriate instruments to combat them. The use of the military is only of limited value because many of the challenges are not susceptible to being remedied by the use of force. A range of other instruments, such as law enforcement, judicial means and the collection of intelligence, are more likely to be relevant in addressing these problems. This means that countries will have to fashion new patterns of cooperation in relation to such issues.

One feature of these new security challenges is that they blur the distinction between internal and external security. During the Cold War, the security threat was easy to discern: the danger of military invasion from abroad. However, the post-Cold War threats tend to merge domestic and foreign policy concerns. Criminal behaviour may penetrate the territory of a state from outside; it may lead to an ongoing threat domestically; it may be perpetrated from outside of the state and it may link up with the activities of indigenous criminal groups. Such behaviour presents major challenges for states to counter because criminal justice systems have previously been structured on the basis of nation-states. To stop such activity may require states to pursue criminals across national boundaries, to cooperate with their neighbours in apprehending criminals, and even conduct prosecutions on a multinational basis.[18] Of the many issues comprising the new security agenda, this study focuses on only one: international terrorism. International terrorism has not been an issue on which either the transatlantic allies or even West European countries have cooperated historically. In the aftermath of the Cold War it was of relatively low salience, and concerns over organised crime, drug trafficking and illegal immigration were all higher priorities. Nevertheless it grew in importance during the 1990s, until the events of 9/11 catapulted the subject of international terrorism to the top of the global security agenda. Secretary of State Colin Powell illustrated the priority Washington attached to this event by stating that 9/11 marked the beginning of the 'Post-post-Cold War world'. The US declared a 'War on Terrorism' and thereby ensured a central place for this conflict in the development of transatlantic security relations.[19]

Terrorism presents a topic that is multifaceted and the subject of endless contestation. This is evidenced by the difficulty of agreeing upon a definition. Some analyses determine an act of terror depending on whether its motivation is legitimate: for example, as part of a struggle for national liberation or based on a political ideology or religion. Others include states as capable of perpetrating terrorism through acts of violence designed to create fear.[20] Even agencies within the US hold slightly different definitions. The FBI's definition of terrorism is 'the unlawful use of force or violence against persons or property to intimidate or coerce a government, the civilian population, or any segment thereof, in furtherance of political or social objectives',[21] whilst the US National Strategy for Combating Terrorism defines terrorism as 'premeditated, politically motivated violence perpetrated against non-combatant targets by sub-national groups or clandestine agents'.[22] The European Council defined a terrorist act as one that sought to compel a government or international organisation to perform an act or to destroy the political, constitutional, economic or social structures of those same actors.[23]

For the purposes of this study, a narrow definition of terrorism will be adopted. Terrorism is understood to be a particular type of action, in which violence is employed for a political purpose. It is conducted by non-state actors against non-combatants, with the aim of creating fear amongst a wider target audience. Terrorism becomes international when it is perpetrated across state boundaries, when it is undertaken by, or targets, individuals of more than one country.

Themes in the book

There are several themes that are explored in this book. The first is that the 'War on Terrorism' presents a unique series of challenges to the transatlantic relationship. Coming as it has after a period in which US-European security relations were languishing, the attempt to build cooperation between the two sides against international terrorism exposes different historical experiences, threat perceptions and strategic cultures. Because terrorism is both a domestic and a foreign policy problem, contending American and European approaches to issues, such as state sponsorship of terrorism and the proliferation of weapons of mass destruction, have been brought to the fore. In the case of foreign policy, transatlantic relations have been taken to the edge of disaster by the differences between leading European states and Washington. Whether European and American approaches to counter-terrorism are converging or diverging will be at the heart of this study.

Second, is the fact that transatlantic counter-terrorism cooperation has been grafted on to a deep-seated and durable security regime. When the Cold War ended, this military security regime was regarded by both sides as too precious to abandon and so it was retained and allowed to adapt to new concerns. This has meant that the prickly questions of fostering new counter-terrorism cooperation are able to draw upon the shared norms and values that matured over several decades in the context of military security. The fact that collaboration against terrorism has been pursued in pre-existing multilateral fora is also grounds for optimism, as these frameworks can help to smooth the process of cooperation. Whether this nascent pattern of cooperation will in turn evolve into a regime in its own right, with its own rules and shared values, is too early to determine. The obstacles to building this pattern of cooperation may come to outweigh the predisposition to work together.

Third, at a time when multilateralism appears to be the object of scepticism, this book argues that organisations matter. They play a major role in guiding and channelling transatlantic cooperation, formalising patterns of action and according them legitimacy. This is not to deny the important role played by bilateral cooperation between the US and each of its European allies in combating terrorism. Bilateral contacts remain very important and it is beyond the scope of this study to explore them in detail. Nevertheless, this book focuses on how transatlantic cooperation is being shaped through organisational frameworks that were designed in an earlier era for purposes other than fighting terrorism.

Fourth, this book attempts to illuminate the tensions that emanate from cooperation between unequal actors. As a superpower, the US has been trying to fashion new patterns of working together with an array of European powers. The US regards itself as the guardian of the international security order in which terrorism has become the foremost priority. With its greater strength and single identity, the United States has been able to shape the counter-terrorism agenda in a clear and determined way. European countries are themselves tied together in a complex mosaic of inter-relationships. The process of building European structures has been proceeding in parallel with the adaptation of the US-European relationship. But such is the association between the US and its allies that it has not been in a position to impose its will upon them. The US needs Europe as a partner in order to offer a legitimate model of counter-terrorism to the rest of the world. The transatlantic relationship is a necessary platform on which to reach out to the wider international community.

Last, transatlantic counter-terrorism efforts have demanded cooperation both in external and internal security matters. By its nature, terrorism crosses the divide between the two spheres of security and requires action across a broad policy field. The events of 9/11 proved to be a watershed in facilitating a multi-dimensional response. Now the two sides of the Atlantic are engaged in patterns of cooperation that extend from the realms of diplomacy, economic sanctions and military power to intelligence sharing, judicial and law enforcement activity, border security and passenger profiling.

1 The transatlantic security regime

The nature of regimes

Regimes are patterns of regularised cooperation between states. As such they are instruments of governance within the international system that enable states to engage in rule-based relationships in which there are expectations of reciprocal cooperation. According to Mayer, this facilitates the creation of an 'intentional social order by self-regulation in international relations'.[1]

For a regime to be said to exist, certain attributes must be evident. In the first place, states must regard a set of issues as interconnected and requiring to be dealt with collectively.[2] The process of defining an issue area is an important precursor to regime construction. Following the delineation of an issue area, a group of states must act together consistently. The actions of these states must be determined by rules and agreements that they have drawn up together. Within a regime, states have the right to expect that fellow members will abide by the constraints laid down by the regime and will refrain from acting in a manner inconsistent with the rules. Lastly, where disputes occur amongst members there should be mechanisms and pre-determined channels for resolving conflicts in a manner that does not put the entire regime at risk.

The requirement that states act together systematically differentiates a regime from an *ad hoc* agreement. Stein, for example, warns against using the term 'regime' to describe all interactions in a sectoral area of the international system.[3] He argues that a regime is present only when there are perceptible constraints on the decision-making of the actors. Regimes presuppose regularised interaction and their establishment and maintenance involves a variety of costs. It must be worthwhile for states to bear the price of creating a regime and ensure it is sustained. If there were a lack of substance to the cooperation then the regime would either not be created in the first place or it would fall rapidly into disuse.

Explaining why states suffer the costs of constructing regimes has absorbed a good deal of attention amongst interested theorists. For states to have interests in common does not necessarily lead to cooperation.[4] Rational choice analysis has demonstrated that sub-optimal provision of collective goods can result from unconstrained self-interested behaviour even amongst actors with shared interests. States may try to benefit from a public 'good' whilst simultaneously avoiding making a contribution. Young[5] notes that the pursuit of individual interests can lead to socially undesirable outcomes, such as the prisoner dilemma, collective action problems, tragedy of the commons and the security dilemma.[6] Game theory would tend to suggest that cooperation would be problematical amongst states with competing interests and this would be compounded by the absence of an enforcement mechanism within an international system that is characterised by an absence of government.

According to liberal theorists, regimes offer a means to circumvent obstacles to cooperation. Based on the assumption that states will be satisfied with achieving absolute gains, regimes enable states to coordinate their behaviour so as to realise common interests. Such public goods might not be achievable if the countries pursued narrowly self-interested policies. Although states remain sovereign actors, regimes provide institutional frameworks for acting together. This assists in building relationships that are based upon the 'legitimacy of rules and their underlying norms', rather than the threat of coercion.[7] In so doing, regimes help to overcome the inherently anarchical nature of the international system.[8] Young endorses this view when he observes that 'conventionalized behaviour is apt to engender widespread feelings of legitimacy or propriety in conjunction with specific institutional arrangements'.[9]

Second, regimes offer procedures and systematic channels of communication. This is vital if states are to overcome the traditional problem of imperfect information impeding their relationships. Regimes help by offering mechanisms for the conduct of state bargaining over designated policy areas. They provide a regularised space for this activity. By maximising the availability of information, uncertainty within the system can be reduced and suspicions clarified. Regimes simplify calculations for states by providing a framework for a variety of interactions and facilitating trade-offs between issues.[10]

Finally, states will be more likely to enter into cooperative relationships because they will have the expectation of reciprocity. States can have confidence that their cooperation will be repaid because the regime serves to constrain the behaviour and options available to other countries. Although regimes are social structures and possess limited power to impose rules, nevertheless states become tied into formalised patterns of behaviour. The long-term impact will be to develop a process of socialisation and feelings of obligation that will reinforce the predisposition towards cooperation. This will render defection from the regime both highly visible and costly, as countries do not want to acquire a reputation for being untrustworthy. Muller supports the contention that states will be socialised by their involvement in the regime and will, over a period of time, feel under pressure to comply with the rules.[11]

Realists and neo-realists reject the view that norms and values have an important role to play in the formation of regimes. The work of Strange, for example, argues that underlying structural realities are based on power and therefore rules and norms are no more than a reflection of who enjoys overriding power within the system.[12] Whilst realists and neo-realists accept that regimes can play a role in coordinating state behaviour and mitigating the worst excesses of the selfish pursuit of interests, they see regimes as only useful in limited conditions. They regard either the pursuit of power or the constraints imposed by the structure of the international system as the key determinants of state actions. States cannot trust one another and must always be prepared for the risk of betrayal, hence regimes must be regarded as weak and brittle. At any moment their allies may judge that their own interests would be best served by a withdrawal of cooperation and possible defection to the side of an adversary. In this situation, relative gains matter and states will be concerned if the countries to which they are attached derive more benefit from the regime than they do. Regimes may be abandoned once they no longer serve the immediate interests of the states involved.

According to this perspective states will always want to preserve their ability to act autonomously or to switch their allegiance to an ascendant power. States will not accept any constraints on their freedom to act independently. Self-help will remain the watchword in a system in which there is no overarching form of government or provider of external security. Krasner points out that regimes are treated as illusory and that states will take rational decisions about their interests irrespective of pre-existing obligations.[13]

Liberal institutionalists reject the realist characterisation of regimes. They believe that state power is mitigated within the framework of a regime and 'rules, routines and practices' develop to underpin the practice of inter-state cooperation.[14] These routines guide their collective behaviour: the norms help to determine their identities, rights and obligations, whilst the rules apply those norms and provide prescriptions for action. This makes it possible for states to work together over a sustained period of time and ensures that the regime is strong and robust. Krasner contends that 'sets of implicit or explicit principles, norms, rules and decision-making procedures' provide the very heart of a regime without which they would not be viable.[15] Young and Keohane concur; the latter adding that regimes may render these rules and procedures explicit or they may remain inferred and based upon observed behaviour.[16] Regimes can just be institutions or agreed ways of doing things, they do not require formal structures. Nevertheless, regimes may evolve from informal patterns of cooperation into formal organisations over a period of time, as behaviour becomes habitualised.

Cognitive theorists have made a contribution to this debate, complementing the liberal institutionalist emphasis on interests. Cognitive theorists help to explain how ideas, norms and values assist the understanding of the evolution of regimes. Actors within states view the world through a prism that comprises their own values and they are drawn towards cooperation with like-minded governments.[17] In the words of Krasner, regimes form when 'expectations converge in a given area of international relations'.[18] A feeling of community and mutual identification may be important factors in a relationship between cooperating parties. Such feelings can result from a shared sense of history, language or linkages between elites, and will reduce the likelihood that states will resort to actions that result in unilateral advantage. Haas acknowledges the importance of cognitivism when he states,

> The real utility of the regime concept is to focus analysis on the multidimensional factors which lead states to engage in regularised patterns of behaviour. The definition demands attention ... to cognitive studies of the beliefs which influence the creation and change of internationally shared norms and principles and national interests.[19]

Liberal institutionalists argue that regimes are most likely to arise when issue density between states is high. States that interact frequently and across a range of issues tend to look for ways to regulate their relationships at a level that is 'beyond the state'.[20] Regimes evolve in specific issue areas to manage this relationship, and the higher the degree of interdependence, the greater the opportunity costs for states of not coordinating policy. The prevalence of regimes amidst interdependent relationships contributes to a self-reinforcing phenomenon. The interdependence between states is reinforced by the manner in which 'value orientations' will converge.[21] As interaction increases, the values and norms of the actors in the regime are likely to be drawn more and more closely together. Haas recognises that interdependence may be a more complex situation than is often thought.[22] He draws attention to the possibilities of asymmetrical forms of interdependence which could lead to variable levels of vulnerability if the relationship between the states were to be changed. He goes on to discuss the possibility of cooperation across multiple issue areas leading to linkages between regimes.

Liberal institutionalists have taken some of these ideas further. They argue that as states hand over competences to institutions to deal with sectoral areas of policy, structures are created that lock-in and formalise patterns of cooperation. This process can have unforeseen consequences. Institutions can encourage cooperative behaviour and thereby modify both state power as well as the ways in which states define and pursue their interests. States are unlikely to be over-ruled but they may be 'socialised' by the regular interaction that occurs within a regime. Institutions can evolve into bureaucracies that develop their own momentum and pursue ideas of their own.

Risse-Kappen provides examples of how membership of an organisation can modify state behaviour. He cites the case of American policy in NATO where a superpower has allowed the views of some of its allies to modify its behaviour.[23] For his part, Keohane is reluctant to abandon the rationalist assumption that states have fixed preferences. Nevertheless, he acknowledges that 'regimes can also affect state interests, for the notion of self-interest is itself elastic and largely subjective'.[24]

Hegemons and regimes

Dominant, or hegemonic, states have a special place in the theory of regimes. They may play a particular role in creating, maintaining and bringing regimes to an end. A hegemon is 'a state powerful enough to maintain the essential rules governing interstate relations, and willing to do so'.[25] It has the power to structure the agenda of decision-making for other states. Inevitably, such states occupy a special position in regime analysis because they can exert a decisive influence on those around them. Hegemonic Stability Theory even goes as far as to suggest that regimes cannot be created or maintained without the presence of a hegemon. Hasenclever *et al.* argue that empirical scholarship has rendered this extreme claim of Hegemonic stability theory invalid, but they nevertheless agree its underlying thesis still enjoys explanatory power.[26]

It is the case, however, that regimes reflect the existing distribution of power and influence within the international system. Even if a hegemon does not create a regime, then the presence of a state more powerful than any others is likely to be a major actor. Haas notes that norms are embedded in regimes and that 'these norms are always an expression of some idea of . . . predictability . . . preferences for a particular "world order"'.[27] States are likely to join a regime if it reflects the distribution of power within the system and if a hegemon is acting as its leading advocate. Such states will not just be making a calculation of their relative costs and benefits, but will be exhibiting conformity with the values of the existing order.

Hegemons may be attracted to the concept of regimes for the very reason that it offers them the opportunity to imprint their norms and values upon other states within the international system. This may be achieved in the form of a multilateral arrangement, instead of having to convince each country individually. A regime may provide a hegemon with the means to reduce the costs of its leadership by pursuing its interests through consensus building and emulation, thereby obtaining widespread adherence at the most efficient cost. Much of the challenge for a hegemon in establishing a regime is about persuading other states of the appropriateness of its ideas. Its power will appear most legitimate when its ideas are accepted by the broadest community of states. True hegemony is when a leader can influence other states into seeing the world through its conceptual lens. Hegemons are likely to be capable of building strong regimes because they can establish authoritative norms and the resulting organisational frameworks will tend to reflect power realities.

A preponderant power will organise the regime in its own interests, but will offer incentives for compliance and threats of punishment to other states to ensure that they abide by its conception of order. A failure to achieve this aim will undermine its legitimacy and result both in the hegemon having to impose its views and sustain them through the imposition of penalties. Gilpin argues that international politics has witnessed a succession of imposed orders.[28] The exercise of physical power, to ensure that the target group remain obedient, is likely to be costly and the hegemon will avoid this whenever possible. Ruling by coercion rather than consent will drain the resources of the hegemon and endanger the longevity of the regime. The values and norms of the regime will be unlikely to take hold and the other members will tend to defect once the power of the hegemon begins to decline. Regimes are about positive benefits just as much as they concern threats of punishment. One of the principal attractions of a regime is that a hegemon can offer important public goods from which a number of lesser states may be eager to benefit. According to Ikenberry, a 'preponderance of power by a state allows it to offer incentives . . . to the other states to agree to ongoing participation within the hegemonic order'.[29] An example of such a public good is security: states may be unable to guarantee it by themselves but they may be able to enjoy it if the hegemon assures their protection. The provision of such public goods provides the hegemon with a vehicle to promulgate its values. A hegemon may be willing to make sacrifices in order to build a security regime, for instance by tolerating 'free riders' that benefit from its provision yet make no contribution of their own. The hegemon may calculate that ensuring security serves its own interests consistently and that over time it will be confident of gaining the cooperation of its weaker allies.

For their part, weak states that participate in a regime may be satisfied that their own interests are being served by membership. A variety of motives can influence their attitude towards the regime. On the one hand, some states may be dependent upon the collective goods that the hegemon provides. They are likely to defer to the wishes of the hegemon in order to ensure the continuation of the regime and they may be very reluctant to defect from the regime even if the power of the hegemon begins to wane.[30] On the other hand, some states may regard membership in the regime as providing an opportunity for them to exert influence over the dominant country. Small states may be able to exercise disproportionate influence within an institution in a way that they would not be able to achieve outside of the framework. Identities, values and norms are likely to be of greater significance within a regime than simple calculations of material power.[31]

Hegemons not only play an important role in creating regimes, but they also have a major part in managing and sustaining them.[32] Keohane notes that 'Successful hegemonic leadership depends on a certain form of asymmetrical cooperation. The hegemon plays a distinctive role, providing its partners with leadership in return for deference.'[33] The hegemon may contribute to leadership in a number of ways. It might be the source of initiatives that keeps the regime relevant in addressing contemporary problems or it might be the reconciler of tensions amongst its members. Young and Osherenko, in their work on environmental regimes, found that leadership by the most powerful state was frequently important in determining both the construction and the parameters of the regime. They discovered that a dominant country was often the mediator between contending factions and that it used its influence and prestige to secure agreements. The absence of a powerful state might have resulted in paralysis for the regime.[34]

A hegemonic power can sustain a regime through a process termed 'constitutionalism'. This approach provides a means to codify the order within a regime and exercise power through agreed channels. According to Ikenberry, a benign hegemon can provide 'institutionalised processes of participation and decision-making that specify rules, rights and limits on power holders'.[35] In effect, the preponderant power is engaging in a process of self-restraint in order to render its leadership more acceptable to its allies. Such action lowers the attraction to other states of counter-balancing the power of the hegemon because it has voluntarily entered into a mechanism of self-control. The weak powers rely on these constraints to prevent the hegemon from acting in ways that would jeopardise their interests. It makes possible the fashioning of a community of states built around shared values and norms. A benign hegemon managing its relationships through constitutionalism is consistent with Young's model of a negotiated regime. This emerges from a process of inter-state bargaining in which there is an explicit contractual base agreed amongst the participants. Each state accepts certain obligations, decision-making systems and enforcement mechanisms.[36] One of the many benefits of such a system is the high degree of legitimacy that it enjoys.

The manner in which a regime has been built and sustained may have a vital influence on what happens to the regime when the power of the hegemon begins to diminish. Hegemonic stability theory contends that such a situation will be the key element in determining the instability of the order. Yet the assumption that a regime will inevitably decline in such circumstances is predicated on the view that the hegemon is imposing its order on weaker states that will quickly desert them once there is insufficient power to coerce them. If the regime reflects only the interests of the hegemon and it has been maintained by threat of punishment, then it is indeed likely to crumble. But if the hegemon has been successful in establishing authoritative norms, and if it has led with the consent of its allies, then the regime may survive, albeit in a modified form. First, there may be a lag time between the decline in the power of the leading state and the decline in the regime. This may enable other states, that have benefited from the system, to step in to keep the regime going. Alternatively, the regime may have developed its own momentum and may have been adopted by a wide community of states. Mutually agreed rules and the willingness of the hegemon to constrain the exercise of its own power is likely to have enhanced the legitimacy of a regime and render other states reluctant to relinquish the goods it has provided. Thus a regime may assist a hegemon in sustaining its leading position even after its own power has declined.

The transatlantic security regime

A security regime tends to be regarded as the most difficult to establish because it involves a core issue: the very survival of the state. With such high stakes involved, states are unlikely to want to take risks by becoming dependent upon the guarantees of others. By its nature security involves high levels of uncertainty.[37] Jervis notes that security usually involves greater levels of competitiveness.[38] However, on the other side of the equation, states find frequently that they cannot ensure their own security. Only by cooperating with other states against a shared problem can their security needs be addressed. Security organisations seek to harness common efforts towards achieving agreed objectives and give states a degree of confidence that their allies will keep to their promises. By entering into binding obligations, states develop a source of influence over the policies of their allies.

Since the end of the Second World War, the relationship between the United States and Western Europe has evolved in a unique way. The bedrock of transatlantic relations has been the shared sense of liberal values, championed by the United States. These values have included a belief in democratic government: free trade and open access to markets and the rule of law. Consistent with the idea of 'democratic peace theory', these liberal democracies have clustered together.[39] Their democratic values have ensured that they have been peaceful towards each other and have harboured no designs against the territories of their neighbours. The common antipathy towards the Soviet Union made it possible to build up strong bonds of cooperation. This western order was constructed around such agreements as the Atlantic Charter, Bretton Woods, the Marshall Plan and the Washington Treaty,[40] and perpetuated through transatlantic institutions.

The security relationship between Europe and the US grew beyond the limitations of a formal military alliance, beyond the legal obligations of a treaty. Deutsch described it as evolving into a 'pluralistic security community'.[41] The absence of security competition between the transatlantic allies – a deeply held assumption by realists – made possible a qualitatively new relationship. Despite the fact that a superpower was a member of NATO and its nuclear weapons were the guarantors of security, decision-making took place under principles of unanimity. Risse-Kappen notes that the NATO Treaty draws attention to the common values and bonds that draw the two sides of the Atlantic together. 'The Western Alliance represents a functional institutionalisation of the transatlantic security community based on common values and a collective identity of liberal democracies.'[42] The expectation of working together to solve problems became entrenched and facilitated the linkage between different issue areas.[43]

Based upon their shared norms and values, the US and Europe evolved a relationship of complex interdependence in political, economic, cultural and security matters. The high density of their interactions enabled a variety of international organisations to develop to manage their relationship. In the economic sphere, despite the inherent competitiveness of the capitalist system, a liberal economic regime was established in trade and monetary relations. Russell Mead has described this as the 'sticky power' that has tied liberal democratic states together.[44] The result was a rule-based environment from which it was hard for European states to disengage and equally difficult for the US to exercise its disproportionate power.

Ikenberry has made a convincing case that the US engineered a successful intra-western post-war bargain: namely, the construction of an American-led order, based around security and economic institutions, in return for allowing its power to be tied down in organisational frameworks. As a *status quo* power, the US acted as a benign hegemon within the west. It exercised its influence through building consensus within multilateral fora, as a way of rendering its power palatable to its allies. Security bargains were negotiated in which the US helped to guarantee the security of countries in return for their membership in an American-led alliance and the provision of bases for US forces. This American-inspired order was not imposed on the Europeans but was negotiated with them to furnish it with constitutional characteristics. Lundestad refers to this policy as 'Empire by Integration' and Cox 'Empire by Consent'.[45] This policy assuaged the fears of European states that they would be dominated by the overwhelming power of the United States. As Ikenberry observes, 'It is precisely because institutions can in various ways bind (particularly democratic) states together, constrain state actions, and create complicated and demanding political processes that participating states can overcome worries about the arbitrary and untoward exercise of power.'[46]

The end of the Cold War presented a challenge to the future of this system. Amidst a period of intense change there was a risk that the calculations of the strategic partners involved could be reassessed. There was no longer the military threat from the USSR that had propelled the transatlantic allies into a position of interdependence in security. Yet the same logic that led the US to lock-in its gains through post-war institutional arrangements continued into the post-Cold War era.[47] Issue density between the two sides of the Atlantic remained high and shared norms and values prevented divergences of interest that might have altered the nature of the relationship.

The organisations on which the Atlantic order had been built during the Cold War did not collapse after 1990. Neo-realists such as Mearsheimer predicted that with the absence of a unifying threat, the organisations would collapse and western inter-state relations would return to rivalry and self-help.[48] But these bleak assessments were not borne out by events, and the organisations that had triumphed during the Cold War, such as NATO and the EC, continued to provide a rule-based environment for cooperation.[49] The durability of American power was a reflection not only of its preponderance but the fact that it was manifested through various institutional frameworks. These contained centripetal tendencies on the part of the Europeans to counter-balance US power. Organisational linkages also ensured the existence of channels to influence American policy-making.

Although there was little danger that the transatlantic relationship would fracture and become conflictual, there was nevertheless a risk that, in security terms at least, it would stagnate. The US was likely to be less concerned with the fate of Europe and more concerned with its other interests in the Middle East and Asia. There was a possibility that the US and Europe would find insufficient grounds to perpetuate their cooperation. It was in this context that attention began to switch to a new security agenda – international organised crime, drug trafficking, and illegal immigration. Not only were such threats viewed as of greater significance with the Cold War over, but they also provided new challenges around which the transatlantic security relationship could coalesce. With these issues raising concerns that impinged on the interests of Europe and the US, it required little justification to 'spill-over' cooperation from hard, military security concerns into new security areas. The two sides of the Atlantic could build upon their shared norms and values and apply these to the task of cooperating against a range of new issues. The long-established military security cooperation provided the infrastructure for this development.

Regimes are hard to create. They comprise complex and interlinked patterns of relationships and hence take long periods of time to develop. As a result, states are reluctant to abandon regimes, especially when they have been successful, and risk trying to create new ones. Not only will states suffer the cost of dismantling a regime but they will have no guarantees that successor regimes will be effective and durable. Within the transatlantic relationship there was a real fear of giving up something that had worked so well whilst at the same time entering into an uncertain future. As a result, according to Keohane, for states it is 'rational to seek to modify existing ones . . . rather than to abandon unsatisfactory ones and attempt to start over . . . regimes tend to evolve rather than to die'.[50] Jervis endorses this view. He argues that regimes become self-perpetuating by encouraging states to invest in the future of the regime; because it would be harder to replace than continue and by developing an institutional permanence.[51]

The transatlantic security regime evolved and mutated after the end of the Cold War. The US and Europe retained their military security regime and adapted it for different purposes. The new security concerns were 'nested' within the existing regime – a process not without precedent.[52] The new security issues were also pursued through the same multilateral fora, such as NATO, the US-EU relationship and the Group of Eight leading industrial countries. Michael Ignatieff has criticised the US for using Cold War era organisations for the management of the post-Cold War system.[53] But this criticism underestimates the difficulty the US would have faced in trying to obtain a consensus about the purposes of new organisations in a world with more diffused and varied interests. It also ignores the fact that these new security issues are inextricably linked to the military security agenda and require the application of some of the same instruments.

International terrorism represented one amongst a range of post-Cold War security concerns. It grew in significance during the 1990s until the attacks of 9/11 brought it to the forefront of the global agenda. As terrorism impacts both on internal and external security policies, it has required states to find innovative ways of working together. The old monolithic threat presented by the Soviet Union demanded the simple commitment of the NATO alliance to act together in the event of aggression. Terrorism, however, presents a different sort of challenge because it is not a single enemy but a diffuse array of actors. It requires a web of cooperation across many fields of activity rather than just the commitment to use force if attacked. This web of cooperation, in order to be effective, needs to be coordinated through multilateral organisations.

Countering international terrorism has demanded collaboration between national actors such as intelligence agencies, law enforcement officers, judicial communities and representatives of internal security ministries. These actors are from policy cultures that have little experience of working across international boundaries: judicial systems, for instance, have always been strictly national in orientation. Cooperation depends crucially upon trust, and this has been a difficult quality to engender between agencies who have been unused to working with overseas partners, sharing information and responding to requests from other countries. The transition from specific reciprocity, where trust exists on a *quid pro quo* basis, to indirect and generalised reciprocity, has been problematic. It was made possible in the case of the US and Europe by a shared understanding of the nature of these new security threats between the two sides. The common transatlantic understanding of the nature of these problems was due to the fact that an epistemic community of security specialists in the law enforcement and intelligence communities existed.[54] These experts played an important part in developing concepts that policy-makers could understand. The chief barrier has been to move from these shared concepts of the problem towards practical patterns of cooperation.

As a hegemonic power, the US has played a special role in facilitating international counter-terrorist cooperation. In spite of its unparalleled strength, the US recognised that it could not defeat international terrorism alone and that it needed the assistance of the wider international community. Europe was considered the natural ally of the US because of the shared values across the Atlantic and the preexisting military security regime. In addition, the re-orientating of that military security regime towards counter-terrorism helped to perpetuate a strong US leadership role on the continent during a period of closer European integration. This leadership role has enabled the US to imprint its priorities upon this sphere of collaboration and to drive it forward. The strength of the US, and particularly its position as the foremost victim of international terrorism since the 9/11 attacks, has accorded it the leverage to fashion collaboration in accordance with America's agenda.

American leadership has not, however, been such that it has been able to impose its model of counter-terrorism. Europe has been in a position to refuse American pressures, and there has never been a hint of coercion in the relationship.[55] Even during the Cold War, when the Europeans were dependent on the US for the provision of military security, the regime that evolved conformed to Young's model of a mixed 'spontaneous' and 'negotiated' regime.[56] It is much more accurate to describe the cooperation as based on mutual interest. It remains to be seen whether the values and norms that the US and Europe shared in their military security regime will be sufficient and transferable to their efforts in combating international terrorism. They will need to come to see threats similarly and be prepared to work in tandem to defeat them.

Transatlantic counter-terrorism cooperation is still at a fairly early stage of evolution. Having developed out of a broader pattern of security issues that included international organised crime and drug trafficking, counter-terrorism was an issue of comparatively late development. For example, counter-narcotics cooperation was much more advanced than counter-terrorism, even justifying the description of a 'regime' in its own right. The US had been instrumental in creating the counter-narcotics regime and putting pressure upon states to conform to its strictures.[57] It was the impact of 9/11 that caused international terrorism to rise to the top of the security agenda, and it is too early to say whether efforts to counter it will assume the characteristics of a regime. The fact that there has been only limited cooperation in the past means that much effort has to be invested in this policy sphere to develop a pattern of rules and norms of behaviour that would justify the title of a regime. What has become apparent is that as the transatlantic allies have attempted to fashion cooperation against international terrorism, they have discovered important differences in their approach. These differences are the subject of the subsequent chapters of this book.

Globalising counter-terror cooperation

The work of Rittberger on regime theory postulates that regimes tend to expand from core groups of states to the wider international community. Once they have been created, regimes set standards that the founders will wish to see replicated beyond the original membership. Rittberger observes that 'international regimes, once firmly established and operative, are likely to have a model-like impact, their principles, norms and rules pointing to possibilities for regulated conflict management in other regions of the world'.[58] These ideas have echoes in the literature on democratic peace. Once a critical mass of liberal states have emerged, they will attempt to diffuse their norms and values through the rest of the international system. In effect, they will seek to socialise others into their patterns of behaviour.

This model of exporting western values to a wider community of states was exemplified during the Cold War. The US and Europe sought to extend their system of political and economic relations, and this was complemented by the desire of states in Asia and Latin America to emulate the western model. For example, the transatlantic economic regime, that was constructed on the principles of capitalist economic relations and contained a variety of principles and regulations, was quickly established as the global standard. This was also true of their military security regime. The US was desirous to enlarge its embrace to countries outside of Europe through such mechanisms as the nuclear non-proliferation regime.

Consistent with this process, the US and Europe are eager to disseminate their counter-terror cooperation to the international community. The transatlantic allies wish to recruit the maximum number of adherents in order both to universalise the norms and values on which their own relationship has been founded and to accord their actions the broadest legitimacy. There will inevitably be differences in the nature of the cooperation that they create with the wider world. The levels of interdependence that underpin US-European relations are not replicated within the rest of the international system. Nevertheless, it is a logical response in order to combat the sort of phenomenon presented by international terrorism.

Globalised cooperation is more likely to reflect the priorities of the western countries that inspired it – thereby conforming to the 'imposed order' described by Young.[59] The level of cooperation that is achieved is likely to mirror the distribution of power and influence in the system. It will be confined to the issue area in question, rather than built on a host of shared values. There is unlikely to be much latitude for bargaining about the nature of the cooperation, once the two halves of the Atlantic have arrived at an agreement. Negotiation has characterised the process by which the US and Europe establish their own pattern of cooperation, but there is a reluctance on their part to unpick those agreements in order to make them more acceptable to other states.

A hegemonic power like the US sees its interests as being served by establishing cooperation with its European allies before pursuing its universality. The US has the most to gain by fostering cooperation that embodies American priorities. This can be achieved most efficiently by adapting the pre-existing military security regime that the US has constructed with its most-like-minded allies, the Europeans, before adapting that to encapsulate counter-terrorism cooperation with the rest of the world. Collaborating with selective partners in stages, before approaching the broader international community, has a better chance of success. Securing cooperation with Europe will increase legitimacy for American policies. Countries, especially those from less developed parts of the world, are more likely to join an existing multi-lateral system than enter into a narrow bilateral system with the

United States. Conversely, tension within the transatlantic relationship is likely to detract from the possibilities of securing broader international cooperation.

Whilst global counter-terror cooperation may more closely resemble an imposed model, it does not follow that all its adherents will have been coerced into membership. Young regards coercion as one possibility, but also sees 'cooptation and the manipulation of incentives' as other strategies.[60] Some states will perceive involvement as a direct benefit to themselves because they will share many of the same values and ideas. Others will become involved because that will embody the values of the prevailing order and states will seek to be in conformity with that order. Another group of states may be relatively indifferent to the issue of counter-terrorism, but they may be wary lest they develop a reputation for non-compliance that could damage their ability to secure western aid in the future. They may fear becoming victims of pressure that could result in them being excluded from the membership of more desirable groupings.

At the other end of the spectrum are those states that are regarded as complicit in the problem of international terrorism. These states are likely to be extremely reluctant to participate in counter-terrorism activities, but they are the very states that the US and Europe will be seeking to involve. States that remain outside, or are uncompliant with its provisions, may detract from the overall effectiveness of the counter-terrorism efforts. Such states may be offered incentives to become involved or they may be threatened with penalties for remaining apart. The US and Europe have at their disposal a range of instruments they can employ against such countries, ranging from diplomatic isolation to economic sanctions.

Global counter-terrorism cooperation will always differ in quality and depth from its transatlantic counterpart. It is going to consist of a looser and less cohesive grouping of states who will participate in some activities and not in others. This will be due to the greater diversity amongst the membership and less of a 'like-minded' association. The agreements reached between these countries may be less ambitious and reflect the lowest common denominator that can be achieved. The tendency to obtain the benefits of involvement without contributing to the costs of sustaining cooperation may be more prevalent. These may be some of the natural drawbacks of a broadly based pattern of international action. The transatlantic allies have to be realistic about these aspects and accept that cooperation on a global basis will be modest. However, they should consider the fact that any level of cooperation is a prize worthy in itself. They may also hope that, over time, this will be strengthened and that more muscular counter-terrorist efforts will evolve.

Conclusion

Transatlantic efforts to combat international terrorism are currently under development. Although still in its relative infancy, this cooperation has developed inside a pre-existing military security regime. It is novel both in nature and in the actors that it involves. To create this cooperation the US and Europe have adapted patterns of security collaboration that they engineered during the Cold War. Its value is to ensure that transatlantic friction and competition in relation to combating terrorism is minimised whilst reciprocity guaranteed. It offers the US an efficient way to pursue its interests and, in turn, assures the Europeans of a way to shape and constrain US power and influence its decision-making. As Keohane argued, the way to assess the significance of international cooperation is to gauge how the behaviour of a government is modified by its existence.[61] There is increasing evidence in the transatlantic relationship that the nascent efforts to counter terrorism are serving to constrain, enhance and modify the behaviour of the two sides.

Counter-terrorism cooperation has arisen in response to a security phenomenon that has grown increasingly alarming. As the threat has risen, the US and Europe have come to recognise that they must work together more systematically in order to contain its menace. The events of 9/11 crystallised this perception. It has resulted in various forms of collaboration being drawn together. Of even greater significance has been the fact that the US has led the drive for enhanced cooperation. Its 'War on Terrorism' has become the principal propellant of this activity.

Cooperation has been pursued through the three key transatlantic frameworks of the US–EU, NATO and G-8. There have also been efforts to internationalise this cooperation. The US and its European allies have sought to obtain global adherence for the policies that they have been promoting. They have used their own agreements as foundations on which to seek universal application of counter-terrorist policies. This promises to be a hard and rocky path, but the US and Europe share the belief that only global efforts will be able to tackle the roots of the problem.

2 Security organisations in transatlantic relations

Introduction

The two halves of the Atlantic interact with one another through a complex web of relationships: bilateral as well as a variety of organisational frameworks. This is one of the most dense and intensive relationships within the international system. The organisational frameworks have arisen in order to systematise cooperation in particular policy areas. The variety in the means of interaction has given the transatlantic relationship great flexibility in addition to underlying strength. Whilst this diversity can present problems of coherence and consistency, it has enabled the US and Europe to adapt their relationship to take account of new issues and challenges.

The survival of organisations such as NATO, the European Community/European Union and the G-7/G-8 after the end of the Cold War demonstrated that they embodied more than the anti-Soviet values that had given rise to their creation. European states believed that these organisations represented their interests in the broadest sense and provided them with vehicles through which they could continue to cooperate with the United States, even at a time when more frictions had entered into transatlantic relations. For its part, the US remained committed to working with its allies, eager not to lose its privileged status within these organisations.

> International terrorism presents the Euro-Atlantic nations with a complex, persistent threat that calls for a multilateral strategic response involving many dimensions of policy and many international actors. No simple approach *and no single institution or channel of international cooperation* can be expected to suffice.[1]
> (emphasis added)

This quotation, from amongst others of the counter-terrorism 'Czar' of the Clinton and first Bush administrations,[2] illuminates the central theme of this chapter. The nature of international terrorism means it has ranged across the pre-existing policy boundaries of the transatlantic relationship. It has required a hybrid form of cooperation including a combination of bilateralism and multilateralism. No single multilateral organisation possessed the range of competences to tackle all of these tasks and no dedicated transatlantic framework has been created for the task. Adapting existing organisations to the demands of combating terrorism was a goal that should not be underestimated. Issues such as the suitability of the organisations to accommodate new roles; the attitudes of key members towards the changes and the stresses and strains that lingered from the original tasks of the organisation, presented real obstacles that had to be overcome. In all of these cases, counter-terrorism cooperation was grafted on to organisations that had been experiencing a process of transition in their own right.

The development of transatlantic counter-terrorism cooperation, containing principles, norms and rules, has found expression both in bilateral relations and multilateral settings. Indeed it has grown from bilateral roots and gradually become multilateralised as the two sides of the Atlantic have expressed confidence that this recent sphere of activity is here to stay. Although multilateralism is the focus of this book, bilateralism is too important to go unmentioned, and it will be discussed briefly in the next section of this chapter.

US-European bilateral cooperation

There has never been a blueprint for the development of transatlantic counter-terrorism cooperation, instead it has evolved on an *ad hoc* basis. In the words of an Atlantic Council report, 'Efforts [at cooperation] have been hindered by persistent tensions over whether bilateral or multilateral arrangements are most effective'.[3] Progress has been achieved incrementally since 1990 and has depended upon the approval of the participating countries. Multilateral cooperation has flowered since 9/11 because of the impact of the attack on the US and the manner in which the Europeans have responded to the Bush administration's War on Terrorism. However, it does not mean that all forms of bilateral cooperation across the Atlantic have been superseded: bilateralism has been vital in the past and continues to be important in the present.

Efforts to combat terrorism have evolved from policies pursued between the US and individual European countries. Cooperation has been constructed from the bottom up, by sub-national actors on both sides of the Atlantic, who have recognised the value of working together against shared threats. Over time, patterns of collaboration have become adopted more widely and have nested within organisational settings. The process of moving from bilateral to multilateral cooperation has followed no pre-ordained pattern, but there have been critical points at which cooperation has been operationalised on an international level. States acting together across the Atlantic ensure policy coordination and greater efficiency. International collaboration facilitates the sharing of information, consultation on policy initiatives, and even joint actions; thereby enabling states to bring their positions and policies into conformity with one another through a process of negotiation or 'mutual adjustment'.[4] Cooperation also tends to increase the ambitions of the participants. The impact of acting together frequently has the effect of driving up standards.

It does not follow that bilateralism will always progress into multilateralism: the former will always enjoy certain attractions. First, some bilateral relationships remain especially close, and those involved will be reluctant to place it at risk by broadening the participation. For example, the sharing of highly sensitive intelligence material may only be undertaken with trusted allies. Second, certain forms of cooperation may involve the interests of a caucus of countries and it would be pointless to try to involve a broader community. This is particularly relevant in operational matters where interest and the requirements of speed may necessitate bilateral arrangements. Third, multilateral agreements can be modest in nature and can bring the risk of exposure to the ebb and flow of the wider political relationship. Cooperation is likely to be invested with a raised political salience once it is taken out of the hands of specialist communities and exposed to the activities of foreign ministries and diplomats.

Counter-terrorism collaboration grew from bilateral linkages between police and other internal security agencies across the Atlantic. Operational powers for combating terrorism reside only in national agencies and therefore practical cooperation has depended upon police, intelligence and judicial agencies working with their counterparts in other countries. In the UK, for example, the 'Police Working Group on Terrorism' was established in 1979 to share operational knowledge with other European police forces. Such cooperation emerges very slowly because these agencies are inherently conservative in nature and are reluctant to share information. Nevertheless, cases that have required collaboration have contributed in the past to building up contacts and a sense of trust. The respect and expectations of reciprocity that have grown up between professionals in the same spheres of work provide a basis on which cooperation can evolve.[5]

Cooperation against terrorism has grown from a number of sources. One in particular has been the shared priority on both sides of the Atlantic to work against illegal drugs and international organised crime.[6] Both narcotics and international crime were designated by the American government as national security threats.[7] This enabled the mobilisation of the full panoply of national resources, ranging from law enforcement and the judiciary to diplomatic instruments and even the armed services. It was not until 9/11 that the threat from international terrorism eclipsed these other threats. There were subsequently strong similarities between the policies adopted by the US and Europe to combat drugs and crime and the measures taken to fight terrorism.[8]

US experience of fighting drug trafficking and international crime meant that it was well acquainted with security challenges that were transnational in nature. The US had realised that it was trying to counteract transnational threats with a law enforcement system that was still bound by a traditional conception of sovereignty. Hence, it took steps to enable its law enforcement agencies to conduct investigations outside of the US homeland. As Winer records, 'the US saw the need to build networks for governments as capable and swift as the networks the criminals use'.[9]

In respect of internationalising its law enforcement activities, the US was considerably ahead of its European allies. This meant that when the two sides of the Atlantic entered into cooperation, a US model of law enforcement was strongly in evidence.[10] As the dominant power within the international system, the US was in a position both to assert its perception of the nature of the threats and its model of how they should be combated. European countries had no choice other than to respond to this American approach. McDonald has commented on this trend of American law enforcement norms and values becoming disseminated amongst its European allies,[11] whilst Nadelmann has referred to the increasing internationalisation of US policing agencies.[12] Transatlantic counter-terrorism efforts were later built on the platform that had been constructed to deal with drug trafficking and international crime.

Evidence of this 'Americanisation' process can be found in the stationing of various categories of US law enforcement personnel throughout Europe. The Federal Bureau of Investigation's (FBI) Legal Attachés, or 'LEGATs', serve as liaison officials in US embassies. Placing these officers overseas enables them to assist with the speed and depth of cooperation when complex transnational criminal cases arise.[13] Similarly, the Drug Enforcement Agency (DEA) has placed agents in Europe in order to facilitate collaboration on cases involving illegal drugs. Although neither the FBI nor DEA officers enjoy operational powers outside of the US, they have contributed to information sharing and the building of networks between police officers on both sides of the Atlantic. The US also seconds some of its attorneys from the Department of Justice to serve in important embassies[14] in order to help to coordinate prosecutions involving multiple jurisdictions.[15] These efforts have ensured that US influence and practices, in relation to countering narcotics and organised crime, percolated into European countries themselves as well as their efforts to act collectively.

The fruits of cooperation between American agencies and their European counterparts can be observed in a number of cases. For example, the phenomenon of Italian-American organised crime led to the development of a close working relationship between the FBI and the Italian Carabinerri. The US approach towards organised crime has been conditioned by its historical experience, based upon a 'Mafia' model of ethnically homogeneous and interlinked criminal groups. These groups have been seen as alien to American society and structured in a hierarchical fashion. This view of organised crime derived from US investigations of its domestic Italian-American crime phenomenon, such as the Kefauver Commission of 1950. Italy and the US worked together to target the principal crime families, their organisations and the flow of contraband goods and drugs that flowed across the Atlantic. A joint US-Italian Working Group on organised crime was established in order to share intelligence information and to discuss optimal detection techniques.[16] The US experience of combating domestic organised crime proved to be especially valuable, and the creation of an Italian witness protection, or *pentiti*, programme owed much to the influence of working with the US Department of Justice.[17]

Germany, like Italy, built up a strong bilateral relationship with the US over a period of time. In the Bundeskriminalamt (BKA – Federal Criminal Police Office) headquarters in Wiesbaden, a computer terminal was installed in September 1997 linked directly with the US National Criminal Information Center.[18] The link enables officers of the BKA to access US police files on criminal suspects and testifies to the close working relationship between German and American police authorities. This collaboration against transnational crime has gone on to form the basis for shared efforts against terrorism. Since 9/11 the German government has authorised substantial extra funding for counter-terrorist efforts, which has been channelled to several agencies including the Federal Border Guards, the BKA, the Bundesamt für Verfassungsschutz (BfV – Federal Office for the Protection of the

Constitution) and the Bundesnachrichtendinenst (BND – Foreign Intelligence Agency).

The pre-existing pattern of collaboration against drug trafficking and international crime has provided fertile soil for the development of counter-terrorist activities. Stevenson notes the importance of bilateralism in American collaboration with Europe although cooperation has deeper roots in some cases than in others.[19] Where a country has suffered from a long-standing problem with terrorism there is more likely to be tradition of working with American authorities. It would be an exaggeration to say that any single country in Europe has cultivated a 'special relationship' with the US in the field of counter-terrorism: mainly because there was insufficient motivation to justify a close dyadic relationship when the traditional threats to European countries had been indigenous.

The UK has traditionally had a close relationship with the US right across the spectrum of security issues and, since 9/11, this has extended to include counter-terrorism. Prime Minister Tony Blair's support for America after the atrocity and the UK's participation in America's military responses has placed the country in the front line of those vulnerable to terrorist attack. The bilateral relationship between Washington and London has been deepened by cooperation over domestic policy and a close working relationship forged between former Home Secretary David Blunkett and Secretary for Homeland Security Tom Ridge.[20] A working group on Homeland Security was created between the two sides and the focus has been upon sharing best practice in domestic counter-terror preparations, joint training exercises, cyber- and physical infrastructure protection, and border and transportation security.

Less well known than the UK-US relationship are the linkages between Washington, Paris and The Hague. France has extensive experience of combating terrorism, arising mainly from its historical links with Algeria.[21] It has possessed tough anti-terrorism laws since 1986 and, following the Al-Qaeda attacks in the US, taken steps to increase the protection of vulnerable targets. Its lead agencies on foreign terrorism have been the Direction de la Surveillance du Territoire (DST) and the Direction Générale de la Securité Extérieure (DGSE) which both liaise closely with their European counterparts.[22] It has made extensive efforts to work alongside the United States, proving the lie to the widespread perception that France is both weak on terrorism and doctrinally opposed to cooperation with Washington.[23] This was demonstrated by the speed with which flights between Paris and America were cancelled after warnings about potential terrorist attack in December 2003. Despite the absence of a major domestic terrorist group, Dutch-American cooperation in counter-terrorism has always been robust, reflecting the strong Atlanticist orientation of The Hague. The Dutch civilian intelligence agency, the Algemene Inlichtingen en Veiligheidsdienst (AIVD), has built up close and privileged cooperation with the FBI.

Bilateralism remains an important strand in US policy towards Europe. Due to its size and strength, the US has always possessed the option of choosing with which countries it wants to maximise cooperation. There has even been the option of playing off European countries against each other. The first visit of the new US Secretary for Homeland Security Tom Ridge to Europe, in which he visited Italy, Spain and Germany but did not go to Brussels, was an example of this US approach. In practice, however, America's capacity to 'divide and rule' in its relations with Europe has been constrained by a number of factors: some reflecting America's own circumstances, others to do with its allies. The chief weakness on the American side has been the plethora of US agencies tasked with law enforcement responsibilities overseas. Having painstakingly built up cooperation agreements with their European counterparts, agencies such as the FBI and DEA have been loath to put this at risk by agreeing to new patterns of collaboration.[24] Competition between the different agencies mitigates the influence that the US can exert overseas.

A bigger problem for the US has been the absence of a culture of cooperation amongst European countries in relation to counter-terrorism. European-wide activity against terrorism is still at an early phase of development and there has been relatively little for the US to build upon. The reasons why European countries are at an early stage of cooperation include several factors. First, national experiences of terrorism have not encouraged European countries to work together as there has been no obvious benefit. Considerations of national sovereignty have been uppermost in this policy area. Internal security has always been an area of great sensitivity and states have feared compromising their sources of information by sharing them with other states.

Second, West European countries have regarded terrorist acts as politically motivated crimes (as defined under the Council of Europe's 'Convention on the Suppression of Terrorism' of January 1977) and have struggled to agree upon a common definition. This has led them to refuse to extradite suspects on the grounds that an accused person might not receive a fair trial or because membership of an organisation is not proscribed in their state. This has left a legacy of distrust amongst European states. For example, Belgium refused to extradite two suspected terrorists wanted by Spain in 1993. In cases where European cooperation has taken place, it has usually been the result of bilateral agreements. For example, France and Spain have built up cooperation since 1984 because of the problem presented by Euzkadi Ta Askatasuna (ETA) which has sought to create an independent state within Spain but that would also include parts of French territory. In 1992 France and Spain cooperated in a raid on a property in Bayonne that resulted in the capture of many of the senior leadership in ETA.[25] In May 1996 evidence of the close relationship between the two countries came when France posted a police attaché officer to its embassy in Madrid to coordinate activities with the Spanish government.[26]

Third, there have been the numerous incompatibilities between the legal and policing systems of European states. Apart from the obvious barriers of language, different legal systems have evolved on the continent. Countries such as France have a Roman law tradition, based on a system of investigating magistrates, whereas countries such as the UK have adhered to a Common Law tradition, that has relied upon the creation of legal precedents.[27] A further source of complexity has been the different types of police forces developed within European countries – 120 according to one estimate.[28] Italy, France and Spain have developed 'gendarmerie' policing traditions, with an armed force organised along military lines and responsible for policing the entire national territory. Germany has developed a federal policing model, which is similar in nature to that of the United States. A third approach, exemplified by the UK, is decentralised with over forty regional police forces granted substantial autonomy.

The US has always been pragmatic in its approach towards cooperation with other countries. Bilateral measures against international terrorism have proved their efficacy over time, particularly in cases where working with a country has best been pursued away from the glare of publicity. Yet in cooperating with Europe the US has been drawn to multilateral as well as bilateral forms of cooperation. The growing international dimension of the problem has demanded a more coherent multilateral answer: a terrorist attack may involve the deaths of nationals from several countries, the police investigation may require evidence from more than one jurisdiction, and suspects may be extradited from multiple territories. Working through organisations presents certain advantages for the US: most notably, the US is able to come to an understanding with a group of European countries rather than negotiate a host of agreements with individual states. Such understandings may enable the US to achieve more than could be gained by separate agreements. Perhaps most importantly, the US has found that its European allies are used to conducting their activities through multilateral frameworks, and unless it can become party to these arrangements then it risks being left out in the cold.

The absence of a dedicated transatlantic framework for addressing international terrorism can be seen as both a source of strength and of weakness. On the one hand, it can be argued to be a weakness because there is a lack of organisational coherence. Because no single organisation is responsible for countering international terrorism, the US and Europe are left to divide this issue between a variety of frameworks. On the other hand, it may be a source of strength because it promotes organisational flexibility. Counter-terrorism has become an issue that may be addressed wherever it is most appropriate and it facilitates overlapping patterns of competence to develop. Terrorism, because of its multifaceted nature, is an issue that does not fall conveniently into a pre-existing framework.

US cooperation with the European Union

Just as West European states were reluctant to cooperate over terrorism in the post-war period, so their principal framework for politico-economic cooperation – the European Community – was slow to develop competences in this field.[29] It was not until June 1976 that the 'TREVI' forum (Terrorisme, Radicalisme, Extrêmisme et Violence Internationale) was inaugurated for interior ministers to discuss their shared concerns relating to terrorism. The forum was conducted on an intergovernmental basis, under the aegis of European Political Cooperation (EPC). This was testament to the sensitivity of states in relinquishing their sovereignty over internal security issues and, as a result, no separate secretariat was ever created. Beneath the level of ministers, TREVI comprised of two working groups, one of which focused on terrorism and comprised senior officials from interior ministries, police officers and intelligence specialists. The other working group was concerned with broader public order matters. As Occhipinti points out, TREVI's activities 'were largely limited to the building of secure communication links among the policing agencies of the member states'.[30]

Despite its relatively humble beginnings, TREVI was an important first step for the EC in creating internal security linkages between member states. The forum was enhanced in 1985 and its remit was extended to drug trafficking and various aspects of international crime. This illustrated once again the important role that these other security challenges, similar to terrorism, have played in driving forward cooperation both within Europe as well as across the Atlantic. TREVI was important in laying the groundwork for more ambitious Community-based structures. An additional working group within TREVI was created, and this put forward proposals that were to form the basis for the European Drugs Unit (EDU) and later the European Police Office (Europol).

By the time the Treaty on European Union had been ratified in November 1993 it was clear that the EU wanted to develop its internal security role as a way of rationalising the diverse efforts of its member states. It was this ambition that drew the attention of the United States and led it to seek actively to enhance cooperation between the two sides. It was clear to American policy-makers that attempting to create a new transatlantic organisation for these purposes was unrealistic. The attraction of the EU was that it represented an organisation of proven pedigree, and the US was eager to be involved at the beginning of its nascent internal security efforts in order to try and shape them in accordance with America's own views.

The EU had emerged from the end of the Cold War unencumbered by the military security responsibilities of organisations like NATO and the Conference on Security and Cooperation in Europe (CSCE). Instead it enjoyed a strong legal base that was ideally suited to dealing with law enforcement and judicial issues. Furthermore, the process of integration has given the EU both a mechanism and a justification for moving forward in the sphere of internal security. Some member states were eager to use internal security as a vehicle to advance their integration process.

The structure of the EU has been a mixed blessing in addressing the complex challenges presented by international terrorism.[31] On the one hand, the three-pillar structure has enabled the Union to deal with both the internal and external dimensions of the security problem. Pillar 1, concerning the economic and trade dimensions of the Community, provides the power to undertake economic sanctions and focus on issues such as money laundering by terrorist groups. Pillar 2, the Common Foreign and Security Policy (CFSP), allows the EU to confront the foreign and defence policy dimensions of terrorism. Pillar 3, the Justice and Home Affairs portfolio, accords the right to develop judicial and police cooperation.[32] On the other hand, the EU has faced considerable difficulties of coordination where terrorism issues have crossed between the remits of the three pillars.[33] For example, den Boer cites how lists of terrorist organisations have been drawn up within Pillar 3, but determining which assets of a group to freeze takes place under Pillar 1.[34] With the decision-making process varying between each of the pillars, the problem has been exacerbated by the fact that the bodies within the EU that deal with these matters – working groups within the Council and the Directorates within the Commission with responsibility for JHA and External Relations – have not always worked smoothly together. The pillar structure tends to promote tunnel vision amongst the various players, encouraging them to focus on their own selfish interests. As the boundaries between internal and external security become increasingly blurred, the separation of issues in Pillars 1 and 2 is frequently regarded as anomalous.

Such factors have contributed to the difficulties experienced by the American government in fashioning a cooperative relationship with the EU. Part of the difficulty has been a fundamental difference in the nature of the two actors. The US is a highly developed federal actor whilst the EU is a complex, multi-level polity. Although there is no denying that America's own large bureaucracies and interagency decision-making processes are opaque to outsiders, they pale in comparison to the EU with its pillars, member states, European Commission, Parliament and Court of Justice. In an attempt to capture its unique construction Calleo calls the EU 'a hybrid confederacy of free states'.[35] It presents a bewildering phenomenon to US policy-makers – even a former US ambassador to the EU confessed that there was a lack of understanding in Washington about the nature of the organisation.[36] Dubois makes a similar point when she describes the machinations of Pillar 3 (after the Treaty of Amsterdam) involving twenty-five working parties, the Intergovernmental Article 36 Committee, the Committee of Permanent Ambassadors (COREPER) as well as the JHA Council of Ministers.[37]

The other major obstacle for the US in attempting to engineer a cooperative counter-terrorism relationship with the Union was that throughout the 1990s the EU was preoccupied with building its own internal security structures. The US was to be found reaching out to the EU, seeking information sharing, improved extradition of criminal suspects and the creation of a transatlantic judicial network. But the Europeans were more concerned with generating their own patterns of collaboration and rebuffed the US advances as premature.[38] The US was effectively told it was too early to enter into a negotiation or, once an agreement had been reached amongst EU members, it was too late to unpick it in order to renegotiate a deal with Washington. This led to considerable frustration on the part of the American government as its overtures for cooperation were repeatedly spurned.

There were also other reasons for the EU's delay. Some member states were reluctant to cede sovereignty over domestic security, fearing that it would add to the momentum of European integration. The UK, for example, opted to remain semi-detached from one of the major security initiatives, the Schengen Convention on internal and external frontiers, because it wanted to preserve its own border controls. Civil liberties concerns also acted as a brake on the process of hardening internal security measures. There was a strong undercurrent of feeling that the EU was paying proportionately more attention to increasing its security provisions as compared to the considerations of liberty and equality of justice. Critics of the Union pointed to its lack of transparency and accountability in the JHA domain[39] and its concentration upon security provisions at the expense of human rights.

The TEU bequeathed Title VI of the JHA portfolio that was ambitious in the issues it sought to address – namely transnational crime, drug trafficking and illegal immigration – but chronically weak in the instruments to achieve those aims. Joint Actions, Common Positions and Conventions were all options that the Union could use to develop police, judicial and border control. Yet inter-governmentalism reigned and unanimity of decision-making was required in all areas. For much of the 1990s, the EU faced a growing array of internal security problems but it lacked the tools to deal with them.[40] Terrorism was not a concern of sufficient importance to drive the process forward and overcome the obstacles. The 'La Gomera Declaration' of JHA ministers in October 1995 was evidence that terrorism was acknowledged to be a threat to democracy as well as economic and social development, but there was a lack of political will amongst the member states to prioritise this aspect.[41]

It was not until the Treaty of Amsterdam in June 1997 that the EU made substantial steps forward in the governance of internal security. Key aspects of the JHA portfolio, such as asylum, immigration and external border controls, were 'communitarised' in the Treaty (Title IV) and Schengen was brought inside the EU.[42] Police and judicial cooperation were retained in former Title VI under intergovernmental strictures, because they were considered too sensitive to be included in Pillar 1.[43] The Treaty declared an 'Area of Freedom, Security and Justice' (AFSJ) in which the right of free movement and the maintenance of a secure internal environment were enshrined as core EU objectives. The Union declared the aim of guaranteeing free movement for its citizens and providing them with a secure and just internal space. The Amsterdam Treaty left the EU with a mixed intergovernmental and communitarised internal security system, but one that offered better prospects for cooperation with third parties such as the United States.

At the special EU Summit at Tampere in October 1999, a road map for future EU priorities in JHA was agreed. There remained a host of weaknesses in the Union's capabilities that were caused by the persistent tension between national interests and the requirements of inter-state cooperation. Nevertheless, a new level of political will was evident. Of particular salience was the decision to pursue the mutual recognition of each other's legal systems. This sought to remedy the inability of members to work together in judicial issues. Rather than try to harmonise their laws, the member states would recognise the existing legal framework of their neighbours. Tampere was designed for a five-year period, and in 2005 the so-called 'Hague Programme' was launched as the next phase of the JHA process.[44]

The most recent attempt to advance the organisational framework of internal security was the drafting of the EU Constitution. This contained measures to improve cooperation between national judicial authorities, improve the management of data relating to law enforcement and tighten up border security.[45] It also sought to abolish the EU's pillar structure. Although the Constitution was signed by heads of state, it ran into crisis when it failed to pass in the referendums on ratification in France and Holland. It is likely that whilst the Constitution itself will be shelved, many of the internal security provisions in the Treaty will be enacted through other channels.

By the time of the 9/11 terrorist attacks, the EU was really only on the threshold of becoming a meaningful internal security actor with a capacity to combat international terrorism. The fact that many member states had not ratified some of the basic international conventions against terrorism was illustrative of the limited progress that had been achieved. The inadequacies of the EU led one commentator to observe that 'It is far from certain that the EU will ever arrive at a fully harmonized horizontal strategy against terrorism.'[46] Nevertheless, the limitations of its internal security system needs to be compared with the beginning of the 1990s when there was practically no system at all. The speed of the EU's evolution has been remarkable and it has begun to take on the semblance of a serious and determined internal security actor.[47] Its intention to create a permanent Internal Security Committee within the European Council is a further illustration of its seriousness.[48]

US-EU foreign policy cooperation

Just as the development of the EU as an internal security actor offered the potential for cooperation with the United States, so did its growing identity in foreign policy. The CFSP built upon the external policy cooperation that had existed in EPC and enshrined it in the intergovernmental Pillar 2. Realising the latent potential in the CFSP was always going to be difficult as it meant finding consensus from the national foreign policies of the member states. Foreign policy has always been a core area of state sovereignty, and the European Community had struggled historically to find areas of common interest.

The US regarded external policy cooperation with the EU as an important objective for two reasons. The first was that American policy-makers saw terrorism as one amongst a range of post-Cold War security challenges that required international cooperation. The second was that America had long regarded Europe as bearing an inadequate share of the global security burden. During the Cold War US officials had periodically chastised the Europeans for neglecting their share of responsibilities and relying on American protection. The issue of international terrorism, amongst others, now seemed to offer the opportunity to get the Europeans to raise their attention from the parochial concerns of their own continent to the global level. Through the vehicle of the CFSP the Union appeared to be changing its role from that of a civilian power into an actor with the full range of competences, including a willingness to exercise politico-military power.

The initial attempt to build foreign policy cooperation between the two sides was undertaken even before the signing of the TEU. It was based on a recognition that the ties that bound the US and Europe had to be renewed in the aftermath of the collapse of communism: that the West now had to be clear what it stood 'for', rather than just what it had stood 'against'.[49] The document that shaped this vision was the 'Transatlantic Declaration' of November 1990. The Declaration talked of 'common goals' between Europe and the US and identified terrorism and drugs as major new security challenges.[50] This represented a first step in trying to prevent the interests of the two sides diverging after the Cold War. However, there was a lack of significant initiatives to give substance to the Declaration. Little was achieved other than sending a signal that both the US and Europe wanted to work with each other and consult on matters of mutual concern.

It was not until the US-EU Berlin Summit in July 1994 that greater substance was imparted to the transatlantic dialogue. Three Senior Level working groups were established, of which one was concerned with CFSP.[51] On 2 June of the following year the US Secretary of State Warren Christopher gave a speech in Madrid in which he proposed the creation of a 'New Transatlantic Agenda' (NTA).[52] At the subsequent

US-EU Summit in Washington, the NTA was operationalised through a 'US-EU Joint Action Plan' (JAP). The NTA institutionalised a dialogue on a number of levels: at the Task Force level of Political Directors meeting four times per year; at a Senior Level Group (SLG), meeting to develop the agendas for summits; at ministerial and at biannual summit levels (after 2000 these became annual). Through these various points of contact it constructed a regularised discussion of issues that were not traditionally regarded as part of the transatlantic relationship.[53] It also contributed to an important process of institutionalising and regularising a relationship of growing importance.

The Joint Action Plan was wide-ranging in scope and related not only to security issues but also to economic relations and democratic values. It provided a list of cross-cutting security challenges, of which counter-terrorism was one.[54] Another was cooperation to halt the global spread of weapons of mass destruction (WMD) and their associated technologies, something that appears prescient in light of post 9/11 concerns. For the American side, it was designed to enlist European support and contributions for American policies that were already underway. For the EU, it marked an attempt to burnish the image of the Union as a global security player and to be treated as an equal by Washington. Many have argued that it was too broad and too diverse. But it did deliberately omit areas of open disagreement between the US and Europe, such as over rogue states, in an attempt to focus cooperation on issues that could be advanced.

In retrospect, few would dispute the view that the NTA delivered disappointing results. Although it was intended to try to build policies by the US and the EU, it has been described as delivering little more than 'enhanced coordination'.[55] The two sides of the Atlantic were pursuing different foreign policy objectives and many of their positions were incompatible. On a more fundamental level, the EU was in the process of building the integrated structures that would enable it to act more effectively in external relations. As for the American desire to focus attention on global problems, the Europeans were reluctant to follow because they wished to concentrate on issues near at hand, such as organisational enlargement, stabilising Central and Eastern Europe and projecting stability to the Mediterranean. The US, with its well-developed set of priorities, found itself becoming deeply frustrated with the limited amount that the EU could deliver through the NTA. The episodic and erratic EU presidencies were a further source of irritation. The US came to feel that the EU was being selective on global issues: concerned where its economic interests were involved but unwilling to shoulder a greater share of the burden of security issues.[56]

Therefore in both internal and external security cooperation it is possible to discern a pattern in attempts to generate cooperation between the US and the EU. In the 1990s the Union was not an organisation with the requisite maturity to be able to respond to American calls for cooperation. The Union had asserted its ambitions to develop its JHA and CFSP portfolios but time was needed to build the necessary policies and structures. Prior to 9/11 there was not the political will to drive forward cooperation in the face of an increasing threat perception. In these circumstances it was unrealistic to expect the United States to treat the EU as a partner in either internal or external security matters. The US regarded the EU as its most important potential collaborator, but only when the Union was ready to assume this mantle.

Transatlantic cooperation within NATO

The role of NATO in counter-terrorism has been part of a complex debate since the end of the Cold War. The strength of the organisation remains its erstwhile role as a bridge between Europe and the US: a point acknowledged in the Istanbul Summit communiqué when it described the Alliance as providing 'an essential transatlantic dimension to the response against terrorism'.[57] But the difficulty for NATO has resided in what it can contribute to combating terrorism and the wider questions about what roles are appropriate for it in a world in which its former purposes have disappeared. The debate has focused around differing conceptions of organising security in Europe: some states have remained committed to maintaining the Atlanticist framework whilst others have argued for greater European self-reliance. Because NATO was the most important forum for transatlantic military security issues during the Cold War, there has been an in-built conservatism about relinquishing its responsibilities. There have remained certain military roles for the Alliance to fulfil, as demonstrated by the conflicts in Bosnia (1992–5) and Kosovo (1999). But simultaneously there has been a perception that the *status quo* was unsatisfactory. As Daalder and Goldgeier comment, 'NATO cannot justify its existence to either Europeans or Americans if it serves merely as a military alliance against external threats'.[58]

A second problem has been the prospective adaptability of NATO to new security concerns. Some have argued that the Alliance would be an inappropriate organisation to assume non-traditional security tasks. The terrorist menace requires not only a potential military response but also for law enforcement collaboration, judicial action and intelligence sharing. In June 2001 the NATO Secretary General Lord Robertson acknowledged the limitations of the Alliance when he stated that it is 'not a police force . . . and because of its nature, it is not terribly well suited to dealing with law enforcement'.[59] Taking on the role of countering terrorism is a difficult one for an organisation not designed for such a mission.

This is not to deny that there may be military aspects to countering terrorism where NATO's strengths are relevant. The armed forces of the NATO members could be employed in a number of contingencies relating to terrorism. One could be the use of military force against a terrorist group: either on home soil or overseas. Most western states have dedicated counter-terrorist forces embedded within their armed forces and these may be assigned to capture or kill terrorists. A second could be the large-scale deployment of forces against a state actively sponsoring or providing refuge for a terrorist organisation. A third could be the use of specialised military capabilities to track and detain terrorist suspects, such as the use of aerial surveillance or the interdiction of vessels at sea. A fourth could be the provision of military forces to conduct peacekeeping and reconstruction tasks in zones of conflict caused by terrorist activities. A fifth could be the training of allied military forces so that they can operate efficiently together. All of these tasks have been conducted by the militaries of NATO states at various times.

Prior to 9/11, NATO acknowledged the risk posed by terrorism but there was no effort to fundamentally re-configure the Alliance around this threat. The NATO Strategic Concept, drawn up in Rome in 1991, did little more than declare terrorism to be one of the security challenges faced by Alliance members.[60] When the Strategic Concept was re-drafted for the Washington Summit in 1999, it was only after pressure from the United States that a reference was made to terrorism.[61] The post-9/11 environment has rendered it impossible for NATO to ignore the centrality of counter-terrorism. The administration in Washington made it clear that the US would consider the utility of the Alliance in direct relation to its capacity to combat terrorism. Despite NATO's pedigree as the dominant Euro-Atlantic security forum, figures of considerable standing such as Richard Lugar, Chairman of the Senate Foreign Relations Committee, made the case that terrorism and associated issues would become the means for determining the value and relevance of the Alliance.[62]

The fact that NATO is ill configured for counter-terrorism has meant that the US has been reluctant to seek recourse to the organisation. Whilst NATO can legitimise operations because of the breadth of its membership, the US has not required the military support of its allies in order to project its power around the world. This attitude has been reinforced by US doubts over the ability of allies to act alongside technologically more advanced American forces. Influential voices in the Pentagon have argued that the US should not constrain its own freedom of action by relying upon formal alliances. Working within an alliance demands building consensus and only conducting tasks on which all can agree. Instead American forces should work with allies depending upon the task in hand. According to this view, America should opportunistically assemble coalitions according to the needs of the situation.[63] From the point of view of America's allies, the strategy smacks of arrogance and a determination by Washington to carry out its objectives regardless of the attitudes and interests of its friends. In the words of Gnesotto, the US attitudes represented the 'transformation of NATO's military value into a sort of vast reservoir from which *ad hoc* coalitions can be formed'.[64]

US attempts to re-focus NATO upon the War on Terrorism resonate with two other long-cherished American ambitions: one of which has been to broaden the remit of the organisation. Since the end of the Cold War the US has wanted its European allies to play a bigger role in controlling the proliferation of weapons of mass destruction. At the Brussels Summit in 1994 the North Atlantic Council drew up an 'Alliance Policy Framework' that sharpened the focus on the dangers of WMD and created two policy groups. The first was the Senior Politico-Military Group on Proliferation (SGP), to focus on the political dimensions of the problem, and the second was a Senior Defence Group on Proliferation (DGP) to investigate the military ramifications.[65] The events of 9/11 enabled Washington to pressure NATO into focusing on these concerns by pointing out the risks of terrorist groups gaining access to WMD. This led to renewed emphasis on the WMD Centre at NATO headquarters, which was established in 1999. The WMD Centre has the job of sharing information, and conducting, planning and coordinating civil emergency responses amongst the member states.

The other American ambition has been to globalise the activities of the Alliance. The fact that terrorism knows no geographical boundaries strengthened the American argument that NATO needed to be capable of conducting operations in any theatre of the world. The US contended that only by developing a capacity to intervene in regions such as Central Asia or the Middle East could the Alliance remain relevant. The success of the US in getting its way was demonstrated at the NATO Prague Summit in November 2002. The Summit signalled a willingness both to adapt the Alliance to new missions and extend its ability to project force over a long distance.[66] The decision to restructure and instigate a 'Transformation Command' was aimed at developing new military capabilities for out-of-area missions.[67] The creation of a NATO Response Force of 20,000 personnel that could be mobilised within thirty days and sustained at long distance for up to a month, was another important step towards fielding rapid reaction capabilities that could be used in the War on Terrorism.[68]

US priorities to broaden NATO's tasks and globalise its ambitions have not found favour with all its European members. France in particular has sought to resist this American agenda. Paris has contended for over forty years that NATO is dominated by the US who uses it to further selfish American interests. France has been determined to keep NATO out of the counter-terrorism role on the grounds that the Alliance should be employed only for collective defence purposes.[69] Its position modified slightly after 9/11 but it has still tried to constrain the additional missions added to NATO's responsibilities. This was evident at the Reykjavik meeting of May 2002 when a compromise form of wording had to be found to bridge the divide between American and French visions for the future roles of the Alliance.[70] The argument from Paris has been that the EU's European Security and Defence Policy (ESDP), rather than NATO, should take the lead in counter-terrorism roles. ESDP was launched under French and UK leadership at the Helsinki European Council in June 1999, and Paris pressed at the Laeken meeting in December 2001 and the Seville meeting of June 2002 for the EU to assume the mantle of the continent's principal security actor. This brought it into direct opposition with the UK, which was sceptical about relying upon the European Rapid Reaction Force (ERRF) and advocated the continuing primacy of NATO.[71] London was willing to see the EU develop a specialised contribution to the War on Terror, such as earmarking police forces, judicial personnel and administrators to contribute to peacekeeping or post-conflict reconstruction efforts, but it was opposed to circumventing NATO.

Yet debates over the primacy of the EU or NATO, in relation to counter-terrorism, ignored the fundamental reality that the EU remained dependent upon NATO for much of its power projection capabilities.[72] The 'Berlin Plus' arrangements made it possible for the EU to compensate for its modest military capabilities by drawing on the assets of NATO, but only on the assumption that the Alliance would have the right of first refusal over engaging in an operation. Clarke *et al.* argue that power realities impose the need for a division of labour between NATO and the EU that allows each to focus on its strengths.[73] Whilst NATO is the foremost organisation in terms of mobilising military power, the EU has a broader array of instruments to call upon such as aid, trade and diplomacy. To a large extent this division of labour has already been achieved, encouraged by the fact that the two organisations have been working closely together in a variety of situations including the EU staff group at SHAPE, the NATO cell in the EU and operations in Macedonia and Bosnia. In June 2004 there was the first joint seminar on terrorism at ministerial level between the EU and the Alliance prior to the Istanbul Summit,[74] and later that same year NATO Secretary General Jaap de Hoop Scheffer called for enhanced cooperation between the two organisations against terrorism.

A division of labour between the EU and NATO does not imply that Europe can relax its defensive preparations. The capabilities of European states to deploy military forces overseas remains very modest,[75] and a growing gap is evident between Europe and the United States. Whilst countries such as Germany and Italy have allowed defence spending to decline, only France and Britain have increased their spending and undertaken the necessary reforms to increase the deployability of their forces. In short, the European members of NATO need to increase the proportion of the national wealth that they devote to defence and rationalise their spending to decrease the level of duplication. NATO's Defence Capabilities Improvement Plan (DCI) was designed to spur the Europeans into rectifying the shortcomings in their defence inventories.[76]

The specific contributions that NATO can make to the War on Terror lie in two principal areas. First, to act in a supporting and coordination capacity when its member states opt to use military force. The Alliance has long acknowledged that its members are the primary actors in combating terrorism, but it has an important role in providing a framework to facilitate these actions. NATO defence ministers tasked the Alliance, under the political direction of the NAC, to prepare a Military Concept against Terrorism. This was duly approved, as Military Concept 472, at the Prague Summit in November 2002, providing guidelines for how force may be used against terrorist organisations.[77] Such an initiative ensures that NATO members will approach the problem with shared military doctrines and will enable the armed forces of the members to be able to operate together. This was complemented by the steps that NATO has taken within its own structure to provide administrative support and coordination to its members. The Alliance established a task force to coordinate work on combating terrorism and placed it under the control of an Assistant Secretary General for Defence Planning and Operations.[78]

Second, NATO can provide support to any of its member states that are victims of terrorist attack. NATO possesses many strengths that may be of great utility: it has experience of civil contingency planning, it consists of several powerful states whose assistance can be coordinated through the Alliance, and it has its own infrastructure and assets that could be made available to a state that had suffered an attack.[79] NATO has been working on its support functions through its Euro-Atlantic Disaster Response Coordination Centre, which was established in 1998. This comprises only eight people but could be enlarged to a staff of forty in the event of a real emergency. Its remit is to coordinate and improve the ability to respond to disasters of NATO members and Partner countries. NATO has also created a Multinational Chemical, Biological, Radiological and Nuclear Defence Battalion to provide specialist support to its members.[80] In the event of a conventional terrorist outrage, most NATO members possess sufficient resources to be able to cope with an emergency without calling for external assistance. Yet in the event that a terrorist group were to use some sort of weapon of mass destruction, then it becomes much more relevant to consider how disaster relief by many NATO nations would be an invaluable source of help.

The contribution that NATO can make to transatlantic counter-terrorism cooperation continues to evolve. The Alliance has been the cockpit in which rival visions of an Atlanticist or Europeanist security policy have been played out. These rivalries emerged around issues unconnected to terrorism, but counter-terrorism became sucked into the debate after it rose to prominence after 9/11. It is the challenge for both NATO and the EU to learn to work closely together and to make the common cause against international terrorism a source of transatlantic unity rather than division.

Transatlantic cooperation through the G-7/G-8

The Group of Seven, now Group of Eight,[81] leading industrial countries is the last of the major organisational forums in which transatlantic counter-terror cooperation is pursued. It is different in nature to the US-EU and NATO fora for two reasons: it is not a complex organisation with a headquarters and a permanent secretariat, and its composition stretches beyond West European and North American states. Instead the G-8 is a more informal and innovative framework, enabling leaders to discuss matters of common interest.

The G-8 brings together some of the leading western states including the US, UK, France, Germany and Italy, and combines them with Canada, Japan and Russia. Its agenda is more eclectic and its aim is to concert policy.[82] It meets at heads of state level but also includes a meeting place for foreign, finance and interior ministers. The involvement of the European Commission since 1981, originally as an observer, has increased the representative nature of the G-8.

The G-8 has become a favoured framework in which to conduct counter-terrorism cooperation: indeed, the seventh series of summits since 2002 focused explicitly on the subject. One reason for this has been the inherent flexibility that member states can bring to the G-8 issues of current concern. The US has valued this attribute particularly because it has been able to engage in a dialogue on terrorist matters with European states who have not been obligated to defend pre-negotiated positions from within the EU. The US was initially reluctant to accord the G-8 a major role, and it vetoed Italy's suggestion for a special summit meeting.[83] But the US gradually came to accept a larger role for the organisation. The second reason has been that the competences of the G-8 have not been limited to a single sphere of policy but range across economic and foreign policy issues. This has enabled the G-8 to tackle the wider ramifications of terrorism, including financial issues, possible state sponsorship and nuclear proliferation. The third reason is that it has offered a forum separate from NATO. For countries such as Russia and France this has been an important consideration. Russia has traditionally been hostile to NATO, whilst France has wanted to avoid reinforcing the role of the Alliance.

The weaknesses of the G-8 are the converse of its strengths. Because it consists of a diverse group of countries, it frequently struggles to achieve a consensus. Countries such as Russia approach many issues from a different perspective and it is difficult to agree on major policy initiatives. When agreement is reached, the G-8 can find the implementation process problematical because it lacks a strong secretariat like NATO or the EU. Much reliance is placed upon the Presidency to push through policies, but each Presidency comes to the G-8 with its own agenda of items that it would like to see advanced. Last, the breadth of issues within the G-8's purview can be a problem. It can lead to the organisation becoming embroiled in topical but transient issues, resulting in a lack of coherence.

Prior to 9/11 the G-8 was employed by the transatlantic allies to try to develop a broad counter-terrorism agenda, such as calling on all governments to ratify the major anti-terrorism conventions. At the Ottawa meeting in December 1995, the European members and the US pressed for agreement on a clutch of practical measures that could be used to inhibit the activities of terrorist groups. Emphasis was placed on promoting intelligence sharing, increasing the security of chemical, biological and nuclear technologies, and highlighting examples of best practice.[84] The Lyon summit of July 1996 drew attention in particular to the links between organised crime and terrorism.[85] The G-8 crime group became known as the 'Lyon Group', and a list of forty recommendations was drawn up for states to implement in order to present a common front against terrorism. These included closer cooperation over the prosecution and extradition of terrorist suspects, greater intelligence sharing, tighter controls over the inter-state movement of individuals, and the exchange of law enforcement and judicial personnel.

After 9/11 the G-8 has devoted much greater attention to terrorism, and has divided its efforts between the internal and external security domains. In the internal security sphere, the meetings between interior and justice ministers of the G-8 have taken on a higher profile. This is an important forum as it enables internal security matters to be discussed by a group of countries that would not normally come together on this issue. Particular attention has been paid to the threat from international terrorist networks and to CBRN issues.[86] In addition, the G-8 foreign ministers' meeting at Whistler in June 2002 announced new resources for aviation security, enabling the International Civil Aviation Organisation to conduct audits of each state's airline security systems.[87]

In the external security sphere, the G-8 has concentrated its efforts on halting the proliferation of nuclear weapons. The US succeeded in gaining broad-based support for an issue on which it had traditionally taken the lead and borne the greatest proportion of the burden. The summit at Kananaskis in July 2002, the first after the 9/11 attacks, discussed measures to prevent the spread of nuclear, chemical and biological technologies. A major source of concern continued to be the risk of leakage of nuclear materials from the states of the former Soviet Union (FSU).[88] The Evian summit in France in the following year also produced a strong G-8 statement of purpose on the nonproliferation of WMD.

One other aspect of the work of the G-8 that is frequently overlooked is its contribution towards monitoring the integrity of international financial systems and preventing the laundering of illicit funds. G-7 involvement in these issues stemmed from the perception of the damage that could be done to international markets and the economies of developing states by corruption and money laundering.

The original source of motivation for G-7 action was the large amounts of money that were being circulated in the financial system by international organised crime and drug trafficking cartels. Since then, identifying the linkages between terrorism and other forms of criminal activity has been a matter of ongoing concern. The Basle Declaration of Principles in 1988 signalled the importance that was attached to this policy area and led to the creation of the Financial Action Task Force (FATF). The FATF, set up under the auspices of the G-7, consisted not only of G-7 members but also countries such as Belgium, the Netherlands, Australia and Spain.[89] Its focus was initially on banking irregularities, but has been widened subsequently to all sorts of financial transactions. (For a more detailed discussion of the work of the FATF see Chapter 6.)

In relation to counter-terrorism, the G-8 is not a framework as important as either the US-EU relationship or NATO. Some of its detractors argue that it should focus on economic issues and not engage in matters such as terrorism.[90] Nevertheless, it provides another forum in which the transatlantic allies can explore the extent of the common ground between them and advance policies that they hope will be taken up by the wider international community. One of the attractions of the G-8 is that it facilitates a form of 'organisational hopping': when more established frameworks are blocked or a radical new idea is being floated, the G-8 provides a place in which this can be pursued.

Conclusion

Transatlantic counter-terrorism cooperation has been developing in the context of pre-existing organisations such as NATO, the EU-US relationship and the G-8. Early forms of collaboration had been present for some time, but it took the catastrophic events of 9/11 to provide the political impetus to expand and systematise the cooperation. Because these new patterns of cooperation have been grafted on to organisations that were designed for different purposes, the resulting activity is sub-optimal in nature. However, the costs and complexity of creating a dedicated organisation to deal exclusively with counter-terrorism was considered prohibitive and unrealistic. With no single organisation to encapsulate these efforts, then it has ranged across various frameworks in an opportunistic fashion.

Amidst this panoply of organisations, the combating of international terrorism has grown most strongly in the context of US-EU relations. This has reflected both the growing importance of the

EU amongst its members and its capacity to offer cooperation to the US across the broadest range of policy fields.[91] NATO has adapted its remit to include global security concerns, but terrorism is not something that the Alliance has been well placed to tackle. This has added greater complexity to the transatlantic relationship because NATO was the traditional repository of the US-European security dialogue. For its part, the G-8 is of less importance but it adds a flexible forum in which new initiatives can be pursued.

The US and Europe have worked together through bilateral as well as multilateral channels. Bilateral cooperation against terrorism enjoys many advantages in being able to build on established linkages between law enforcement and intelligence agencies on either side of the Atlantic. Yet the transatlantic allies have found that bilateralism needs to be supplemented by multilateralism. In a world of rapidly changing priorities, states need to work together in frameworks that enable the largest number of actors to align their policies. Common sets of standards need to be agreed and those states that are reluctant to raise their standards need to feel the pressure of their peers. Because the countering of international terrorism demands a diverse range of issues to be targeted simultaneously, multilateral cooperation can provide added value. Furthermore, multilateral frameworks represent the values of their members and offer the prospect of holding interstate relations together when crises loom.

3 Contrasting threat perceptions

Introduction

The security threat posed by international terrorism is very different to that which dominated transatlantic relations during the Cold War. The USSR and its Warsaw Pact allies presented an overarching military threat that put at risk the territorial integrity of Western Europe. This justified European dependence on the United States, for no other country had the ability to counterbalance the Soviet Union. By contrast, the threat from international terrorism is much more diffuse: the enemy is shadowy and a simple military response is inappropriate. The fact that the risks are difficult to calculate has contributed to disagreement between the two sides of the Atlantic. It is ironic that whilst common threat perceptions used to underpin the transatlantic relationship during the Cold War, they risk dividing them today.

The challenges presented by international terrorism are becoming harder to calculate because its nature has been changing. In the words of Haas, 'Before states can agree . . . on how to deal collectively with a specific problem, they must reach some consensus about the nature and the scope of the problem.'[1] In the past, terrorism was an instrument used by the weak against the strong in order to achieve a political objective. Shootings, bombings, kidnappings and other acts of violence were designed to create a sense of insecurity amongst a target population, thereby pressuring governments and attracting the maximum degree of publicity. A terrorist event was designed to send ripples radiating outwards to a wider community. The amount of damage caused as a result of the violence and the extent of the casualties was usually a secondary issue compared to the desire to influence public opinion. With the end of the Cold War, many of the Middle Eastern terrorist groups went into decline as their state sponsors, such as Libya and Syria, curtailed their support.

Writers such as Hoffman have argued that a 'new' form of terrorism has been emerging over the last decade.[2] This terrorism has a different rationale, usually a religious motivation, that aims to destroy those who are deemed to oppose the spread of that belief system. Such terrorism seeks to inflict the highest levels of casualties upon its enemies and is not constrained by the need to gain public approbation.[3] The perpetrators are often heedless of their own safety and actively seek martyrdom in the service of their cause. Raufer notes several other trends in relation to contemporary terrorism. These include its de-territorialisation; an increasingly hybrid nature that is partly criminal and partly political and, finally, its increasing lethality.[4]

The fact that such terrorists are willing to cause as much damage as possible to a society raises the issue of their potential access to weapons of mass destruction. This is where the boundaries of the subject of international terrorism become blurred and link up with the more traditional security agenda focused on the proliferation of WMD and 'states of concern' that are hostile to western interests. Some countries might be capable of developing WMD and could make the technology available to terrorist groups.[5] Asmus and Pollack note this change between old and contemporary experiences of terrorism: 'This threat is not just terrorism of the sort many countries, particularly in Europe, have known in past decades. It is the interweaving of terrorism, weapons of mass destruction, and failed and rogue states from Marrakesh to Bangladesh.'[6]

Militant Islam

International terrorism is not restricted to one ethnic group or even one religion; rather it is an instrument of choice by several types of movements around the world. Nevertheless, terrorism perpetrated by 'Islamists' – namely those carrying out a political project based upon an extremist understanding of the Koran and the teachings of the prophet Mohammed – are deemed to be the principal source of threat to the West. Muller justifies this choice on the grounds that 'the number of terrorists of the Islamic faith is larger . . . it is the only religiously motivated terrorism that has managed to create a transnational, globally organised network'.[7]

Militant Islam has grown from a number of sources, and it is beyond the scope of this book to explore them in detail. One source has been indigenous radical groups that have advocated a 'holy war' or 'jihad' against non-believers.[8] This call for a religiously inspired conflict has served to define their own identity and demonstrate their rejection of the value system of the societies from which they have emerged. Al-Qaeda ('the base') is an illustration of such an organisation, stemming from the Wahabbi movement in Saudi Arabia. It has been successful in acting as the facilitator for jihadist violence by disparate groups of fighters around the world.[9] Its leader, Osama bin Laden, issued a 'fatwa' – or religious edict – in 1998 declaring that it was the duty of all Muslims to kill citizens of the United States. The targeting of America has been due to a number of factors. Its status as the leading exponent of the values that Islamists reject has made it a focus of their hatred.

Many of the Islamist groups are not centrally controlled but maintain loose linkages based upon a common ideological standpoint. The extent of these linkages and the material support that flows between them is a subject of contestation in the literature.[10] Pillar describes bin Laden as being at the centre of concentric circles of Sunni radicalism: the inner circle over which he has direct control; outer circles in which his organisation may only have made a financial contribution; and finally of distant circles in which he may only be an inspiration.[11] The fact that the groups are structured around cells of highly dedicated individuals has presented a particular problem for western intelligence-gathering agencies. According to Simon and Benjamin, 'The looseness of these networks, and the way in which the cells within them coalesce, makes identification, penetration and disruption of the groups extremely difficult'.[12] The head of the UK domestic intelligence service, MI5, described Al-Qaeda as being the antithesis of the old hierarchical and structured organisations of the past.[13]

Militant Islam has also received an impetus from hard-line governments that have shared some of the jihadist ideals. The theocratic governments in Iran and Sudan have sought legitimacy by calling for a world-wide Islamic revolution in which countries are governed according to the guidelines of the faith. Such countries have been willing to provide support to armed groups that either employ a strategy based on terrorism or are prepared to use violence against the opponents of their regimes. Even Saddam Hussein's Iraq provided support to the families of Palestinian suicide bombers in the territories occupied by Israel. This was probably less about Islamic fervour and more of an attempt to be seen as a leader in the Arab world.

The grounds on which Islamists justify their radicalisation over the last two decades relates to a series of injustices that have been perpetrated against Muslims. One of the injustices relates to the repressive, secular governments in countries such as Algeria and Egypt which have failed to deliver good governance and economic prosperity to their peoples. Poverty and unemployment among the young have been important, but not exclusive, sources of recruitment for Islamist groups.[14] Another sense of injustice has derived from conflicts around the world in which Muslims have been the principal victims. The Soviet invasion of Afghanistan in 1979 sparked the beginning of the Mujahideen resistance that later provided a host of well-trained and well-armed warriors willing to fight on behalf of their faith in various parts of the world. The long-running conflict over Kashmir has been a major grievance, as has more recently the plight of Muslims in Bosnia fighting ethnic Serbs and those in Chechnya fighting the Russians.

This sense of injustice has been turned against the West, and particularly the United States, based on a perception that they have been inactive in protecting Muslims from aggression and persecution. The West delayed intervening with decisive force in the Bosnian conflict and did little to restrain Russian atrocities in Chechnya. In the case of the Palestinians, the US has made no secret of its support for the state of Israel and has provided weapons and financial aid to that country against Arab states in the wars of 1956, 1967 and 1973. As for authoritarian regimes in Muslim countries, many have enjoyed western support and economic assistance. The Saudi Arabian government was willing to allow a US military presence to reside on its soil, despite the fact that some of the holiest sites of Islam are situated within the country. In the 2003 war against Iraq, the US led a coalition of western countries that invaded the sovereign territory of an Arab state and removed Saddam Hussein from power.

The 9/11 Commission Report argues that the threat to the West comes in two forms.[15] The first is Al-Qaeda, whose strength has been degraded since the American and European responses to the 9/11 attacks. The second is the network of radical Islamic groups who have been motivated by the success of 9/11 and incensed by the US conflicts in Afghanistan and Iraq. These two groups seek to inflict the maximum pain on western societies and cause them to withdraw their presence from the Arab world. These groups also seek the overthrow of pro-western Muslim regimes and the instigation of religiously pure Islamic governments.

The European experience of terrorism

The transatlantic allies share a common opposition to terrorism not least because they recognise that they are all potential targets. However, they have different historical experiences of the phenomenon and this has influenced how they have responded to the contemporary threat. Even within Western Europe, experiences of terrorism have varied and this has contributed to divergent attitudes amongst countries.

Some countries in Europe, such as the Netherlands and Belgium, have been fortunate to avoid any real experience of domestic terrorism. Other countries such as France, Spain and the UK have had significant, on-going difficulties. Spain suffered with Basque terrorism until its decline, after 1990, to a sporadic level of violence for the rest of that decade.[16] The UK faced a determined and highly professional adversary in the form of the Provisional Irish Republican Army (PIRA) until the Good Friday Agreement in 1998. Since then it has only experienced occasional acts of violence from splinter groups such as the Real IRA. French support for the Algerian government in its conflict with the Armed Islamic Group (GIA) led to terrorism in France, especially prevalent in 1995 and 1996. Germany experienced some terrorist problems as a result of its large Kurdish and Turkish communities, but this declined in intensity in the 1990s. According to Chalk, 'it is only those states which have suffered extensively from the problem of terrorism that have developed any meaningful sense of urgency for firm collaborative endeavours'.[17]

The result of European experiences of terrorism was that it was regarded primarily as a domestic issue – only Palestinian terrorism in the 1970s impacted more broadly on the continent. This accounts for the different approaches of states towards addressing the problem as each formulated their own methods and priorities. It contributed to an unwillingness to cooperate together. European states sometimes refused to extradite individuals accused of terrorist crimes on the grounds that those crimes were political in nature. By the 1990s even indigenous European terrorist groups were declining, and international movements were not judged to be a major threat. An illustration of this perception was a JHA Council debate on terrorism in November 2000 that was devoted almost entirely to the Basque problem in Spain. Europe was reluctant to align itself too closely to the US in counter-terrorism because America had become the foremost target of extremist Islamists. Terrorism was seen through some European eyes as the price America paid for its activism in the Middle East and its overt support for Israel. Furthermore, European governments were wary of putting in jeopardy their access to Middle Eastern oil.

The European appreciation of the threat from international terrorism altered after 9/11.[18] There was a desire in Europe to influence America's response. Governments on the continent were fearful that a counter-terrorism crusade on the part of the United States could result in it becoming detached from its long-standing ties with European allies. UK Prime Minister Tony Blair was the chief spokesman for this perspective, but he was supported by prime ministers Silvio Berlusconi of Italy and Jose Maria Aznar of Spain. Tony Blair expressed his misgivings to a group of diplomats in London in January 2003 when he said that in relation to international terrorism, 'America should not be forced to take this issue on alone'.[19] The other factor accounting for the change of attitude was the *modus operandi* of the 9/11 attackers. The sophistication and planning of the bombers and the death toll that they inflicted was sufficient to stir out of their relative complacency even those European states that had little experience of domestic terrorism. Den Boer notes that the impact of 9/11 resulted in 'The EU's discourse on terrorism . . . moving from state-based terrorism to globally dispersed terrorism'.[20]

There was widespread recognition that Europe was especially vulnerable to this form of international Islamist terrorism. Some of the perpetrators of the attacks on New York and Washington had been resident in Hamburg, illustrating that Europe had been a benign environment in which to prepare their operations. Terrorist suspects were apprehended subsequently in Spain, the UK, France, Belgium and Italy, and the authorities revealed that intended attacks in Europe had been foiled.[21] If any doubts about the seriousness of the threat to Europe remained, then they were dispelled by the 11 March 2004 attacks on the railway network in Madrid, which killed over 200 people, and the 7 July 2005 attacks in London, which killed over forty people. The Madrid bombings were evidence of the links established by Al-Qaeda with Islamists from North African countries such as Algeria and Morocco. Spain was probably targeted because of the support of its government for the US-led wars in Afghanistan and Iraq. The London bombings illustrated the potential radicalisation of domestic Muslims who had grown up and made their lives in the UK.

The discovery of cells of militants in European cities has thrown the spotlight on the broader issue of large Muslim immigrant populations resident in Western Europe. In the Netherlands there are 1 million Muslims, in the UK 1.5 million, in Germany just over 4 million and in France 6 million.[22] Many of these people have integrated themselves into these countries, secured good jobs and comfortable lives. Yet other immigrants, especially those from poorer countries such as Pakistan and Algeria, have suffered from racism and discrimination and struggled to find economic opportunities. The assertion of their culture and religion has provided a means to express their identity, but some have proceeded to reject any concept of integration.[23] This, in turn, has caused resentment within western society that interprets such outward expressions of piety as the strict Islamic dress code as a rejection of its own values.

Roy refers to the phenomenon of 'diasporic radicalisation' in which Muslim immigrants, who have failed to prosper in their new societies, become increasingly alienated.[24] What proportion of these immigrant populations share sympathies with extreme Islamist groups has been hard to determine. A Dutch Member of Parliament, Geert Wilders, who started a new political party that argues for tougher state policies towards Islamic radicals, estimates that 10–15 per cent of the Muslim population may be sympathetic to jihadist ideology.[25] The fact that the US has embarked upon a 'War on Terror', that is equated by critics as a 'War against Islam', adds fuel to fears that greater militancy may be forthcoming from Europe's Muslim populations. Certain commentators have opined that Europe has been slow to realise this threat to its domestic security.[26] In the words of Fukuyama, 'Europeans are threatened internally by radical Islam in a much more severe way than Americans are in terms of their external threat'.[27] Stevenson contends that 'Europe clearly has a serious transnational Islamic terrorist problem'.[28]

It is no secret that the domestic intelligence services in Europe have altered their priorities so as to focus more of their effort on watching Islamic radicals. France, Britain, Italy and Spain have been sharing intelligence on radical Islamists suspected of attending training camps overseas.[29] Mosques, in which there are imams who have a reputation for inflammatory preaching, are being monitored. An attempt has been made to target pockets of extremism before it can affect a wider religious community. For example, in the UK, the radical cleric Abu Hamza was arrested and accused of inciting violence and encouraging Muslims to train overseas for jihad. The Dutch intelligence service, the AIVD, acknowledges that religious tension is a growing problem within its own society. This takes the form of both independent militant cells undertaking acts of violence and the stirring up of enmity between Muslims and the rest of society.[30] Tensions within the Netherlands have been exacerbated by cases of violence carried out against people who have criticised Islamist culture, such as the murder of the controversial film maker Theo van Gogh.

Europe has come to recognise that it is particularly vulnerable to this form of threat. Its open borders and tradition of immigration, its single market and its complex mix of law enforcement bodies and legal systems, make it a relatively easy target for Islamist violence. As the threat crosses the old divide between internal and external security,

Europe has been forced to come together and to find new means to address the challenge.

The American experience of terrorism

Unlike many of the leading West European states, the US has been fortunate in having limited experience of domestic terrorism. That is not to say that there have been no examples of terrorism on US territory in the past. There were the activities of the Weather Underground in the late 1960s and early 1970s,[31] bombings by extreme religious groups, attacks on abortion clinics,[32] and incidents carried out by the Earth Liberation Front and the Animal Liberation Front. However, such attacks have been infrequent and localised and the US has not had to combat a sustained terrorist campaign by a disaffected group. The bombing of the Oklahoma Federal Building in 1995, by a militia group vehemently opposed to the government, was the first major terrorist attack by American citizens.[33] A foretaste of what was to come took place in 1993 when there was a bomb attack on New York's World Trade Center. The bomb inflicted serious damage but it failed in its intention to topple the twin towers. The attack was conducted by an Islamist organisation and represented a major attempt to inflict harm on US territory by a transnational group.

Because there had been so few terrorist attacks on American soil, there was an underlying perception in the body politic that its homeland was invulnerable. Thus, the 9/11 attacks had an even greater impact on the American psyche than might have been expected. In the 1980s and the 1990s only 871 US citizens had died in attacks attributed to terrorism.[34] In the 9/11 attacks 2,783 people were killed, making it the largest terrorist atrocity ever recorded. In addition, the attacks took place in the nation's capital and in its foremost city, and destroyed the symbol of its leading position in the global trading system as well as severely damaging the headquarters of its armed services. No comparable blow had been struck against the American homeland since the strike on Pearl Harbor in 1941, and that had been made by a foreign government on the military forces of the United States; not by a transnational actor on civilians.

The US has experienced terrorism more as an overseas problem than a home-grown one. In the words of Vice President Al Gore's assistant for national security affairs, Leon Fuerth, 'terrorism was a problem elsewhere in the world'.[35] Throughout the 1980s and 1990s, the US has suffered from a series of grievous attacks on its citizens, property and interests – the 1983 bombing of the US embassy and the marine complex in Beirut; the 1986 bombing of a discotheque frequented by American servicemen in Berlin; the 1996 bombing of the Khobar Towers in Saudi Arabia; and the 1998 bombing of the US embassies in Africa. By 1998, of the 273 terrorist attacks that occurred in that year, 40 per cent of them were directed against the United States.[36] The US had become accustomed to regarding terrorism as a foreign-inspired phenomenon. That experience has been instrumental in shaping America's response, relying upon external policy instruments to counter the threat.

This experience also conditioned America's attitude towards terrorism in Europe. The US regarded terrorist attacks in Europe as a national problem for those governments rather than a shared threat. The US had limited experience to offer and was not minded to provide cooperation to the countries affected. The occasional forays into the terrorist problems of European countries tended to reflect the interests of particular presidents, such as Bill Clinton's interventions in the politics of Northern Ireland in the mid-1990s. It was therefore an irony that the 9/11 attacks on the United States led it to call on its European allies for a mobilisation against international terrorism.[37]

There was a sense at the end of the 1990s that the threat to the United States from terrorism was increasing and that a new level of priority was warranted. For example, the Hart-Rudman Commission on National Security in the Twenty-First Century warned of the growing risk of a major attack on US soil.[38] Similarly, the National Commission on Terrorism in 2000 called for more determined steps and higher funding to meet the challenge. It argued that the President should impose sanctions on countries not wholehearted in the fight against terror and went so far as to name allies of the US, such as Pakistan and Greece.[39]

The Clinton administration could not be accused of neglecting the danger posed by international terrorism. Indeed, Richard Clarke heaped praise on the industry of the Clinton period. He went on to castigate its successor, the Bush administration, on the grounds that he, the Counter Terrorism Coordinator at the National Security Council, was unable to obtain the attention of key officials right up to the time of the Al-Qaeda attacks.[40] President Clinton pursued an energetic course in raising awareness of the risks of terrorism. In his address to the UN General Assembly on 22 October 1995 Clinton called for a common fight against terrorism and placed it in the category of one of the foremost security challenges facing the world, along with crime and drug trafficking. With numerous terrorist incidents taking place in the 1990s, the US government was more focused on the threat from international terrorism than most of its allies. After the attacks on the US embassies in Africa, the US exercised a military response against Afghanistan and Sudan. It also proceeded, under Presidential Decision Directive-63, to allocate over $10 billion to the protection of key infrastructures both within the US and overseas. Terrorism changed from being treated as a tactical to a strategic problem that required considerable new assets and the coordination of government responses.[41]

After the 9/11 attacks, the Bush administration reacted swiftly. Now that the US had been struck on its own soil, a military response conducted overseas was deemed to be insufficient. On the one hand, the US began planning a military operation against Al-Qaeda in Afghanistan. This was viewed as the first step in a wider war against international terrorism.[42] Bush refused to say that this was a war against Islamic terrorism because he was fearful of appearing to target Muslims and alienate Muslim states that would be vital allies.[43] On the other hand, the US began to develop a strategy for the defence of its homeland: a project without precedent in American history.

The state sponsorship of terrorism

State sponsorship of terrorist groups has concerned the United States for some considerable time. As the dominant power within the international system, America has been hostile to states that reject its leadership and seek to advance ideologies and interests inimical to the US.[44] Since the end of the Cold War some of the countries that used to receive Soviet patronage, such as Iraq, Syria and Libya, were cut off from that material support. They have been forced to survive within an international system increasingly dominated by American power, and have been deterred from challenging the *status quo* overtly. Two options have presented themselves to former sponsors of terrorism. One has been to turn away from this sort of activity. There has been evidence of groups, such as the Popular Front for the Liberation of Palestine, suffering a significant downturn in their support. Alternatively, some states have increased their support because terrorism has offered a means to inflict pain on the US through asymmetric means, at a time when America has been unassailable in conventional military power.[45] Iran, for example, whilst not a major beneficiary of former Soviet funding, has nevertheless tried to continue to wage a covert conflict against the state of Israel and its American backer.

State sponsorship can add significantly to the capabilities of terrorist groups and can take many forms. Direct support might result in the provision of weapons or training bases in which recruits can be equipped with the skills to execute their activities. Afghanistan, for example, provided bases for Al-Qaeda in which between 10,000 and 50,000 individuals were trained. Indirect support might result in the provision of finance, communications, logistics or even refuge from retaliation. States may provide these various forms of assistance because they share similar ideologies with terrorist organisations or because these groups can be used as instruments against the country's enemies.

Yet it is important to bear in mind that state sponsorship also provides opportunities for combating terrorism. Contact with state sponsors can serve to bring terrorist groups out of the shadows and into the limelight. Counter-terrorist efforts can focus on influencing state sponsors who might be more vulnerable to threats of coercion than terrorist groups. Closing down the support base and infrastructure of terrorist groups can be a powerful weapon in the hands of the international community. One of the problems of any counter-terrorism strategy involving the military is the absence of high-value targets to attack. But state sponsors of terrorism are likely to possess targets of value, and by either striking or threatening to strike at these, pressure may be put on the sponsors to alter their behaviour.

The attention paid by the US towards these so-called 'rogue' states or 'states of concern' increased in the 1990s. This was evident from the first Clinton administration when National Security Adviser Anthony Lake wrote an article in the journal *Foreign Affairs*.[46] In essence, this was a statement of administration policy towards these countries. Lake argued that by rejecting the precepts of the existing international order these states presented a threat to the US. He contended that these states were international pariahs that presented a variety of dangers. First, they threatened the security of their neighbours, such as in the case of North Korea's threat to South Korea. Second, they abused the human rights of their own people and challenged the values of the international system. Third, they could provide terrorist groups with access to ever more dangerous categories of weapons.

The US has sought, since the beginning of the 1990s, to confront such states and pressurise them into altering their policies. The mechanism by which the US government has designated states as sponsors of terrorism has been the Export Administration Act of 1979. An annual certification of countries is conducted by the US Department of State, and those regarded as incompliant with the Act are barred from trading or receiving all forms of American assistance. The economic penalties that the US can bring to bear are extensive: ranging from restrictions on trading, technology transfer, foreign assistance, export credits and guarantees and foreign exchange transactions, to economic embargo. Under the International Emergency Economic Powers Act, the President can declare an issue to be a threat to national security and then impose economic sanctions on a state.[47]

Post-9/11, the US has placed greater pressure on those states it suspects of supporting terrorism, demanding that they give up all means of assistance and the offer of sanctuary, and abide by the international counter-terrorism conventions. The promulgation of a national strategy for counter-terrorism was an unmistakable signal to state sponsors that the US intended to act forcefully and decisively with those that aligned themselves with terrorist organisations.[48] In his address to Congress just after the attacks President Bush declared that 'Every nation, in every region, now has a decision to make. Either you are with us, or you are with the terrorists.'[49]

Europe has diverged with the US over policy towards alleged state sponsors of terrorism. Rather than isolating and punishing countries, Europe has tended to believe that dialogue and multilateral pressure is likely to prove most fruitful.[50] They have been much more willing to engage in diplomatic relations with governments treated as pariahs by Washington.[51] Europeans have sought ways to encourage state sponsors to disassociate themselves or to rein in groups that they can influence. European policies should not be read as being indifferent to the phenomenon of terrorism. As Hoffman notes, 'It would be misleading to see Europe's comparatively conciliatory position on state-sponsored terrorism as reflecting a laissez-faire attitude toward indigenous or regional threats'.[52]

Failed states

'Failed states' are a different category of actors pertinent to the debate about sponsorship of terrorism. These are states where there has been a breakdown in governance and the maintenance of law and order and territorial security. Prior to 9/11 these states were seen as representing problems of lawlessness, an inability to satisfy the needs of their people and the risk that they might degenerate into civil conflict. The Clinton administration sought to address some of the root causes of state disintegration and even intervened in the case of Somalia. Post-9/11, these states are seen in a different light, as providing a potential permissive environment in which terrorists could thrive.[53]

The European Security Strategy, published in December 2003 at the European Council,[54] also acknowledged the importance of failed states but exhibited a different emphasis to the US position. The Europeans are more predisposed to see these states as victims. They argue that the risk presented by these countries derives from their fragility; that they needed to be assisted to prevent them from becoming political vacuums. European states have been prepared to become involved in nation-building and post-conflict reconstruction, in areas such as the Balkans, West Africa and Afghanistan. This has reflected European beliefs that resources, investment and even peace-keeping operations can help to tackle some of the root causes that lead states to collapse.

This reflected some of the thinking of Robert Cooper, the chief architect of the European Security Strategy. Cooper had long warned that the international system was becoming more polarised between states of different levels of development. Cooper divided the world into categories of 'pre-modern', 'modern' and 'post-modern' states. He argued that 'pre-modern' states were slipping further behind, in terms of prosperity and good governance, than the 'modern' and 'post-modern' states and that the risk of conflict would increase from these weak and unstable countries.[55] He drew attention to the risk of pre-modern states impacting on the security of the post-modern, as a result of being unwitting hosts of armed groups rather than as inherent threats in their own right.

The US, in contrast to the Europeans, has tended to focus on the danger that could emanate from these countries. Terrorist groups might feel confident that they were not at risk from law enforcement or judicial prosecution because of the collapse in the effectiveness of the agencies of the state. Alternatively, criminal groups could gain political power and enter into cooperation with terrorist groups for financial gain. The Bush administration has feared that failed states could provide a sanctuary from where terrorists could project threats into the West.[56] The US has been unwilling to share the European focus on these states as the hapless victims of outside pressures, and has been sceptical about the viability of nation-building. Many of the ideologues within the Bush administration have been suspicious that participation in grand notions of nation-building would result in excessive burdens being placed on the shoulders of the American government.

Terrorists and weapons of mass destruction

The greatest concern over international terrorism has been that a state pursuing a clandestine WMD programme could make that technology available to a terrorist group. The inherent complexity of developing a nuclear weapon and the difficulty of procuring the necessary components, such as fissile material, has made the task of producing a functioning device an enormous obstacle to a terrorist organisation. Thus, the most likely manner in which a group could gain access to such technology would be through a state sponsor.

The Clinton administration made strenuous efforts to alert the international community to the risk of a state making such technology available to terrorists. This was highlighted as early as December 1993 in the 'Defense Counterproliferation Initiative' that sought to develop American capabilities to overcome this danger.[57] The administration argued that the nexus between terrorism, WMD and states of concern was the foremost threat to international security.[58] This assessment was enshrined in Presidential Decision Directive 39 and was reinforced by the subsequent experience of 9/11. The ruthlessness of the hijackers, determined to destroy the maximum number of non-combatants, illustrated graphically the danger that would exist if such individuals had access to a nuclear weapon. In such circumstances, non-state actors would have acquired the destructive capability that has hitherto only been available to a small number of countries. This would fundamentally alter the nature of the threat posed by terrorism. Freedman has called this prospect 'Superterrorism' whilst Muller termed it 'Megaterrorism'.[59]

President Bush, speaking to Congress in 2002, picked up this theme and used it to justify a new hard-line American approach towards states of concern. He argued that states that had traditionally been hostile to the interests and allies of the US could furnish terrorist groups with the capacity to inflict enormous damage upon America. He alleged that Iran, Iraq and North Korea 'and their terrorist allies, constitute an axis of evil . . . By seeking weapons of mass destruction, these regimes pose a grave and growing danger. They could provide these arms to terrorists, giving them the means to match their hatred.'[60] The 'National Security Strategy', announced by the White House in 2002, identified the threat of rogue states arming terrorists with WMD as the key security challenge facing the United States. The threat posed by terrorists obtaining such technologies was reinforced by the 'National Strategy to Combat Weapons of Mass Destruction', which focused almost exclusively on this scenario.[61] A fundamental re-appraisal of America's foreign policy priorities was based on a hypothetical risk.

On this issue there have been differences between US and European threat perceptions. Prior to 9/11, the possibility of terrorists acquiring WMD from state sponsors was thought unlikely in Europe. Yet the importance that was attached to this issue by the Bush administration caused European governments to re-consider the matter, if only to avoid being too far out of step with Washington. The European Security Strategy acknowledged the risks of WMD falling into the hands of terrorists but set it in the context of a range of other security challenges, including organised crime and environmental degradation. The Europeans were prepared to go some way towards the US position but not to embrace it fully.

However, a certain degree of scepticism is appropriate in relation to this threat. Falkenrath *et al.* argue that two schools of thought have been present in relation to the possible use of WMD by terrorists: those that thought it inevitable and those whose complacency ruled out the prospect altogether.[62] No evidence has ever been found that points to a state being willing to make a nuclear weapon available to a terrorist group. The difficulty even for governments of mobilising the capability to construct such awesome weapons, should not be under-estimated. Should a government succeed in doing so, despite the existence of the nuclear non-proliferation regime, then it would be an enormous risk for that government to give this technology over to a sub-state group. Muller argues against such a scenario on several grounds.[63] First, the state would be relinquishing a supremely important weapon into the hands of individuals over whom it might have little control. Second, with an inability to control the terrorist organisation, the state would always be at risk of having the weapon turned against itself. Third, western countries might be able to trace a nuclear device back from the terrorist group to the state that provided the weapon. This would leave the state sponsor vulnerable to the devastating retaliatory capabilities of countries such as the United States, the United Kingdom and France.[64]

This opens to challenge the simple assumption that the threat derives from states hostile to western interests. In reality, the most significant danger to date seems to have come from the Pakistani nuclear scientist, A. Q. Khan, who sold technology to anyone capable of paying sufficient money.[65] It was ironic that Pakistan, ostensibly an ally of the West, was the country that enabled the Khan network to flourish, although President Pervez Musharraf claimed this was done without the knowledge of his government. Conversely, Libya was a country that was seen as a major supporter of terrorism as well as a state seeking to acquire WMD. But the government of Qhaddafi subsequently abandoned its weapons programmes, invited outside inspections of its facilities and renounced its support for terrorism. This illustrates how simplistic assumptions about threats can prove to be erroneous.

Another assumption that is open to dispute is whether nuclear weapons are the most likely instruments of mass destruction to become available to terrorists. Biological or chemical weapons are actually at greater risk of falling into the hands of sub-state groups. These weapons require relatively limited technological sophistication and financial resources to produce. Such capabilities are frequently referred to as the 'nuclear weapons of the poor'. In the words of one specialist, biological agents are the 'weapon(s) of choice for both state and nonstate actors seeking to inflict maximum damage while minimising the risks of detection and retaliation'.[66] Such weapons may not be used on a large scale but they could cause panic amongst a civilian population. Evidence from documents in Afghanistan show that Al-Qaeda was interested in developing such weapons and that some of the jihadi training camps were providing individuals with instruction in chemical and biological warfare techniques.

The US has taken the threat from chemical and biological weapons seriously because of its experiences during the Cold War.[67] In 1973 it negotiated and signed the Biological Weapons Convention (BWC) in which all sides agreed to dismantle their stockpiles and research facilities connected with biological weapons. In spite of this, the Soviets built up a massive, covert stockpile of biological weapons that the US did not discover until after the end of the Cold War. This demonstrated the comparative ease with which such weapons can be hidden. The US has taken the view that a state sponsor of terrorism could pursue a secret weapons programme that would not be known to western intelligence agencies. This might make it more attractive for a state to provide such a capability to a terrorist group, as it would facilitate the means to deliver a major blow against the West whilst publicly disavowing any weapons programme.

The principal obstacle to the efficient employment of either biological or chemical weapons remains 'weaponising' the substances, dispersing them effectively and controlling the results so that the perpetrator is not harmed. The attempt by the Aum Shinrikyo sect to release Sarin gas on the Tokyo subway in 1995 illustrated the difficulty of using such agents as indiscriminate weapons. The anthrax attacks in the US in 2001 and the discovery of ricin in the UK confirmed the seriousness of these threats. In January 2002, President Bush responded to the new situation by authorising $2.9 billion of spending for bio-terrorism preparedness.[68] This was twice the figure that the Clinton administration had allocated to nuclear, chemical and biological preparations.[69]

Two other forms of terrorism that have hitherto been neglected but are gradually receiving increased attention are radiological weapons and so-called 'cyber' attacks. The former is a bomb in which radiological material is packed around a conventional explosive device. Although there would be no fission or fusion reaction, the explosion would cause radioactive contamination which could render the centre of a city uninhabitable for decades.[70] Such a 'dirty' bomb presents a much more likely possibility than a nuclear explosion because of the relative profusion of radiological materials, such as in hospitals or universities, compared to the problems of obtaining enriched plutonium.[71] The seriousness with which this threat is taken is attested to by the decision of the European Council, in December 2004, to examine ways in which the EU as a whole could increase its readiness to deal with radiological attacks.[72]

Cyber-terrorism involves the deliberate targeting of computer services that provide a range of vital services. These include agricultural and food production systems, power generation, banking and computer networks and health care. The damage can be inflicted by hacking into them, by overloading them with fraudulent electronic messages or corrupting them with viruses. Although this form of activity is usually conducted at an individual level, if it is supported by the resources of a state, then it may become particularly damaging. Advanced western societies have come to recognise their vulnerability to this threat.[73] The seriousness with which this issue is viewed is demonstrated by the fact that the Clinton administration requested $2 billion for cyber-security in 2001, and the US has proceeded to draw up a dedicated 'National Strategy to Secure Cyberspace'.[74] In contrast, the Europeans have been much slower to take the threat of cyber-attacks seriously. It was not until December 2004 that the European Council decided to set up a programme to protect the critical infrastructures of European states.[75]

The post-9/11 War on Terror has led to a group of issues being bundled together. This has caused perceptions of threat to be undifferentiated and unclear.[76] There has been a tendency to conflate terrorist groups, whose access to WMD would be extremely problematic, with states seeking to develop WMD for their own security needs. This has brought two implications for the transatlantic relationship. One has been the divergence of view between the US and Europe. The other has been that all potential threats have been treated as in need of urgent solutions, which may in the long term prove to be unsustainable.

Strategic culture

To explain differences in threat perceptions and the responses that they evoke between European states and the US, it is necessary to look at the differing politico-military cultures of the two sides. The concept of 'strategic culture' is associated with states as they are the legitimate wielders of force in the international system. Strategic culture arises from a mixture of sources: the historical experience of the people of that state; the material power of the country; its domestic political system and the contemporary international environment.[77] Although contested and imprecise, it is a useful concept for understanding the cognitive process through which countries consider the use of coercion. In the words of Toje, 'strategic culture provides a framework in which an actor approaches the questions of threat (or use) of force – and the broader question of hard power capabilities as policy resources'.[78]

The United States possesses a clear and easily identifiable strategic culture. Domestic influences that have shaped its strategic culture include the right of its citizens to bear arms, the belief in American exceptionalism and the prestige accorded to its armed forces. In the twentieth and twenty-first centuries, its superpower status has been a decisive factor, and has steered America away from the path of isolationism to intervene decisively in two world wars and then engage in a prolonged military stand-off with the Soviet Union. America's leadership within the West, and its alliances and commitments in the Far East and Middle East, gave it responsibilities that it sought to underpin with the threat, or use, of military power. Its position since the end of the Cold War has been one of unparalleled strength – a 'hyperpower'[79] – and was demonstrated by its domination in the two Gulf wars. The confidence the US has derived from its military superiority has only been tempered by its historical suspicion of being dragged into foreign wars, its searing experience in Vietnam and its hesitation to become mired in military commitments that have no clearly defined end goal.

By contrast, it is not possible to talk about a European strategic culture.[80] NATO has been the purveyor of an Atlanticist strategic culture by virtue of the overarching presence of the US. One reason for the absence of a specifically European strategic culture is that a sense of continental unity only emerged in the latter half of the twentieth century. Security matters were excluded from the process of European construction until the Treaty on European Union, where it was mentioned only in aspirational terms.[81] It was not until 1999 that the EU decided to create its own military instruments with the European Rapid Reaction Force, a Political-Security Committee and Military Committee and Military Staff. Even after their creation, the so-called 'Petersberg' tasks that define the actions that the EU would undertake are inherently modest in nature.

Second, the national strategic cultures of European states have persisted and they remain both vibrant and varied. At one end are the strategic cultures of countries such as the United Kingdom and France. These states possess highly capable military forces, including nuclear capabilities, with proud traditions that cover the full spectrum of defence tasks. The range of military operations involving France and the UK since the end of the Cold War, from Bosnia to Kosovo to Sierre Leone and the Congo, belie the accusation that European states are pacifist in nature. These countries have frequently used force themselves, and supported the US use of force against Al-Qaeda and the Taliban in 2001. At the other end of the spectrum are countries, such as Ireland and Austria, which have historically been wedded to policies of neutrality and have only deployed forces in peacekeeping operations. Germany has maintained large armed forces but adhered to a unique strategic culture based on the principle of a 'citizen in uniform'.[82]

In short, a cohesive European strategic culture remains to be built – something that is now the subject of pressure from various quarters on the continent. There is disagreement over whether a coherent strategic culture could be created within the EU. Detractors of the EU argue that there are too many differences between the national strategic cultures of European states. Freedman, for example, posits that it would be impossible to weld the views of the member states together in the absence of a coherent foreign policy.[83] Advocates of an EU strategic doctrine believe that it could be built in stages; that the instigation of the ESDP, and the experience of actual military operations, is contributing to building such a culture. They argue that the drafting of the ESS was a major step forward and that the EU should proceed to draw up a strategic doctrine and a European Defence White Paper.[84]

The fact that Europe lacks a cohesive strategic culture, unlike the United States, helps to account for the differing priorities of the two sides. In regard to threat perceptions, Everts notes that where the US sees threats to its security, the Europeans talk about 'challenges' and 'risks'.[85] The Europeans believe that these risks should be addressed through political cooperation and the allocation of resources. They are distinctly uncomfortable with a US approach that appears eager to resort to the use of military power. Different threat perceptions are also partly explained by structural inequalities. The disparity in power between the transatlantic allies is pushing them apart over how to respond to international terrorism. Neo-conservatives in the US endorse this perspective and argue that the Europeans are ignoring threats because of their relative military weakness. Kagan opines that 'The incapacity to respond to threats leads not only to tolerance. It can also lead to denial.'[86] He goes on to say that the two sides of the Atlantic occupy contrasting positions:

> Americans are from Mars and Europeans are from Venus. They agree on little and understand one another less and less. . . . When it comes to setting national priorities, determining threats, defining challenges, and fashioning and implementing foreign and defence policies, the United States and Europe have parted ways.[87]

Because of its unparalleled power in the world and the absence of counter-balancing constraints, the US is predisposed to the use of hard power. The US has faith in the symbolic value of force: in signalling resolve within the international community and as a means to deter future attack. Its military gives the US a global reach and ensures that no targets are beyond its ability to strike. America also believes in the efficacy of military power: both in attacking the sanctuaries of terrorist organisations and punishing state sponsors by destroying assets of value. Framing the struggle against international terrorism as a 'war' has enabled the US to privilege and justify its own response. By militarising the struggle, the US has been able to assert its model of counter-terrorism and mobilise its population. The traumatic experience of 9/11 has given America the political will to use force internationally, to strip away the constraints that hitherto made it a reluctant interventionist.

The Europeans do not tend to see terrorism as something on which war can be declared – rather, as a long-term challenge that needs to be managed. In their view, military power is an ineffective instrument in countering terrorism. Their long experience of fighting terrorism within national contexts has convinced European countries that force is a blunt and indiscriminate tool to try and employ against elusive and disparate targets. In their view, it leads frequently to simplistic solutions and to mistakes that cannot be rectified. European preference for treating force as an instrument of last resort has been shaped by their historical experiences. After the catastrophic results of two world wars, European states are justifiably averse to conflict. They have become 'post-modern' in nature; seeking to resolve differences through negotiation and the building of international regulatory organisations.[88] The Franco-German *rapprochement* is evidence of the way in which European countries have transcended the military rivalries that used to plague the continent. They also know from bitter experience how difficult it is to fashion a satisfactory peace after the cessation of hostilities.

They are aware that time and money are necessary to resurrect a functioning state after a military conflict.

In the words of Archik, 'Most EU members continue to view terrorism primarily as an issue for law enforcement rather than a problem to be solved by military means'.[89] European governments see terrorism as something that can only be dealt with through a multi-pronged strategy that recognises its complex nature. Europeans see the main instruments for fighting terrorism as being the use of civilian means: law enforcement cooperation, the prosecution of terrorists before criminal courts and the sharing of intelligence. Law enforcement and prosecution occur after an offence has been committed, demand high levels of proof and respect geographical boundaries. They differ in nature and timing from the use of military force.

The debate over the pre-emptive use of force epitomises the conceptual cleavage between Europe and the US. The Bush administration has argued that in the light of the potential use of WMD against the US, it would be too late to use force in retaliation.[90] It sends a signal that the US will not sit back and watch a potential adversary build a nuclear or bacteriological capability. This possibility has led the US government to move away decisively from its former strategies of containment and deterrence: the latter makes little sense when transnational actors may not be persuadable by the traditional cost/benefit analysis that the US deployed hitherto to deter the Soviet Union. Preemption was always an option for the US but now it has been elevated into a doctrine of US security policy.[91] In his speech at West Point, President Bush declared, 'the war on terror will not be won on the defensive. We must take the battle to the enemy. . . . In the world we have entered, the only path to safety is the path of action.'[92]

The Europeans have expressed profound misgivings over the new American policy direction towards pre-emption. They fear that such a stance will undermine the legitimacy of American actions. International law accepts that a state has the right to use force in self-defence but it does not allow for the use of force in an anticipatory fashion. Critics have accused the Bush administration of confusing pre-emption, based on the concept of an imminent threat, with prevention.[93] A preventive strategy assumes that a state can predict an enemy's intention and should have the right to use force in an anticipatory manner before a threat materialises. Such a strategy would require perfect intelligence of the enemy's intention and would be liable to abuse. In addition, European countries have been alarmed at the signal this sends to the wider international community. It makes it possible for other states to use this argument as a pretext to undertake aggression.

Nevertheless, in spite of their concerns, the Europeans have been forced to react to American policies by virtue of the leading role that the US has played in combating terrorism.[94] The hegemonic status of the US has meant that Europe has had no choice other than to modify its stance. This was exemplified by the European Security Strategy. First, the document made a concession towards US views by acknowledging the growing importance of global, as compared to regional, security issues such as nuclear proliferation and failed states.[95] Second, the ESS accepts that the use of force may be an instrument of last resort in dealing with new security challenges. It does not go as far as US national security documents in embracing the language of war in relation to counter-terrorism, but it signals a shift towards US priorities.[96]

Another major transatlantic difference is over the importance attached to multilateralism. European support for the role of international organisations reflects the part that they have played in overcoming the historical enmities on the continent and reconciling antagonistic states. Europe has built its post-war success on pursuing the peaceful resolution of disputes through diplomacy, building consensus and adhering to the rule of law.[97] These are the norms and values that are at the heart of European' integration, and they are consequently the norms and values that the Europeans seek to export to the wider world.[98] To borrow a phrase from Nye, this is a constituent part of the 'soft power' with which Europe is richly endowed, as compared to the 'hard' military power in which its capabilities are modest.[99] The ESS calls for 'effective multilateralism'. This was a concession to the US in accepting that not all multilateralism serves its intended purpose. The Europeans' desire to demonstrate the legitimacy of their actions by working for the broadest degree of international support. Wherever possible, the use of force should be approved by the United Nations.

Of course, to argue that the US is committed only to the use of force, in dealing with terrorism, is a caricature.[100] In reality, the US employs the full panoply of its capabilities. The National Strategy for Combating Terrorism recommends that the US draw upon 'every instrument of national power – diplomatic, economic, law enforcement, financial, information, intelligence, and military'.[101] This is consistent with its policy of treating terrorism as a threat to national security, requiring the active engagement of all US agencies. It is not the case that the US only uses force in relation to terrorism. Yet this has become a powerful perception in the minds of its European allies, leading even informed commentators such as Muller to allege, 'an almost single-minded emphasis of the United States on the military instrument'.[102] Because the US has the ability to use force, and because it has done so in relation to Afghanistan in 2001 and Iraq in 2003, the perception has arisen that the US only uses military power. The need to redress this misperception was acknowledged by the 9/11 Commission Report. While accepting that the first phase of America's strategy was correctly focused on the Taliban and Al-Qaeda, the Report recommended that 'long term success demands the use of all elements of national power'.[103]

The US has actually crafted an integrated plan for countering terrorism in a manner that no other European state has replicated. The extent and coherence of the plan reflects an attempt to compensate for the absence of such a strategy before 9/11. The National Strategy for Combating Terrorism is designed to be an integral part of the overarching National Security Strategy. Its emphasis lies in two areas: first, drawing together all the instruments of policy; and second, designing a layered security strategy that provides defence in depth. The outer circle of defence brings together US diplomatic, military, economic and intelligence assets. Diplomacy is designed to pressure states into ending their support for international terrorism, backed up by economic sanctions and the targeting of the financial infrastructure of terrorism. Military assets provide the option to use force, complemented by America's unrivalled intelligence capacity. Law enforcement officers based overseas extend the reach of the American legal system.[104]

The next circle is designed to identify and neutralise threats before they arrive at US borders. The conceptual framework for this activity was derived from the Office for Homeland Security in the White House and embodied in the US National Strategy for Homeland Security. Part of this role has been assigned to the US military, under the designation 'homeland defense', not only dealing with distant threats, but also in providing military assistance to the civil authorities.[105] US Customs, the Immigration and Naturalization Service and the Coast Guard have been incorporated into the Department of Homeland Security (DHS) since November 2002, first under Governor Tom Ridge and then, in the second Bush term, under former Assistant Attorney General Michael Chertoff. The DHS has identified several priorities, including: hardening transport security, tightening immigration procedures, screening cargoes entering US ports, and making provision for recovery after catastrophic attack.[106]

In bringing together twenty-two previously separate agencies into the DHS, the US undertook the biggest reorganisation of the federal government since 1947. It was an attempt to rectify the inter-agency rivalry and lack of information sharing that had detracted from America's security in the past.[107] Critics have questioned the effectiveness of the changes. Flynn, for example, notes that although sizeable sums of money have been allocated to homeland security – President Bush asked Congress for $37.7 billion for the year 2003 – the figure is small compared to the enormous spending on the US military.[108] Others have questioned the wisdom of creating such a leviathan as the DHS, and suspect that it will enable turf battles to continue within the context of a bloated bureaucracy. Another criticism is that inadequate attention has been paid to fusing together the efforts of various levels of government.[109]

The final, inner circle of defence comprises federal and state law enforcement agencies and the creation of networks to involve the private sector. The responsibility of the agencies within the inner circle is to prevent terrorist attacks within the US and to protect critical infrastructure. Much of that infrastructure, such as power plants and chemical companies, belong to private companies and can only be protected with their acquiescence. Furthermore, state authorities have the responsibility to plan for the relief and reconstruction effort after a major terrorist attack.

The European response has not been as sweeping or deep-seated as that of the US. Some European countries have taken steps to tighten their border controls, and more intelligence information is shared than in the past. In addition, member states of the EU have taken collective measures to enhance their shared security. Yet there has not been the sort of reordering of government that has been witnessed in the United States, and there has been no attempt to set up the equivalent of a Homeland Security agency. Asmus has argued that the EU should rethink this policy. '(T)he new frontline of defense must be transatlantic homeland security. There are few areas in which the need for transatlantic cooperation is more self-evident. . . . The EU . . . needs to create its own Office of Homeland Security.'[110] The contending approaches of the US and Europe towards internal security and the cooperation that has developed between them is the subject of Chapter 4.

Conclusion

Although the shock to the US of the 9/11 attacks cannot be denied, nevertheless much of the threat analysis was present in American thinking long before that tragedy. It was evident from speeches made by the President and officials during the Clinton administration that the US had come to see the principal threats to its security as emanating from a complex nexus of international terrorism, states of concern and weapons of mass destruction. What happened after 9/11 was the prioritising of these threats: a domestic attack upon the United States resulted in the reordering of its foreign policy. From the terrorist attacks that were visited upon the US the political energy was derived to address these threats with determination and widespread domestic support. Whereas under the Clinton administration the US used force in retaliation to attacks, under Bush it moved to using force proactively.

The US has perceived itself as the guardian of the international security order in the post-Cold War era. As the most powerful actor within the system it took upon itself the authority to shape the agenda. By declaring a 'War on Terrorism', America arrogated to itself the manner in which international terrorism would be countered. Whilst drawing on the full range of American diplomatic, economic and law enforcement tools, the terminology of war has privileged US military superiority. As a result, terrorism has become the defining international security issue and America the architect of the response. This has made it harder to work in harmony with Europe. In the past, limitations on European power meant that Europe relied upon the US to manage global security concerns. Now the US is calling for Europe to follow the American lead and take on its share of extra-European security threats.

European threat perceptions did not change as radically as those of the US after 9/11.[111] This was principally because the continent was not the victim of the attack, but even after the Madrid bombings, European countries still regard themselves as less likely victims than the United States.[112] Europe seems to have assumed a more pragmatic response to the threat of terrorism. Unlike the US, which now yearns for invulnerability and absolute security, Europe appears to be content to manage the risk. Stevenson argues that the US and Europe now disagree about 'whether preventive and precautionary measures should be adopted more on the basis of vulnerability in light of the potential capabilities of terrorist networks, or on threat-driven analyses of terrorist objectives and modus operandi'.[113]

The EU Counter-Terrorism Coordinator Gijs de Vries remarked that there are 'inevitably . . . differences of perspective between us [the Europeans and the US]'.[114] There is now evidence that the threat perceptions of the two sides are beginning to grow closer together.[115] The need to respond to the US War on Terrorism has steered Europe closer to American positions. The European Security Strategy has demonstrated a narrowing of the divide over the key differences of the use of force and the potential for linkages with WMD. As the two sides of the Atlantic seek to broaden their patterns of counter-terrorism cooperation, they will need to work towards shared perceptions.

4   Internal security cooperation

Introduction

There was little evidence of transatlantic internal security cooperation prior to the 9/11 attacks. This reflected the fact that there was relatively little demand for such cooperation. The two sides of the Atlantic were focused on different problems and there was no pressure from either side to focus on this area of activity in the absence of a shared sense of threat. Yet over the last five years cooperation in internal security has flourished.

Because West European experiences of terrorism had been predominantly national in nature, there was only limited collaboration between these states, let alone with the US. Many individual European states had well-developed internal security apparatuses for combating terrorism, but comparatively little effort had been invested in trying to build inter-state structures. Internal security capacities have been developed substantially since the impact of 9/11 and considerable effort has been invested in working bilaterally with the US.[1] Yet 9/11 highlighted the need not only for transatlantic internal security cooperation to develop *per se*, but for it to be engendered at a European level with the US. A fundamental shift has occurred in which both sides of the Atlantic have recognised the importance of working together through organisational frameworks.

NATO has not been an appropriate framework in which to develop transatlantic internal security cooperation: it has no remit and its strength has always resided in external security. The G-8 has enjoyed greater relevance in this regard and some initiatives have been pursued under its aegis. Yet by far the greatest amount of cooperation has been conducted within the US-EU relationship. The EU's model of internal security – originally constructed to meet the challenges of international crime and illegal immigration – has been adapted to cope with the threat from international terrorism. At a special European Council

Meeting on 21 September 2001, shortly after the attacks on the United States, the EU agreed upon a 'Road Map' of priorities in combating terrorism.[2] The Road Map established sixty recommendations that were to serve as a guide for the Union's counter-terrorism efforts.

Compared to Western Europe, the US had further to travel in the field of internal security. Because of the perceived absence of a domestic terrorist threat, the US had neither the structural architecture nor the policies in place to address the new situation. As a result the Bush administration was forced to develop a rapid response from a low base. This helps to explain the plethora of changes in US internal security provision that have occurred over the last few years, ranging from domestic legislation and new law enforcement powers to the creation of the Department of Homeland Security. The implications of these activities for America's European allies have been significant.

At a meeting on 21 September 2001 between the US Secretary of State Colin Powell and the EU Troika, comprising of Louis Michel, Javier Solana and Chris Patten, the transatlantic allies began to sketch out the future pattern of their cooperation.[3] This was followed up a month later when the White House communicated a list of measures it wanted to be taken by the EU.[4] Counter-terrorism was moved to the very heart of US-EU relations. The seriousness with which US requests for cooperation with the EU were treated was demonstrated by the fact that American representatives were admitted into some of the key EU meetings on internal security: the Police Chiefs Operational Task Force (PCOTF),[5] the CFSP Counter-Terrorism Working Party (COTER) and the third pillar Working Party on Terrorism.[6] Five issue areas became the focal points for cooperation between the two sides.[7] The first was closer police and law enforcement cooperation. The second was judicial collaboration, particularly over the extradition of terrorist suspects. The third was information sharing and granting each side access to criminal databases. The fourth was cooperation over border and transport security – a vulnerability that had been exposed by the 9/11 hijackers. Fifth, the US and Europe agreed to work together to target the sources of funding that financed terrorist operations. Each of these five areas will be assessed in detail.

Police and law enforcement

The US has long wanted greater cooperation with the law enforcement agencies of the EU. The American government has recognised the efficiency gains it could achieve by negotiating agreements with the EU as a whole rather than each individual member state. It has watched with interest as the Union's own agencies, such as Europol, have developed and has sought to influence this process. But the US has been aware of the obstacles that have stood in the way of moving from a bilateral pattern of cooperation with individual European states to one in which the US cooperates within a multilateral framework.

The sphere of law enforcement has presented particular challenges for transatlantic cooperation because of the different powers invested in the police by the two sides. In the past the US has been willing to invest its law enforcement officials with greater powers than its counterparts in Europe.[8] The difference in transatlantic attitudes may reflect the fact that the US experienced a bigger problem with domestic organised crime and drug trafficking than West European countries, and gave its police forces stronger powers through the 1970 Racketeer Influenced and Corrupt Organizations Act (RICO). Membership of certain organisations was proscribed, criminally derived property or assets could be confiscated, access to suspects' bank accounts was permitted and police forces were able to use *agents provocateurs* and electronic surveillance techniques such as telephone tapping.[9]

McDonald makes the interesting observation that after 9/11, the US wanted cooperation with the EU to extend to broader 'criminal matters' as well as terrorism.[10] This raised suspicions on the part of European governments that the US was employing terror as a wedge to secure other forms of cooperation. The reality of the situation was that the US saw the issues as linked. For example, an Atlantic Council report recommends that transatlantic cooperation in criminal investigations should be expanded to impede terror networks that increasingly connect with other types of crime such as drug trafficking.[11] It is possible to identify a range of measures that have been taken to counter terrorism that will also be relevant against crime: for example, US-EU action against money laundering, the sharing of intelligence information and new extradition arrangements.

There has been a hardening of police powers across Europe over the last few years in an attempt to counteract the threat from international terrorism. The UK, for example, has increased police powers in relation to the search and arrest of suspects, the freezing of assets and the confiscation of property and the right to obtain telephone and email records from telecommunications companies.[12] Similarly, Germany has increased the right of access by its law enforcement officers to personal data, as well as given greater powers to conduct surveillance through telephone communications and electronic mail. France has possessed strong counter-terrorism measures for some time, including wiretaps and extensive powers to arrest suspects. Nevertheless, there remains a gap between the ethos of the transatlantic allies. The fact that the Americans and Europeans differ in the powers they invest in their police forces is a factor of considerable importance. Evidence that can be used in a prosecution differs between the two sides, raising the fear that a case in a European court could be undermined if it was based on material derived from US authorities.[13] For example, evidence obtained from electronic surveillance or from the use of *agents provocateurs* by American law enforcement officers would be inadmissible in a UK court. This has meant that transatlantic police cooperation has required careful and deliberate management. It has also meant that lawyers attached to the judicial departments of each side are cross-posted into capitals so as to ensure that the requisite expertise is on hand to prevent cases being undermined.

After 9/11, changes in the US have increased concerns on the part of European governments. US legislation has increased the power of law enforcers to initiate wiretap surveillance, trace mobile telephone numbers and obtain credit card information. Furthermore, in relation to terrorist suspects, there has been a broadening of the grounds on which search warrants may be obtained, individuals can be deported and foreigners held for up to seven days without charge. These measures have drawn criticism from some European governments. The US Ambassador to the EU acknowledged this problem in December 2001 when he said that 'Differing legal systems and approaches to the protection of civil liberties, both among EU Member States and between the US and Europe, have hampered full collaboration'.[14] The 'EU-US Declaration on Combating Terrorism' in June 2004 committed both sides of the Atlantic to try to resolve some of the differences between them over the 'appropriate' use of various investigative techniques.[15]

A further source of consternation in Europe was the decision of the American government to end the separation between information obtained by the law enforcement and intelligence communities. Many European countries have legislation forbidding them from using material gained through intelligence agencies for the purpose of pursuing criminal proceedings.[16] Drawing on clandestine sources of information frequently contravenes domestic laws, making it problematical to cross-examine witnesses. The issue goes to the heart of two different sorts of cultures: one based on law enforcement and judicial process – which leads to demands for accountability and civil liberties – whilst the other is based on national security and intelligence agencies. Law enforcement focuses on making cases for criminal prosecutions, as compared to intelligence agencies which concentrate on the prevention of harm to the state. Both sides of the Atlantic have wrestled with the problem of how to make information derived through intelligence channels compatible with the demands of law enforcement.

In July 2003 the FBI ended the separation, or 'wall', that had hitherto existed between investigations into suspected terrorist activity that relied on intelligence gained under the US Foreign Intelligence Surveillance Act (FISA), and material gained through law enforcement techniques such as interviews and search warrants.[17] The ending of this separation made intelligence material available for criminal prosecutions (designated '315 classifications'). The full range of investigative techniques, such as electronic surveillance of telephones and emails as well as a person's movements and place of work, have been made available in suspected cases of terrorism. In addition, many thousands of intelligence files were reviewed in the period following the 9/11 attacks.[18] American police forces are now required to inform intelligence agencies if they acquire sensitive information in the course of a criminal investigation. Centres have been created to serve as clearinghouses for information and analysis.[19] The result has been a culture shift within the policing and intelligence communities of the US.[20]

One source of satisfaction for the US in seeking closer law enforcement cooperation with Europe was a breakthrough in the development of a working relationship with Europol. This had been a long-term aim of the American government because, although Europol was never intended to have the power to conduct actual investigations or make arrests, it was designed to conduct strategic analyses of crime, crime trends and threat assessments, as well as facilitate the exchange of criminal information and maintain important criminal databases. The American law enforcement community was eager to obtain access to these databases and had entertained high hopes for cooperating with the agency. But the US had become frustrated by the long time taken to bring Europol into being. The Europol Convention was eventually signed in July 1995 but even then, because of wrangles amongst the member states, it did not enter into force until October 1998.[21] Its remit was also slow to develop: it was not until 1999 that Europol was given the right to become involved in matters pertaining to terrorism.[22] US enthusiasm had to be tempered because of the slow pace at which the agency was developed and the modest resource base with which it was endowed.

As far as the EU was concerned, the US was a long way down the list of countries with whom Europol was considering cooperation. However, as a result of the 9/11 attacks, the US was allowed to leapfrog to the front of the queue. The Director of Europol, Jürgen Storbeck, signed an agreement with the US Ambassador to the EU, in December 2001, which facilitated the exchange of strategic and technical information, such as analyses of patterns of criminal activity and information on suspected criminal assets. It permitted the exchange of liaison officers, so that a US representative was based at Europol offices in The Hague, and enabled the US to participate in 'Joint Investigation Teams'.[23] This concept sought to create teams of law enforcement officers and representatives from Europol and member states to work together on terrorism cases that were transnational in nature.[24] The US had expressed a particular interest in being associated with this initiative. In December of the following year, the initial understanding between Europol and the US was followed by an agreement of even greater significance to exchange personal data.[25]

The success of the transatlantic allies in securing a US-Europol relationship has been tempered by three factors. The first is the practical reality that Europol has little expertise in the sphere of counter-terrorism and its resources are small in comparison to agencies such as the American FBI.[26] The FBI initially exchanged liaison officers with Europol's Counter-Terrorist Task Force but the representative was withdrawn in August 2002. The US had grown to be disillusioned with the lack of substantive progress that Europol had achieved in counter-terrorism.[27] It was not until the Madrid bombing in 2004 that interest was revitalised in the Counter-Terrorist Task Force idea, and at the Troika meeting in The Hague in September the US announced it would re-assign its representative to Europol.[28]

The modest size and resources of Europol has meant that even interaction with European national police forces and intelligence agencies has been patchy. Europol remains dependent on the information that it receives from its member states, but scepticism from the latter about the utility of Europol has led to a general reluctance to share fully. This has been in spite of the directive from the European Council for member states to pool all useful intelligence material with Europol.[29] A thorny problem has proved to be the unwillingness of intelligence agencies to share national material that they fear will be compromised when put in the wider Union domain. The heads of the intelligence services of the largest EU countries, France, Germany, Spain, the UK and Italy, meet regularly in the Counter-Terrorist Group, within the Council, to share information, but their attitude towards Europol has been disappointing.[30]

The second drawback has been the tension created by the reluctance of some US law enforcement agencies to prejudice their bilateral relationships with European states in order to work with Europol. In the case of the FBI Legal Attachés and the Drug Enforcement Agency (DEA) representatives, they risk cuts in their privileged presence overseas if it appears that there is duplication between their interaction with member states and with the EU. This bureaucratic resistance to change is exemplified by the way in which the FBI and DEA have responded to requests for information by the recently created Europol Liaison office in the European Commission in Washington.[31] The responses have been channelled back not through the Europol Liaison office or even through the Europol headquarters in The Hague, but through European national representatives located in the embassies in Washington.[32] At best this represents inertia; at worst it is an attempt by some of the large US law enforcement agencies to protect their own established patterns of bilateral cooperation. At a time when European states have been attempting to consolidate the progress made by Europol, this has been a cause for dissatisfaction.

The last problem has stemmed from American concerns about the reliability of the ten countries that acceded to the EU on 1 May 2004. Part of the value to the US of a liaison relationship with Europol was the latter's role as the hub of a continent-wide criminal information system. By entering into information sharing with Europol the US was gaining a foothold in a larger network from which it would otherwise be excluded. But paradoxically, this access carries risks for the US because it is sharing information with the newly acceded states from Central and Eastern Europe in whose law enforcement systems the US has little confidence.[33] Reciprocity will mean that the US will have to respond to requests for sensitive data from these countries, just as it would from West European states. Officials in Washington have expressed misgivings that sensitive information on US citizens suspected of criminal offences could leak from judicial systems and place prosecutions at risk.[34]

Thus, since 9/11 there has been a breakthrough in forging law enforcement cooperation between the EU and the US. In the case of the US-Europol agreements they represent the most wide-ranging undertakings entered into by Europol with another country. Yet for all its innovation, the limits of transatlantic cooperation have swiftly become apparent. The EU has been unwilling and unable to progress cooperation with Washington faster than its members have been willing to work together inside the Union.

Judicial cooperation

A similar pattern of opportunities and limitations has been replicated in transatlantic judicial affairs. The political imperative to respond to the new level of terrorist threat after 9/11 led the US to put pressure on the European side. There was an expectation amongst Americans that judicial matters were an area where the EU could act effectively and where transatlantic agreement could be realised. There was a pre-existing 'Justice Dialogue', begun in 1998, between officials of the US Department of Justice and their counterparts in EU Justice and Home Affairs.[35] But zealous American domestic security measures after the terrorist attacks on New York and Washington unnerved European governments and rendered them wary of entering into full cooperation with the US.

Philosophical differences over matters of justice have led commentators and practitioners alike to express concern over the desirability of the EU to work too closely with the US. The retention of the death penalty in some American states has been the most salient difference,[36] but US penal policy has also been the subject of criticism. The US has responded by pointing to what it regards as the unjustifiably light sentences handed down in European countries for the most heinous of offences, as well as the ability of terrorist suspects to gain refuge under asylum laws.[37] American officials have been particularly strong in their condemnation when their citizens have been murdered in European countries and the perpetrators have received sentences short of life imprisonment.[38]

Transatlantic cooperation has been forced to contend with the problem posed by the diversity of European judicial systems and legal processes. There was evidence of this diversity in the terrorist legislation on the statute books of the EU members at the time of 9/11. Only six countries, who themselves had suffered in the past with domestic terrorist problems, possessed legislation dedicated to this purpose. These were Germany, Italy, Spain, Portugal, France and the UK,[39] and only the latter four had determined a satisfactory definition of terrorism.[40] Cofer Black has argued that several European countries are in need of dedicated counter-terrorism legislation and also need to reassess their standards of evidence that are currently placed unrealistically high.[41] Countries such as the Netherlands did not have counter-terrorist legislation but took steps after 2001 to introduce such provisions. Other countries, such as Belgium, have not passed counter-terrorist legislation nor criminalised membership of terrorist organisations.

This contrasts with the plethora of far-reaching counter-terrorism legislation that has emanated from Washington. It underpins the arguments of some commentators that the legislative gap between the two sides of the Atlantic has been widening over the last few years.

Archik, for example, points to the constraint that has been imposed upon European legislation by the European Convention on Human Rights.[42] The experience of the UK bears this out. The UK government's derogation from the European Convention, in order to hold foreign terrorist suspects indefinitely in detention, was condemned comprehensively by its own Law Lords.[43] The Home Secretary, Charles Clarke, responded by ending the special status of foreign terror suspects and instituting a system of house arrest for both national and foreign detainees.

No comparable constraint existed on American legislation and, in the absence of domestic counter-terrorism laws prior to 9/11, the Bush administration rushed through the 'Uniting and Strengthening America by Providing Appropriate Tools Required to Intercept and Obstruct Terrorism Act', otherwise known as the USA PATRIOT Act. This Act made numerous enhancements to the law enforcement machinery and mandated closer cooperation between US federal agencies. It created new federal crimes relating to terrorist attack on public transport, harbouring terrorists and providing them with material support; it toughened federal money laundering laws and increased powers to prevent entry into the US.[44] Furthermore, it permitted the confidential use of informants, the use of surveillance and search warrants and the imposition of long prison sentences in order to help to obtain information through plea bargains. In the eyes of its critics, the Patriot Act has granted powers that are too extensive to law enforcement officers and has undermined the cherished civil liberties of American citizens.[45] The reaction in Europe has been one of apprehension, on the grounds that the US has over-reacted to the threat of terrorism.

Nevertheless, just as securing cooperation with Europol was heralded as a breakthrough in the transatlantic relationship, so there have been four areas of judicial policy that the two sides have treated as important successes since 9/11. The first was an EU agreement on a common definition of terrorism. This issue had hitherto been a major obstacle because, with member states adhering to different understandings of terrorism, it had been hard to agree on counter-measures and problematical to cooperate internationally. A draft agreement was reached in December 2001 and this entered into force in June of the following year.[46] This has made possible cooperation between EU states as well as with third countries.[47] As well as defining the types of crimes that comprise terrorism, the agreement also determined the penalties that should be imposed for terrorist offences. As member states could not agree on a full range of penalties, only two offences were delineated. Leading a terrorist group was liable to a sentence of at least fifteen years whilst financing its operations was liable to a punishment of at least eight years. Other terrorist offences were left to member states to determine the appropriate tariff.[48]

The second issue was the creation of a European Arrest Warrant (EAW). The EAW designated thirty-two offences, punishable by at least three years' duration, on which a warrant for arrest could be issued in one European country and the accused arrested and held in another country. The Arrest Warrant promised to speed up the process of extradition on a continent-wide basis and ensure that offences no longer need to be exactly the same in the state in which the crime is committed and the state surrendering the suspect (the principle of dual criminality). After considerable debate a Framework Decision on the EAW was agreed in June 2002.[49] The potential value of the EAW for the US was clear. It addressed the thorny problem of extradition, and the US had struggled in the past to obtain suspects from European jurisdictions. The warrant represented a leap beyond the principle of the mutual recognition of laws, agreed at Tampere, towards a model of legal harmonisation within the EU, which might ease US difficulties in working with the EU in the future. Last, there was the prospect of spill-over from this success to other initiatives. Indeed, after the experience of the EAW, the European Council decided to proceed with a European Evidence Warrant to replace the mutual legal assistance arrangements between member states.[50] This would be an ambitious step because a country's court would have the power to demand that another country provide evidence.

The third success was the creation of Eurojust, a body of European public prosecutors with the powers to coordinate criminal cases that transcended the boundaries of EU members. Eurojust accorded with an American vision for collaboration between prosecutors on both sides of the Atlantic, and there was contentment that an American liaison magistrate had been agreed with the new body.[51] Eurojust was to focus on the same crimes as Europol and the two agencies signed an agreement under which they would share information. But there was substantial disagreement from the outset as to whether Eurojust would serve only to coordinate cross-national investigations or whether it would be able to initiate both investigations and prosecutions.[52] It was eventually agreed that it would only have the power to request states to initiate investigations, but these debates took time to resolve[53] and as a result Eurojust did not begin its work until the end of 2002. However, the fact that Eurojust has held meetings designed to bring together prosecutors from across Europe who work on anti-terrorist cases has pleased the US because this is exactly the sort of activity in which it wants to participate.[54]

The last source of satisfaction in transatlantic judicial relations has been the negotiation of a Mutual Legal Assistance Treaty (MLAT). The MLAT concerned a range of judicial issues that the US was eager to enhance with Europe. One was the extent of the evidence that could be shared for criminal investigations and prosecutions and better knowledge of the rules that guided the actions on either side of the Atlantic.[55] A second was the streamlining of extradition arrangements; an issue of great sensitivity in Washington and something that caused harm to relationships when it went wrong. A third was the creation of central points of contact between US judicial authorities and their EU counterparts. This enabled US authorities to send requests for information on such things as individual bank accounts and, through the mechanism of the Patriot Act, reciprocate with European requests.[56] The US had initially hesitated about negotiating an overarching MLAT with the EU because it feared that this might impact negatively on the existing bilateral MLATs that had been signed with nine of the member states. For example, some of the agreements already in place sanctioned the extradition of EU nationals to the US, and the American government was unwilling to give these up in a multilateral accord.[57] The US came to the view that it could achieve added value through an agreement with the EU and that this would supplement rather than supplant the pre-existing treaties. The 'Agreement on Extradition and Mutual Legal Assistance' was eventually signed at the EU-US Summit in Washington in June 2003.

However, securing judicial cooperation with the EU has not come without its drawbacks for the US. The chief problem has been the amount of time it has taken for the EU to implement these agreements, or even those amongst its own members. Delays have resulted from slow domestic ratification processes or from doubts about the legal processes of allies. The outcome has been a sense of frustration and disillusionment. No mechanism has existed to oversee a state's importation of EU provisions into its own national legislation, and there have been no sanctions to deploy against laggards, other than naming and shaming them. This is consistent with the EU's wider position on countering terrorism: solemn declarations followed by severe delays, causing observers to conclude that there exists an absence of will to bring the measures into effect.

Problems with the speed of the EU's implementation process were exemplified in the cases of the MLAT and the European Arrest Warrant. In the MLAT, the treaty was signed on behalf of the EU and the US but then had to be implemented individually between the American government and each of the European signatories. The US found that the implementation process became bogged down in domestic legislative processes and in civil liberties considerations. In the case of the European Arrest Warrant, the Framework Decision was adopted in June 2002 and should have been in force by the end of that year. But eight member states dragged their heels and by as late as July 2004 it was not fully enacted.[58] Some of those eight had the means to enforce the warrant against foreign nationals on their soil but had failed to pass legislation in time enabling their own citizens to be tried in another country.

Transatlantic intelligence sharing

Intelligence sharing presents a unique issue in transatlantic internal security cooperation. The sensitive nature of the information, the difficulty of obtaining it and its vulnerability to being compromised makes intelligence a precious commodity that states share only with great reluctance. Added to this has been the fact that the US enjoys a global dominance in intelligence gathering because of its enormous resources and multiplicity of agencies. The rationale for the US to share intelligence with its European allies, at least on face value, is difficult to make.

Bilateralism, rather than multilateralism, has been the watchword for post-war intelligence sharing. Information may be shared with one country, but not with another, thereby rendering it difficult to build up broader patterns of dissemination. The US has recognised the value of sharing information but it has done so through close bilateral relationships with allies. Certain European countries have established a privileged intelligence relationship, namely the UK, France and Germany, and this has given them a vested interest in ensuring that the relationship continues.[59] Since 9/11 the level of bilateral intelligence sharing has increased manyfold, made possible by long-founded relationships and mutual trust between intelligence officials on both sides of the Atlantic.[60] As Clarke *et al.* note, 'most cooperation between governments will necessarily be bilateral and primarily amongst law enforcement and intelligence agencies'.[61]

Yet paradoxically, counter-terrorism requires intelligence sharing beyond the traditional model of bilateral relationships. Timely and accurate intelligence is the vital ingredient in fighting terrorism and, for it to be effective, it must be pooled. Ways must be found by countries to disseminate information to the widest number of recipients in order to raise the general awareness of the threats. Only by the building up of a picture from the sharing of fragmentary pieces of information can target nations have any hope of anticipating a terrorist attack. The failure of the US Central Intelligence Agency (CIA) and the FBI to cooperate effectively over information on the 9/11 attackers before the event is a powerful example of the tragic costs that can result.[62] The 9/11 Commission Report called for more US intelligence sharing with allies and for more resources to be invested in human intelligence sources. It pointed to the fact that 'Intelligence and security cooperation continues to be problematic because there is a fundamental tension between an increasingly networked world, which is ideal terrain for the new religious terrorism, and highly compartmentalised national intelligence gathering'.[63]

The challenge for the transatlantic relationship has been to find a framework in which intelligence can be shared multilaterally. There are enormous advantages for both sides if they can obtain information from single, central sources rather than engage in cross-cutting bilateral contacts. This need not mean that all information be shared with all parties: certain intelligence might go to a particular country on a 'need to know' basis, if there were indications of a threat to that state. But trust is something that takes a long time to foster, and the transatlantic allies have wrestled with the problem that there is no obvious framework in which to share information. The 'Berne Group', established in 1971, has traditionally been the forum for six of the main West European countries to pool intelligence across a broad range of issues. After 9/11 an offshoot of the Berne Group was developed into the 'Counter-Terrorist Group' (CTG) as a transatlantic forum with a particular focus on counter-terrorism. Information is collated not only on terrorist suspects and their movements but sources of financing, sources of arms and training, patterns of activity and countries willing to offer refuge. The CTG comprises all the West and East European states plus Norway and Switzerland and is therefore separate from the EU. Its first meeting took place in The Hague in November 2001.[64]

Nevertheless, the CTG remains an *ad hoc* intergovernmental framework and the creation of an effective interface between the US and EU has been more problematical. This reflects one of the historical shortcomings of the EU – the absence of a body to collate information on internal security threats, to analyse them and then prioritise responses. At the time of the EU 'Action Plan on Organised Crime' in 1997, attempts were made to find a mechanism by which intelligence could be gathered together from various agencies at a national level and fed through to the EU.[65] Success in this endeavour was patchy: there was evidence of the old problem of member state reticence in sharing information. When the US put pressure on the Union after 9/11 to improve the exchange of intelligence information across the Atlantic, then its weakness was exposed. The EU made a commitment, as part of its Anti-Terrorism Road Map, to share information to the greatest extent possible but it was left to create the necessary mechanisms to fulfil this pledge.[66]

The most ambitious proposal to redress the intelligence weaknesses was made by Austria at the JHA Council in February 2004, when it proposed the creation of a European Intelligence Agency to pool information on terrorist suspects.[67] This reflected the tendency among EU states to respond to a problem by setting up a new structure rather than making the existing machinery work more effectively. What was eventually agreed at the European Council was a more modest plan for an intelligence body to be integrated into the Council Secretariat.[68] The Joint Situation Centre (Sitcen) will play host to a unit dealing with internal intelligence. This will involve the allocation of a representative from the interior ministries of member states and will draw on intelligence derived from the Counter-Terrorist Group.[69] The aim of this body is to conduct threat analyses for the Union, paying special attention to the radicalisation of Muslim communities in member states.[70]

The Joint Situation Centre will thus have a future capacity to receive, analyse and disseminate intelligence on both external policy issues, as part of the European Security and Defence Policy, as well as internal security. This is an important step forward, both in recognising the inextricable link between internal and external security and according the EU an independent capacity to analyse threats. Although in its infancy, Sitcen addressed a long-standing source of European weaknesses.[71] With NATO constrained to the field of external military security, there was no established European organisation serving as a focal point for internal security information. The Joint Situation Centre also provides a European perspective on external policy separate from NATO where the views of the United States always weigh so heavily. The EU is no longer dependent upon just the information and analysis that NATO is willing to provide.

If the EU has experienced a rocky road in creating the structures for transatlantic intelligence cooperation, then it would be fallacious to assume that the US has experienced a smooth path. The US has faced some of the same pressures for reform, only from a different standpoint of making its bloated intelligence agencies work together effectively and end unnecessary competition.[72] Post-9/11, the FBI has reacted to criticism of its own performance in two ways. First by changing substantially the balance of work it undertakes so as to focus more specifically on terrorism. Second, to use its intelligence gathering both to inform its activities and to share information throughout its own structure.[73] Taken together, these measures have required the FBI to shift away from its traditional law enforcement culture towards a greater emphasis on intelligence and national security matters. In response to recommendations of the 9/11 Commission Report, two further changes were imposed upon the US intelligence agencies. A National Counter Terrorism Center (NCTC) was established, including personnel from all the major intelligence agencies, and superseding the Terrorist Threat Integration Center. Moreover, an overall National Intelligence Director was accepted by the Bush administration in August 2004, after some initial reluctance, replacing the role of the Director of Central Intelligence. John Negroponte, the former US ambassador to the UN, was appointed to the post in February 2005.

Fostering practical intelligence cooperation between the US and the EU brings together very different cultures, as illustrated by the divergences over the issue of data protection. Questions over how information about individuals is shared, used and stored have become contentious matters.[74] Because European governments hold relatively large amounts of information about their citizens and because they have been required to enter into cooperative arrangements with other European states, they have been careful to lay down clear guidelines and appoint an Independent Data Protection Commissioner in each member state. Consequently, the EU approach to data protection has been enshrined in an extensive series of regulations.[75] The US approach towards data protection, in contrast, has grown up more pragmatically through statutes and through precedents established by courts. Comparatively little data on citizens is held centrally by the US government and its attitude towards data protection has been more relaxed than that of Europe. This has led Europeans to criticise what they have regarded as the inadequate US framework for the protection of personal data. The US government has countered by arguing that European regulations are overly strict and impede vital law enforcement requirements.[76] This has made the concluding of transatlantic agreements over data sharing immensely complex.

Two examples highlight the friction that has been generated in US-European relations. The first was the attempt by Europol to share personal information, such as names and addresses of criminal suspects, with the US. The fact that the agreement took a whole year to negotiate was testament to the controversy it provoked. Europol had adopted a Data Protection Policy in September 1999 but the US side lacked a central body with the right to control personal data.[77] Information in the US judicial process has to be available within the court system, at both federal and state level, and it is therefore difficult to give definitive guarantees about how data will be used. This situation was incompatible with Europol's guidelines, and there was also pressure from countries such as Germany and Austria who themselves had stringent rules on data protection. The result was an impasse between Europol and the United States that threatened to undermine the prospect of meaningful counter-terrorism cooperation. It was not until the US government gave reassurances about the use of personal data that the impasse was broken and an agreement was signed.

The second example of data protection sensitivities was the 'Passenger Named Record' (PNR) agreement. The passing of the US 'Aviation and Transportation Security Act' of 2001 required airlines flying across the Atlantic to provide information on their passengers in advance of their arrival.[78] The information, taken from reservations and departure control, concerned people's finances and their dietary requirements. This was a source of consternation to European governments and the European Commission because it offered the potential to profile passengers in order to determine who might present a security risk.[79] There were no mechanisms for individuals to find out the data being held on them or challenge its accuracy. It was also not clear whether sensitive data on individuals could be made available to third countries if it was judged that their security might be in jeopardy. The use of information in this way contravened the EU's privacy directive. Nevertheless, European airlines were made aware that failure to meet these new American regulations could mean that they would lose their permits to fly passengers to the US. The European Commission, responding to an issue of commercial confidentiality, felt that it had received inadequate warning by the US of this provision. The result was a protracted and testy negotiation.

The US and the Commission eventually resolved the PNR issue by delineating the categories of information that could be shared. A formal agreement was signed in May 2004. However, the European Parliament mounted a challenge to the agreement, contending that the amount of information that was being collected, retained and transmitted to the US was more than was necessary. There was dissatisfaction with both the reassurances given by the US and the way in which the agreement had been reached. Representatives of the European Parliament as well as national legislators were unconvinced that there was sufficient accountability over the way in which understandings were reached with the US.

Whilst the existing US-EU agreements are considered useful, it is the potential benefits of future agreements that have aroused American interest. The variety of mechanisms that the EU is developing for data storage and sharing offer the prospect of the US gaining access to enormous quantities of information pertaining to law enforcement, immigration and asylum. Two examples are the Schengen Information System (SIS) and the Europol databases. The SIS is a computer database comprising 14 million records on the movement of criminal suspects across European borders, as well as the movement of stolen cars and firearms.[80] It stores basic information about individuals and a description of their features: it is complemented by the Supplementary Information Request at the National Entry (SIRENE), which contains photographs and fingerprints, and the EURODAC database which holds the fingerprints of asylum applicants. Although the SIS was set up to combat illegal immigration, it has become an instrument of great value in countering crime and terrorism.[81] This illustrates one of the unresolved tensions in data protection; whether information procured for one purpose can be used for another.[82] The US has made no secret of its desire to be able to gain information from the SIS, and furthermore it has sought access to its successor system, the Schengen Information System II, which will provide an integrated and interoperable database that includes the ten new EU members. In terms of Europol, the US has been eager to access two of its three computerised databases: one of persons suspected of committing crimes within Europol's remit of responsibility, and the other of people who might testify or assist in investigations.[83] The US has been keen to see a European Council decision of December 2004 enacted, by which Europol will be informed of all national investigations relating to terrorism. This will give the US one point of contact for finding out what terrorist investigations are underway in the territories of the twenty-five EU members.

One other European development in which the US has expressed particular interest is the so-called 'Availability Principle' concerning the sharing of law enforcement information between member states.[84] The principle would be to give access to other European law enforcement agencies on a basis comparable to those applied to the country's own authorities.[85] The Dutch Presidency of the EU, in preparing the 'Hague Programme', proposed making all databases accessible to the various police forces of member states by 2008.[86] The rationale was that if the providers of data were given the confidence that there would be tight controls on its availability to other European colleagues, then they might be more willing to share what they possess. Technology could offer a way forward by ensuring that certain categories of information could only be granted to specified individuals according to strict accessibility protocols.[87] Some European states have begun to establish their own arrangements which could serve as pilot projects for a scheme encompassing all EU members. Spain, France and Germany, for example, have agreed an information exchange between their police records.[88] Such measures as these have caught the attention of US law enforcement agencies eager to be involved in attempts in Europe to share information more freely, especially on the exchange of criminal records.

According to a study by the Center for Strategic and International Studies, 'intelligence and law enforcement cooperation between the US and Europe is, by general consent and in general, excellent'.[89] This obscures the very real tension that has been felt on the part of the EU as it has struggled to respond to American requests for greater sharing. Differences in the standards adopted by the two sides have resulted in prolonged negotiations as EU officials have wanted to be assured that the information they transfer to America will be handled carefully. In addition, Europeans will judge the utility of cooperating with the US by the amount of information that flows the other way, from America back to the continent. There have been grumblings in Europe that the US has pressed for and obtained a one-way street in information exchange.[90]

Transatlantic cooperation over border controls

The issues of more effective border controls, document security and the exchange of visa information were highlighted by the events of 9/11. The hijackers had been able to move between western countries with relative ease, despite the fact that some of them were listed on databases as dangerous individuals. They had not been forced to enter the US clandestinely: rather, they had transited legally from Europe. In trying to address these vulnerabilities there was the risk that the threat from terrorism would be conflated with many lesser problems such as illegal immigration and unfounded asylum applications. Guild notes how terrorism has increasingly become linked with other issues of border security, not least through the introduction of new technologies, such as fingerprinting, which allow entrants into national territories to be identified and tracked.[91]

The 9/11 Commission Report was damning in its condemnation of US border security prior to the terrorist attacks. Its investigation concluded that there was neither a counter-terrorist capacity built in to the US border security system in 2001, nor was there a satisfactory immigration system capable of screening out dangerous entrants into the US.[92] Consequently, the US has undertaken a thorough reform of the architecture of its immigration system. The 'United States Visitor and Immigrant Status Indicator Technology' (US VISIT) programme has been introduced and placed under the control of the Department of Homeland Security. US VISIT has concentrated its efforts on more stringent inspection of documents at US borders, the profiling of passengers to attempt to identify security risks, tighter controls on student visas and the swift deportation of individuals found to have violated US entry laws. Visa waiver countries have been given time to develop systems which are compatible with the US before it is applied universally. Visitors from countries that already require a visa to enter the US have been expected to implement this new system.

The ten states that acceded to the EU in May 2004 have found themselves on the wrong side of the visa waiver divide. Even though by 2007 the new members will have acceded to Schengen, this will not qualify them for visa exemptions to the US. As Lebl notes, Poland and the Czech Republic were angered by the manner in which they were being treated by the US, and the latter appealed for help to the European Commission.[93] The Commission has made representations to the US,[94] but there was an irony here as the EU was already discriminating against those countries by the fact that they were being kept temporarily outside of Schengen.

The US pressured the EU to respond to its demands for tighter border security. Amongst the recommendations contained in the 'Road Map' of 21 September 2001 was a commitment on the part of the Union to develop an integrated border management strategy, tighten the safety measures of its many airlines and crack down on passport and visa fraud.[95] However, the EU has not attempted to disguise its unease with the approach of the US towards enhancing its domestic security. The US has made it clear that it wants to exercise extra-territorial control over the movement of goods and people departing from Europe to the US. This has been the concept underpinning the Passenger Named Record initiative, and it is a principle that the EU has found difficult to accept. Furthermore, there have been traces of coercion in American attitudes towards Europe. The National Strategy for Homeland Security of July 2002 made it clear that the US would be unwilling to let countries enjoy privileged access to their territory unless they implement the same sorts of security measures as the US.[96]

One of the ways in which the EU has attempted to take forward its plans for enhanced territorial security has been through the establishment of a European Borders Agency. The Agency would be designed to manage the Union's external borders, assist in the training of personnel, undertake risk assessments and help states in returning illegal immigrants to their home countries. The European Commission made a proposal to set up the European Borders Agency in November 2003 with the role of coordinating the activities of member states and to ensure the uniform application of the Schengen provisions. By May of 2005 the Agency was operational with its headquarters in Warsaw.[97] Attempts to complement the creation of the Agency with a corps of EU border guards have not met with the same success. Although such a corps would be designed to assist rather than replace national authorities, nevertheless the parameters of what some member states are willing to see communitarised has proved an insuperable obstacle.

Three issue areas related to border security have been the source of transatlantic tensions. The first was the debate about armed officers or 'sky-marshals' on passenger aircraft. Under the Aviation and Transportation Security Act, American companies were expected to increase the security on commercial aircraft, including the provision of sky-marshals and the screening of passengers. The US wanted to be able to demand similar requirements for European carriers, namely that flights, considered to be at high risk, were provided with armed, plain clothes officers. In the background was an implicit threat that the US would revoke the licences to fly to the US of those European companies that did not comply. When this was raised at the end of 2003 the EU complained that the US was trying to impose a policy upon them and had failed to consult sufficiently in advance. The issue was eventually resolved when some European airline companies agreed to provide armed officers and others agreed to enhance their ground-based security.

The second issue has been the security of shipping containers that enter the US. Nearly 7 million containers transit through America's ports each year and the US is part of a global transportation system that is both time sensitive and vulnerable to disruption. There were fears that containers could be used to import a deadly cargo into America, such as a radiological or nuclear device or even a biological weapon. In November 2002 the authorities responded to concern by launching the US Container Security Initiative (CSI), which enabled checks and the sharing of information. The CSI was initiated on a bilateral basis with seven key European countries who were providing the majority of the containers transported to America. US Customs Service officers were stationed in European ports and the US agreed to provide special access to its ports by those countries in the

CSI scheme.[98] But it was quickly realised that there were implications for the EU's internal market provisions. The European Commission began to take legal action against those countries that had established these arrangements on the grounds that it was responsible for ensuring fair competition.[99] An agreement was duly signed between the EU and the US on 22 April 2004 which replaced the bilateral agreements between the US and the EU member states.[100]

The third area of tension has been the issue of biometric identifiers in passports and identity documents. Biometric identifiers may take many forms, such as the recording of facial features, the scans of irises or fingerprints, but they provide ways to catalogue the unique characteristics of each human being and make it very difficult for identities to be disguised. The US set the requirement for two biometric identifiers to appear in passports for entry onto their soil by October 2004. The EU had already begun to grapple with the issue of biometric identifiers but felt that it was being rushed into provisions because of unilateral steps that were being taken in Washington. It also expressed concern at the data protection implications.[101] Under the EU Visa Information System (VIS) the personal details and photographs of persons will be stored on the system by 2006, whilst fingerprints and other biometric data will be stored by 2007. In 2004, the US Congress agreed that the date for implementing biometric identifiers for visa waiver states be extended by a year. The JHA Council in October 2004 concurred in introducing a facial image into passports within 18 months and fingerprints within 36 months.[102] This enabled both sides of the Atlantic to implement a system that met the required standards of either side and could be realised by the target date.

Each of the examples of transatlantic tension exhibit a similar source. Ideas were incubated inside the US bureaucracy without a clear understanding of the implications that they would have for Western Europe. The US government has been ineffective in communicating its thinking on homeland security to its allies. This has left the EU reacting to a US-inspired agenda, such as on travel documents and airline passenger information. Failure to reach an agreement has carried with it the risk that the US will proceed regardless and a serious disruption to the relationship will ensue.[103]

In the light of these tensions a significant initiative was agreed in November 2003. The EU and the US established a forum entitled the 'High Level Policy Dialogue on Borders and Transport Security'. This met first in April 2004 in Brussels and will meet biannually. It draws together the US Departments of State, Justice and Homeland Security with the EU Directorate General for JHA and the European

Commission offices dealing with the US, plus the EU Presidency and the Counter-Terrorism Coordinator. It focuses on issues in the first pillar pertaining to transport and immigration and marks an attempt to build cooperation from an early stage through the sharing of ideas. It is intended to enable the EU and the US to become aware of the plans of the other side and thereby build the procedures, tailored to their own needs, that will work and be compatible. In the words of Jonathan Faull, the European Commission Director General responsible for internal security, 'we [the transatlantic allies] should be frank with each other about ideas in the early phases of their gestation so that we have time to consider the implications for all of us on what is being planned'.[104]

Targeting of terrorist financing

The US and Europe have come to regard the targeting of finances as an important way to counter terrorism. The laundering of money from illegitimate sources and the transferring of funds around the world to facilitate terrorist activities renders these actors vulnerable to tracing and interception. This area of counter-terrorist activity was neglected in the past, due to a number of factors. First, there was an absence of clarity as to whether the laundering of money should be the subject of attention or whether it should be the criminal offence that accompanied this activity. Second, the international financial system suffered from inadequate policing mechanisms to trace the vast sums of money that were moved and then laundered around the world. Last, certain western countries were profiting indirectly from money laundering and were reluctant to stop this abuse of the system. The US was critical of some of its European allies for maintaining banking secrecy laws that enabled them to profit from illicit funds and for tolerating off-shore tax havens such as the Cayman Islands and the Virgin Islands. The Europeans have responded that US actions on money laundering have been far from exemplary. A report from the Financial Action Task Force on countries implementing its provisions placed the US in the third tier, below a host of European countries.[105]

The new level of threat from international terrorism altered the equation, and targeting the financing of these activities became an additional weapon in the armoury of western states. It represented a practical area of activity on which both sides of the Atlantic could cooperate, and it offered the opportunity to work together within more than one forum: the US-EU relationship as well as the G-8. The principal objectives have been, first, to freeze the assets of organisations linked to terrorism; and second, to increase the transparency of financial transactions so that terrorists find it harder to conceal their operations.[106] In October 2001, just a month after the attacks on New York and Washington, the Financial Action Task Force met in Washington and decided to use existing anti-money laundering mechanisms to target terrorist financing.

Some critics would argue that employing anti-money laundering as a means to counter terrorism was no better than a marriage of convenience; in the sense that it was an action that governments could be seen to be taking regardless of its dubious value. Concentrating on money laundering might be an effective strategy to combat international organised crime and drug trafficking, where huge criminal profits may be uncovered and where the strategy originated, but it is arguably of little use in dealing with terrorism, where the money might be from legitimate sources. Targeting the money that funds such activity is particularly difficult, because, as Pillar notes, 'Terrorism is fundamentally different from other leading transnational problems . . . in that big flows of money are not intrinsic to the operation'.[107] The EU traditionally restricted money laundering agreements to the sphere of drug trafficking but, after urging from Washington, it passed a directive that broadened the ban to include all types of international criminal activity.[108]

The US cajoled its European allies into tightening their provisions against money laundering.[109] In October 2001 the US Congress approved the Bush administration's 'International Money Laundering Abatement and Anti-Terrorist Financing Act', which established a system of regulation that extended beyond the major banks. A month later EU finance ministers followed this American lead. (As of August 2005, the EU has passed three Money Laundering Directives.) The obligation was placed on all sorts of professions to participate in reporting suspicious financial transactions exceeding $10,000, including *bureaux de change*, wire transfers, cash couriers and hawalas.[110] Regulations have been introduced for firms offering financial services. Moreover, sanctions will be imposed against states that permit their territories to be used as havens for illegal profits.

The US has been exasperated by the same sorts of weaknesses exhibited by the EU in anti-money laundering as those in other forms of internal security cooperation. EU member states have been willing to sign up to a host of commitments but they have often been poor in taking the necessary steps to implement them.[111] Agreements have stood idle, awaiting ratification by groups of states. Amongst these has been the UN 'Convention on the Suppression of the Financing of

Terrorism' and the Framework decision of July 2003 relating to money laundering.[112] In the case of a Framework Decision on the freezing of assets, agreed in March 2002, it was to have been implemented by the end of that year, but even as late as mid-2004 there were still states, such as Greece and Luxembourg, that had not enacted its provisions.[113]

There remain differences of emphasis between the US and Europe over combating terrorist financing. However, it has been a significant achievement to make this an important and very public sphere of regular transatlantic cooperation. The illustration of that achievement was forthcoming in June 2004 when the US and the EU agreed to hold a regular dialogue on the subject of terrorist financing.[114]

Conclusion

Although the history and natural inclination of the US has been to cooperate bilaterally with European countries, the widening competences of the EU have made it both an increasingly attractive and necessary partner for America in internal security matters. It has been necessary in the sense that EU member states have taken on obligations to act collectively and they are ever more constrained in entering into bilateral arrangements with a country such as America. The US-EU relationship has enabled new patterns of collaboration to evolve and standards to be raised, providing added value to a policy area where little existed in the past. Some may argue that the achievements to date have been modest. Yet they represent a recognition that terrorism can only be defeated by a community of states, and that they are the foundations on which more ambitious plans can be laid. The multilateral context has helped to provide momentum in attempts to work together, at a time when the broader transatlantic relationship has experienced unprecedented strain.

Both sides of the Atlantic have been developing a model of internal security. Despite starting from a low base, the US model has developed very fast because it has been adapted from measures that were designed to confront other types of threats, such as organised crime and drug trafficking. For example, the key provisions of the Patriot Act were in existence prior to 9/11 and the US used these to fashion a broad package of measures.[115] Added to the federal nature of its political system and the traumatic impact of 9/11, the US was able to propel legislation forward with great alacrity. The European model has been slower to develop, reflecting the multiplicity of national interests within the EU and the complexity of securing agreement amongst twenty-five states. Through a variety of measures, such as the

European Arrest Warrant and developing Europol and Eurojust, the EU has increased its ability to cooperate meaningfully with the US.

The speed of its own developments has enabled America to drive forward the process of cooperation with the EU. Europe has been reacting constantly to US initiatives but it has not had an American model of counter-terrorism imposed from the outside. There is too much evidence of US frustration in its relationship with Europe to support such a view. America has offered a model to Europe of how it believes cooperation should be pursued, but agreement rather than coercion has been the norm. The EU has continued to harbour a range of concerns about American policy and has been hesitant to enter into some agreements, such as over personal information sharing in Europol and PNR. It has expressed reservations over the implications of American actions for civil liberties and the different cultural values of Europe.[116] Two other anxieties have been uppermost in European minds: the risk that the US could try to use terrorism as a justification to force greater cooperation from EU; and the fear that there will be insufficient reciprocity from Washington in information exchange.

The difficulties of developing transatlantic internal security cooperation have been evident in numerous examples of tension. The US has felt exasperation at the slow pace at which EU decisions have progressed. It has also been frustrated by the apparent 'gesture' politics of some European states – the signing of agreements that are not implemented. This has been echoed from within the EU. In March 2004, EU Commission President Romano Prodi was openly critical of states that had not enacted provisions on JHA in the six key texts that were vital to the fight against terrorism, namely the EAW, Joint Investigation Teams, Money Laundering, Eurojust, Legal and Police Cooperation Measures against Terrorism, and the Framework Decision on the Definition of Terrorism.[117] The appointment of an EU Coordinator to fight terrorism, Gijs de Vries, following the Madrid attack, was an acknowledgement of this problem.[118] For its part, the EU has been critical of the bureaucratic wrangling that takes place in Washington and the open competition between intelligence agencies. The cultural differences of the two sides of the Atlantic have made cooperation challenging.

Nevertheless, as the transatlantic allies have fashioned new ways of working together, they have grown to understand some of the inherent complexities faced by the other side. The process of mutual learning has helped them to appreciate that they would be better served by frequent and early consultations before either side launches a major initiative. This message was implicit in a speech in 2004 by the outgoing JHA Commissioner, Vitorino, when he said of transatlantic cooperation that 'As we work together, we need to know what you are doing'.[119] The 'High Level Policy Dialogue on Borders and Transport Security' and regular exchange visits between senior officials dealing with internal security in the US and EU is evidence that better cooperation is being sought on both sides.

5 External security cooperation

Introduction

There is a paradox in transatlantic security cooperation. In the field of internal security there is evidence of increasing multilateral cooperation, whilst in external security the reverse is the case. The US has moved away from patterns of multilateral cooperation that characterised the Cold War era and has grown to favour bilateral cooperation with particular European allies. This is a reflection of two factors. First, because of its power the US has always possessed a choice over with whom to work: international organisations or individual European governments. The limitations of the organisations, and the problems of obtaining consensus from diverse clusters of states, have always been powerful arguments against multilateralism. Conversely, the inherent strength of the US, the ease of working within bilateral relationships and the opportunity to build coalitions of like-minded states, has been a powerful attraction. Second, US attitudes have changed substantially since 9/11, to a greater extent than those of Europe. Where the US was reluctant to intervene in international crises during the 1990s because it did not perceive its vital interests to be at stake – such as in Bosnia – now the US regards the War against Terror as central to its interests. As a consequence, it has been wary of allowing its power and global reach to be constrained by the attitudes of its European allies, particularly when they add only marginally to US capabilities.

An added source of complexity has been the fact that the traditional vehicle for conducting transatlantic external security cooperation, NATO, has been ill suited for counter-terrorism tasks. As was discussed in Chapter 2, NATO's competences in the military security of Europe have not been especially appropriate for dealing with the shadowy adversary of international terrorism. Yet the alternative framework of the European Union has been constrained by its under-developed Common Foreign and Security Policy; a Security and Defence Policy that has only been in existence since 1999; and a dependence on NATO for the use of infrastructure and military assets. In the light of these limitations, US scepticism about the added value of multilateralism has not been difficult to understand.

Indeed, European states themselves have adopted a similar approach during times of crisis. The most powerful European countries, such as the UK, France, Germany, Italy and Spain, have made their own offers of cooperation with the United States in the midst of the War on Terrorism. They have sought to coordinate their views amongst each other, but they have avoided pursuing multilateral efforts through either NATO or the EU. They too have reasserted the importance of their separate national interests and, by their actions, have shown themselves to be sceptical about notions of European common interest, cohesion and solidarity.

Confronting state sponsors of terrorism

The 1990s demonstrated the contrasting approaches of Europe and the United States towards state-sponsored international terrorism. Fearing the linkage between state sponsors, terrorist groups and WMD, the US argued that countries needed to be confronted and threatened with heavy penalties for putting the prevailing security order at risk. In the minds of friends and foes alike was the experience of April 1986 when the US had unilaterally used force against the Libyan government of President Qhaddafi. After the Reagan administration had obtained evidence that Libya was behind the bombing of a discotheque in Berlin frequented by US servicemen, 'Operation El Dorado Canyon' had been unleashed in which US carrier-borne aircraft, and bombers based in the UK, attacked three target complexes including Tripoli and Benghazi. The US had signalled from this attack that it was prepared to employ its military power against countries that supported or perpetrated terrorism.[1]

Each year the US has drawn up a list of those countries it regards as major terrorist sponsors.[2] Libya was thought to provide training and arms for various Middle East factions, although this diminished following the US attacks of 1986. Syria and Sudan were considered to be lesser sponsors; the latter was seen as an active supporter until around 2000 when it closed down training camps on its territory. North Korea figured on the US list primarily as a nuclear proliferator. Cuba was accused of fomenting instability in the Caribbean, but its status had more to do with history than its current activities. In

October 1999, UNSCR 1267 demanded the giving up of Osama bin Laden from Afghanistan and threatened the imposition of sanctions. Two states that were placed in a special category at the top of the list were Iran and Iraq. Iran was accused of supporting the movements Hezbollah and Hamas, as well as the Popular Front for the Liberation of Palestine (PFLP). Since the Gulf War of 1990–1 the US had marked down Iraq as a threat to regional stability, a country committed to obtaining WMD and a provider of support to certain groups such as Mujahedin-e Khalq. As a consequence the US followed a policy of 'dual containment' towards Iran and Iraq, seeking to limit their ability to export their ideas and influence in the region.[3]

The extent to which state sponsorship of terrorism remained a major problem was the subject of contestation in the 1990s. Many analysts were of the opinion that terrorist groups had changed in nature because of the paucity of sponsorship after the end of the Cold War. The new types of terrorism arising in the 1990s, characterised by religious motives, were less in need of state support.[4] According to the Director of the CIA, state sponsorship was in decline.[5] Even states such as Libya and Iraq were believed to be decreasing their support for groups around the world. Ambassador Sheehan, the US Coordinator for Counter Terrorism, testified to Congress in 1999 that 'Libya and Iraq remain on our list of state sponsors. . . . But their direct sponsorship of terrorist acts has diminished'.[6] In contrast to this assessment, Pillar argues that state sponsorship has remained vital to effective terrorism. He takes issue with the prevailing wisdom that terrorists need states less, and is not convinced that powerful terrorist groups only seek to act from the territory of 'failed' states.[7]

European attitudes towards such countries diverged from those of the United States. There was near universal condemnation of the US attacks on Libya: France had even refused US warplanes the right to over-fly its territory in execution of the raid. Only the government of Margaret Thatcher had supported the strikes and had permitted the use of UK bases. European countries have thus been much more reticent about using force or supporting the use of force against states accused of sponsoring terrorism. They have wanted to be sure of the legitimacy of an action before lending their support. Europeans have been prepared to countenance the use of force if it appears to be proportionate to the aggression and if it is in accordance with Article 51 of the UN Charter on self-defence. This is not to say that the Europeans have always implacably opposed the US employment of its military against states of concern. In August 1998, for example, following the terrorist attacks on the US embassies in Kenya and

Tanzania, President Clinton authorised military action. Tomahawk cruise missile strikes were conducted against alleged terrorist bases in Afghanistan and the al-Shaifa chemical plant in Khartoum, Sudan. A federal jury in New York issued an indictment for the arrest of the suspected instigator of the plot, Osama bin Laden.[8] In this case, there was a high degree of support from European allies for the US policy of retaliation.

European governments have preferred to offer positive incentives to states of concern to reform their behaviour. They have regarded sanctions and the threat of coercion as blunt instruments that tend to reinforce rather than reform errant behaviour. This has led European countries to engage in trade, diplomacy and cultural contacts with governments that the US has branded as pariahs. For example, in regards to Libya and Iran during the 1990s, individual European states as well as the EU pursued regular interaction, supported with trade incentives, in an attempt to promote changes in policy.[9] The EU professed that it wanted to strengthen the hand of moderates and reformers within those countries and undercut the arguments of hardliners. The policy was called a 'critical dialogue' on the grounds that the Europeans were not afraid to point out the wayward behaviour of these states, including aspects of their foreign policies and records on human rights.

Critics of the European critical dialogue have argued that it amounts to appeasement – a word calculated to stir the consciences of continental governments. Many of the most fervent critics have been in the US Congress, an actor that is frequently overlooked in analyses of American counter-terrorism policy, but one that has enjoyed enormous influence. The Congress put pressure on the Clinton administration to compel European governments into taking a harder approach towards states accused of supporting terrorism. They argued that European policy was based not on principle but on selfish interests. European governments were charged with being more concerned to protect trading advantages and investment – including the sale of high-technology and dual-use items – rather than security.[10] As the US took steps to isolate dangerous countries, they contended that Europeans refused to demonstrate a sense of solidarity and instead stepped in to take advantage of lucrative contracts that resulted from American disengagement.[11]

The differences in European and US approaches were highlighted most starkly in the case of the Iran/Libya Sanctions Act (ILSA). This Act was imposed by Congress upon a reluctant Clinton administration in 1996 and it was designed to put pressure on European governments that had not followed the American approach towards these states. It caused great resentment in Europe because it tied US extra-territorial legislative provisions to a comprehensive array of sanctions against Iran and Libya. Any western company that traded with either Iran or Libya, over a $20 million threshold, would be liable to being sued by a US company. The value of the suit would reflect the value of the property the US company had lost from the sanctioned country. In addition, visa restrictions would be placed on the entry into America of executives from the European companies concerned.[12] In 1997 the French company Total, along with Malaysian and Russian companies, won the right to invest in the Iranian petrochemical industry, and it looked as if the provisions of ILSA were about to be applied.[13] There was universal condemnation in Europe of the American position; even the UK government joined the European Commission in opposing ILSA's extra-territorial dimensions.

A transatlantic crisis was in the offing as the EU threatened to take the United States before the World Trade Organization (WTO). Intensive discussions occurred under the aegis of the New Transatlantic Agenda, and in May 1998 the crisis was defused when President Clinton waived the imposition of penalties on European companies.[14] America backed down, in the knowledge that a WTO ruling was likely to be unfavourable.[15] Nevertheless, it left a legacy of bitterness on the US side. They believed that Europe had attempted to profit from a situation that America had considered to be a matter of principle and, in doing so, had helped to prop up an unsavoury government in Tehran. This grievance was exacerbated by a German court ruling in April 1997 that implicated the highest levels of the Iranian government in the Mykonos murders of Kurdish dissidents in Berlin in 1992.[16] This appeared to confirm the American view of the vicious nature of the government in Tehran. Although EU governments withdrew their ambassadors from the country for a period of time, the US regarded the European response as little more than symbolic and far short of what was necessary to cause Iran to reconsider its policy towards the West. In American eyes this was another example of an age-old problem – namely European governments relying on the US to police the world and ignoring security concerns that were not within their immediate spheres of interest.

The European response to 9/11

Expressions of outrage by Europe in response to 9/11 were genuine and heartfelt. There was a real sense of solidarity with the US after the severity of the attacks and the magnitude of the loss of life. NATO famously responded by activating its Article V collective defence guarantee in which the European members of the Alliance offered support to the US.[17] It was a sad irony that the only time in which this guarantee has been invoked was the opposite way around that everyone expected. There were countless offers of help to the US government, ranging from the use of ports and airfields in Europe to the mobilisation of armed forces.

The experience of 9/11 confirmed US perceptions that its foremost threat was from international terrorism and associated state sponsors. The US made it clear that it would draw no distinction between the terrorists who committed the attacks on American soil and those who gave them refuge.[18] The US regarded state sponsors as of equal danger to the terrorists they supported because they might potentially provide them with the most lethal weapon technologies. The state sponsors also provided a more tangible target than the terrorist groups themselves – as President Clinton's retaliation against alleged terrorist training camps in Afghanistan in 1998 had demonstrated. The Bush administration was forthright in declaring that it would call state sponsors to account and the US arrogated to itself the right to use force pre-emptively. In an address to the nation, Bush stated, 'In this conflict there is no neutral ground. If any government sponsors the outlaws and killers of innocents, they have become outlaws and murderers themselves.'[19]

The initial anxiety in Europe was that the attack on its soil might lead the US to over-react and use force indiscriminately around the world. An unconstrained American response risked doing great damage to western relations with Islamic states. In light of this, Chancellor Schröder of Germany assured the US of the support of his country but warned America against undertaking 'adventures'.[20] When it became apparent that the US response was going to be measured and calculated, the relief in Europe was almost palpable. Various European capitals exhorted Washington to respond to the attacks in a way that would harness the greatest sense of legitimacy and the authority of international law. The EU called for 'the broadest possible coalition against terrorism, under the United Nations aegis'.[21]

There was no disguising the fact, however, that the US-led War on Terror was divisive within Europe. The fact that the EU's Common Foreign and Security Policy represents little more than a collection of the national foreign policies of the member states was exposed by the crisis. There was a lack of unity within the EU and the major states each sought to enhance their bilateral relationships with the US. The

Union focused upon internal security cooperation with the United States through Pillars 1 and 3, whilst Pillar 2 was neglected.[22] The US amplified this tendency amongst the European powers by focusing on its relationships with individual states and disregarding the EU as a whole. Grant notes that when the Belgian Prime Minister went to the US at the end of the year to speak on behalf of the EU, the key members of the US administration could not even find time to meet with him.[23]

The best example of the assertion of European national policies was in November 2001, when British Prime Minister Tony Blair hosted a dinner at Downing Street in the midst of the US military action in Afghanistan. Because of Blair's closeness to the Bush administration, this dinner was designed to share information and try to coordinate positions amongst the leading European powers. Invitations were extended to Chancellor Schröder of Germany and President Chirac of France. Yet other European leaders became aware of the meeting and felt excluded by the 'Big Three'. Italian Prime Minister Silvio Berlusconi, Spanish Prime Minister Jose Maria Aznar, and Dutch Prime Minister Wim Kok all insisted on attending. Invitations were later sent to the Belgian Prime Minister, whose country occupied the EU Presidency, and Javier Solana, the EU's High Representative. This was illustrative of the competitive approach that emerges between European countries during times of crisis.

France and Britain, both with strong global perspectives due to their power and history, nevertheless represent the opposite ends of the spectrum in relation to foreign policy cooperation with the United States. The French have long been wary of cooperation with America as they have viewed Washington as advancing its own selfish interests under the guise of working on behalf of the West. France has argued that Europe needs to build up its power base in order to be able to pursue its own interests and should not be dependent upon America. A stronger Europe, according to Paris, would facilitate a more equitable relationship with the US. After 9/11 President Chirac and Foreign Minister de Villepin argued that military operations should be confined to Afghanistan.[24] The US largely ignored these French arguments in the period following the military success in Afghanistan. Yet French policy remained consistent, and it was this that came to haunt Franco-US relations in the aftermath of the conflict against the Taliban.

Britain has stood at the opposite end to the French position. Prime Minister Tony Blair argued that the US and Europe had to pull in tandem in order to overcome the new level of threat presented by international terrorism and state sponsors. There was fundamental agreement in Britain with the American focus on terrorism and WMD as the foremost threats to international security,[25] and a determination to act before threats materialised. Dunne talks of a 'resurgent Atlanticist identity which is shaping British security strategy after 9/11'.[26] There was certainly a desire to be a close partner of American policy and to prevent a mood of unilateralism taking hold in Washington, based on the view that European countries would leave the hard foreign policy issues to the US. Where there were differences between the US and Europe, Britain sought to act as a transatlantic bridge. It was a tenet of British policy that its own interests, as well as those of Europe, would best be served by transatlantic unity of thinking and action.

The war in Afghanistan

The war in Afghanistan was an example of a conflict in which the Europeans supported America's decision to use force. The US issued an ultimatum to the Taliban rulers in Afghanistan that they must surrender all members of Al-Qaeda and its leader Osama bin Laden. The refusal of the Taliban to accede to these demands provided the justification for the use of force and the requisite legitimacy required by European governments. 'Operation Enduring Freedom' commenced on 7 October 2001 with the aim of either arresting or destroying Al-Qaeda and toppling the government in Kabul from power.

The US chose not to act through NATO, but to undertake a largely unilateral policy. The offer of help from NATO was gratefully received in Washington but the decision was made only to accept background support for the American campaign. NATO naval assets were sent to the eastern Mediterranean to enable US vessels to be withdrawn in support of Operation Enduring Freedom; five E-3 advanced warning and control systems (AWACS) planes were sent from the NATO pool to police the east coast of America under 'Operation Eagle Assist', and NATO nations took over the protection of US facilities in Europe. But the Alliance as a whole was not called on by the US. The operation in Afghanistan was planned and conducted out of US Central Command, under General Tommy Franks, rather than by the NATO Supreme Allied Commander at Mons in Belgium.

The US chose to depend on no other ally. After the difficult experience of the Kosovo conflict in 1999, when the US had been required to obtain the agreement of its NATO allies for the manner in which it fought the war, in this circumstance the US chose to act alone. This was in part understandable because the Al-Qaeda attacks had only been perpetrated against the US and because its massive military strength meant that it did not need assistance to crush the Taliban. Yet it also reflected a deeper undercurrent of thinking in the Bush administration about the flexibility and malleability of international relationships. In September 2001 US Deputy Secretary of State Richard Armitage spoke of choosing allies with whom the US wanted to work, whilst US Defense Secretary Donald Rumsfeld stated that he envisaged the military task determining the coalition.[27] There were indications from senior figures in the Bush administration that the US would choose its allies according to the tasks it wished to undertake, rather than be locked into formal alliance arrangements that would circumscribe its freedom of action. In the event of crises, the US should assemble *ad hoc* groupings of states that shared its priorities and were able to make useful contributions to military tasks. The implications of this thinking were that America had no fixed allies, only shifting patterns of interests.

On a bilateral basis, several European countries made contributions to the US operation against the Taliban. They provided mainly special forces personnel and support aircraft, notably refuelling tanker aircraft for US strike operations. Some naval forces were also engaged, such as Royal Navy submarines firing Tomahawk cruise missiles as part of 'Operation Veritas'. But offers of forces from countries such as Spain, Italy, the Netherlands and Poland were simply not taken up by the US.[28] This was partly a reflection of the sort of war the US chose to fight: one in which long-range airpower was used with devastating effect, whilst for ground troops the US relied upon the rebel 'Northern Alliance' and special forces. It was also partly due, as Serfaty notes, to the swift collapse of the Taliban which left little fighting on the ground other than chasing the remnants of Al-Qaeda into the mountainous terrain of Tora Bora.[29] Nevertheless, the upshot of the campaign was that the Europeans played only a marginal role in the victory.

It was not until after the conflict that the US turned seriously to the Europeans for a major contribution. An International Security Assistance Force (ISAF) was assembled under a UN mandate to maintain security in the country, and the UK initially took the leading role, with the support of troops from France, Germany, Denmark, the Netherlands, Belgium and Portugal. The US reduced its military presence in Afghanistan, although it maintained some military operations as part of 'Operation Enduring Freedom'. It was apparent that American attention was switching to Iraq accompanied by increasingly bellicose noises.[30] In August 2003 this impression of European control was further reinforced when NATO was given command of ISAF. NATO, with German operational command, concentrated initially on the security of Kabul and then gradually moved to extend its control into the countryside with the creation of Provincial Reconstruction Teams.[31]

It was hard to avoid the impression that the US had been uninterested in European involvement in the military campaign in Afghanistan, but was eager to hand over the laborious task of post-conflict stability and reconstruction to its allies and the UN. This was a familiar source of tension between the Europeans and the Americans. With its overwhelming military firepower, the US has proved decisive in military interventions. Yet the US has sought to extricate itself rapidly from post-conflict reconstruction and has left it to European countries to shoulder the lion's share of the peacekeeping and the financial investment.

One area of European contribution that went on behind the scenes was the diplomatic support for US actions conducted with a variety of states in Central Asia, the Middle East and North Africa. This diplomacy was designed to assist the US effort and build a broad coalition against terrorism. It was undoubtedly of help to the US that Europe utilised its contacts with regions of the world in furtherance of this endeavour. EU Troika visits, for example, were made to Saudi Arabia, Iran and the states of Central Asia, whilst NATO used its contacts, through the Partnership for Peace programme, with states such as Morocco, Tunisia and Algeria. British Prime Minister Tony Blair made an energetic round of visits which took him to Russia and Pakistan in October 2001 and then on to sensitive countries such as Syria. France also undertook such efforts on the part of the US with those countries with which it enjoyed close relations.[32]

Some of the goodwill that the US had enjoyed from Europe was dissipated in the conduct of the conflict in Afghanistan. Another source of transatlantic tension appeared after the conflict ended, over the issue of how the US was treating its prisoners. President Bush made it clear that the scale of the attack on the US was tantamount to an act of war, albeit one that was carried out by non-state actors.[33] In the light of this interpretation that the US was at war, the President signed a Military Order on 13 November 2001 relating to the detention, treatment and trial of non-US citizens. 'Enemy combatants', judged to be members of Al-Qaeda, were transported to 'Camp X-Ray' at Guantanamo Bay in Cuba to be held there indefinitely. The US government had chosen this location because it represented a sort of legal limbo, outside the normal jurisdiction of US federal courts. The US argument was that these were dangerous individuals on whom the US had insufficient, or inadmissible, intelligence evidence, on which to convict them, but they nevertheless needed to be incarcerated.

Many European countries have been deeply critical of the US approach towards prisoners on Guantanamo, arguing that it debases America's own traditionally high standards of justice. They have regarded it as illustrative of the differences in standards that circumscribe the potential for closer transatlantic cooperation. Europeans contend that the damage done to the US image by being perceived to practise injustice, outweighs the gains it makes in individual cases. As Gijs de Vries, the EU Counter-Terrorism Coordinator, stated in evidence before the US House of Representatives in 2004, 'Violating the rule of law in the fight against terrorism is not only morally undesirable but also ineffective in the long run'.[34] It was not until the autumn of 2004 that the US Supreme Court intervened in the matter and ruled that those held in detention had the right to have their cases reviewed. Such reviews will be undertaken by military tribunals, to the chagrin of European countries.

The Iraq war and its aftermath

It soon became clear that as the conflict in Afghanistan was drawing down, American attention in its War on Terror was shifting to other theatres.[35] The US was no longer thinking and acting as a *status quo* power; instead, it perceived itself to be under threat, and in possession of the means and the political will to confront these threats.[36] This was exemplified in President Bush's address to Congress in January 2002 when he talked of an 'Axis of Evil' threatening international security.[37] Three states were identified as comprising this axis: Iraq, Iran and North Korea. Bush declared in his speech that 'We will not permit the world's most dangerous regimes and terrorists to threaten us with the world's most destructive weapons'.[38] Iraq became the principal focus of US security policy.

This focus on Iraq reflected the priorities of key figures within the Bush administration. A group of neo-conservatives, or so-called 'Democratic Imperialists', such as Paul Wolfowitz and Douglas Freith within the administration and Richard Perle outside, argued that America should use its power to remove tyrannical governments around the world that threatened America's interests and allies.[39] They argued that the fall of the Baathist government in Iraq would create a beacon of democracy in the Middle East that could act as the harbinger of change. The neo-conservatives enjoyed support from conservative nationalists within the government, such as Defense Secretary Donald Rumsfeld and Vice President Richard Cheney. They also had the ear of the President, whose father had tried to undermine Saddam Hussein after the Gulf War of 1990–1 and had suffered an assassination attempt in Kuwait in April 1993. The hatred within the Bush administration for Saddam was almost visceral; indeed Wolfowitz and Rumsfeld had argued for attacking Iraq almost immediately after the events of 9/11.[40]

The US came to argue that defeating Saddam was an essential part of the War on Terror. An extensive case was made before the invasion of Iraq that Saddam was determined to acquire WMD and that he had lied and evaded the attempts of the post-1993 UN inspection system that had been established to disarm the country. There was incontrovertible evidence that Saddam had tried to sustain covert weapons programmes that had subsequently been discovered, but what was unclear was the level of effort that had continued after UN weapons inspectors had been barred from the country in 1998. President Bush demanded that Iraq undertake a transparent exercise in disarmament. The US administration went on to draw a link between Iraq's weapons programmes and its support for terrorism,[41] alleging that Iraq 'aids and protects' Al-Qaeda.[42] It was asserted that Iraq might develop WMD that it would then place in the hands of international terrorists such as Al-Qaeda. This view was not unique to the administration of Bush. His predecessor, President Clinton, had made a similar warning in 1998 and called for a change of regime as part of the Iraq Liberation Act.[43] Nevertheless, this linkage was something that European countries disputed, and it was an allegation that the 9/11 Commission later declared to be unfounded.[44] The Bush administration used the rationale of state sponsorship of terrorism and the threat of WMD to justify the use of force towards a country with whom it had long experienced an antagonistic relationship.

In preparing for a showdown with Iraq, the Bush administration sent two important signals to its transatlantic allies. The first was that while the US was desirous of their support, it was not a pre-condition for American action. Bush announced that although the US 'will constantly strive to enlist the support of the international community, we will not hesitate to act alone, if necessary'.[45] This was consistent with the thinking of the US government up to that point in time; that America needed to have freedom to act, to be able to use its unparalleled strength without the constraint of allied opinion. US national interests would not be subordinated to the demands of leading alliances.[46] This American approach was justified publicly on the grounds of exercising its inherent right of self-defence.[47] The implication was that allies took too long to convince and mobilise, at least in a multilateral forum, and therefore the US might have no choice other than to assemble a coalition that could counter the near-term threat.[48] The European Parliament complained in 2002 that it was 'deeply concerned by the rising unilateralism in US foreign policy and the lack of interest in close consultation and cooperation with the European partners'.[49]

The US was advancing a model for conducting its War on Terror in which it led and expected its allies to follow. This was a very different model of leadership to that which the US had proffered during the Cold War, in which consultation had been extensive. Wallace observes that 'European governments are therefore faced with a harsher choice in responding to the reassertion of American leadership . . . a choice between "followership" . . . or resistance to American leadership'.[50] Nelson concurs in this assessment, arguing that the US was seeking not 'burden-sharing, but identity subservience'.[51] It fell far short of the 'partnership' that had been aired by leading figures within the US administration.[52] Counter-terrorism had become the yardstick by which the US would assess the utility of all its existing patterns of cooperation, a crude form of reductionism that many of its allies were unwilling to accept. Rather than invest the time and diplomatic effort to convince other countries of the rightness of its cause, the US chose to act according to its own priorities. When leading countries in Europe, such as Germany and France, expressed objections to US policy, Defense Secretary Rumsfeld dismissed them as the unimportant views of 'Old Europe'.[53]

Inequalities in power between the US and Europe convinced senior policy-makers in Washington that they had little to gain in waiting until their allies were convinced of the need to remove Saddam Hussein from power. Issues were painted in black and white terms so that there was no room for alternative ideas. European countries must accept part of the blame for this, because they had allowed their defence capabilities to fall to such a level that enabled the US to ignore them. The fact that they had relied on the US, hitherto, to provide for their security meant that they possessed limited military capabilities to offer to Washington. The US was right to be sceptical about the 'added value' that its allies could make available.

The other signal that the US sent to its transatlantic allies was its willingness to use force pre-emptively to counter perceived threats. Important questions were raised by this stance: from where was

America drawing its authority to use force against Iraq, and how reliable was the intelligence upon which its calculations were based? There was clearly a risk that the world's only superpower was employing the pretext of pre-emption to use coercion against a state it had long despised. America was changing the rules of the multilateral order that it had been instrumental in creating, and this is what caused such offence in Europe. No longer would the UN Security Council be the forum in which the use of force would be sanctioned. Now the US was arguing that it had the right to choose when it was correct for it to act. In so doing, it was giving authoritarian states an excuse to use force when it suited them.

Over the case of Iraq, divergences in transatlantic attitude had been evident for some time.[54] The US and Britain, since the first Gulf War, had been the leading supporters of sanctions as a way of punishing Iraq and limiting the resources it could direct towards military programmes.[55] The 'oil for food' policy enabled Iraq to sell its oil but controlled the disbursement of funds so that the money was spent on foodstuffs and medicines for the population. Through the 1990s a gradually diminishing group of countries policed the 'No Fly Zone' in Iraq, between the 33rd and 36th parallels, until eventually only the US and Britain performed the task. Periodically, US and British air strikes were inflicted on the country, usually in retaliation for Iraqi attempts to target aircraft policing the zone. In December 1998, 'Operation Desert Fox' subjected Iraq to four days of bombing of its suspected weapon sites, after the ejection of the inspectors from the UN Special Commission on Iraq (UNSCOM). These strikes became a source of tension between Washington and various European capitals because the action was judged to be heavy-handed and an insufficient incentive for Iraq to reform. France withdrew from policing the No Fly Zone on these grounds, and other European states grew reluctant to find Iraq in material breach of her UN obligations, in case the US interpreted this as a pretext to use force.[56]

By the end of the decade the sanctions regime had become highly porous, despite the best efforts of the US and Britain to shore it up. Sanctions had failed in their intention of removing Saddam, who had found ways to circumvent them, particularly through illicit sales of oil. The sanctions had come to be regarded as a heavy burden upon the Iraqi people, causing high levels of infant mortality and widespread suffering. The US adopted 'smart' sanctions as a way to relax the broader range of restrictions that were hurting ordinary people whilst tightening controls over goods that could increase the coercive power of the government.[57] Many European countries argued that sanctions should be lifted altogether. Yet the US was suspicious of the motives of governments like France and Germany, believing that they were eager to profit from contracts with Iraq and were seeking to recoup loans that they had made earlier to the government in Baghdad. As the US confrontation with Iraq escalated after the beginning of 2002, the gap between the transatlantic allies widened. France and Germany were the European countries leading the opposition to the American policy: in Germany's case this was a dramatic reversal of its erstwhile closeness to the US. Both France and Germany questioned the whole assumption as to whether Iraq was relevant to the War on Terrorism, especially the linkage between Saddam Hussein and Al-Qaeda.[58] They feared that the stance could actually stir up more terrorism and worsen relations with Muslim countries.[59] President Chirac expressed strong misgivings about the unilateral approach of the Bush administration, over its failure to sustain a dialogue with its allies, and the problem of legitimacy associated with circumventing the UN Security Council and pushing for war. France did not rule out the use of force against Iraq, but argued that all avenues needed to be exhausted first, including giving more time to the UN weapons inspectors.

There was no unity amongst the European positions, however. Several countries shared the hard-line US approach towards Iraq, as exemplified by the open letter that was signed by the UK, Spain, Italy, Poland, Portugal, Denmark, the Czech Republic and Hungary at the end of January 2003. British policy had shadowed that of America from after the Gulf War, including over sanctions and the periodic use of force. Tony Blair shared the fears of the Bush administration that WMD would eventually reach the hands of terrorists, and he believed that the international community had to prevent this danger before tragic consequences ensued. Although the British did not believe in an Al-Qaeda link with Iraq, they did fear that terrorists and states with WMD might work together in the future. In a speech to the Parliamentary Labour Party in February 2003 Tony Blair said that 'People say that you are doing this because the Americans are telling you to do it. I keep telling them it's worse than that. I believe in it.'[60] Despite these protestations, it was also a priority for the British government that a transatlantic split over war with Iraq be avoided. Tony Blair worked tirelessly to try and reconcile the positions between the Bush administration and its European critics, but found himself boxed in by the decision of the White House, as early as the spring of 2002, to remove the government in Baghdad. The Prime Minister was successful in working with moderate voices in the Bush administration, such as Secretary of State Colin Powell, to convince President Bush to use the United Nations to justify its policy towards Iraq. The passing of Security Council Resolution 1441 in November 2002 mandated the return of weapons inspectors and gave Iraq one last opportunity to disarm comprehensively. The differences between the major European states ensured that there was no attempt to use the EU to try and fashion a common response to the crisis. The CFSP was paralysed once more by divergent perspectives amongst the leading European states.[61] Some accused the Bush administration of pursuing a deliberate policy of 'divide and rule' towards Europe over the Iraq war.[62] Such an interpretation neglects two important factors. The first was that the Europeans had already demonstrated their own capacity to generate division amongst themselves; there was little need to blame the US. Second, it presumes that anything more than a token European contribution towards the war was important to America. In reality, the US was confident that it could overcome the weakened Iraqi armed forces in a relatively short space of time. Europe could add few military capabilities to those of the US and a conflict that involved allies was likely to complicate American military planning.

NATO, like the EU, was sidelined by the cleavages both across the Atlantic and between its European members. The US made no secret of its lack of interest in the Alliance and did not really attempt to carry opinion in the North Atlantic Council. An extra blow was struck to the Alliance when the US requested, in January 2003, that it consider offering help to Turkey in the event of a war with Iraq. France, Germany and Belgium opposed the request on the grounds that it made conflict more likely. A crisis was created by the fact that the Alliance was prevented from fulfilling its obligations to a member when there was a military threat. The crisis was resolved when NATO's Defence Planning Committee reached a compromise by agreeing to send only defensive equipment to the government in Ankara. Yet damage had been done to confidence in the Alliance.

The transatlantic relationship was torn apart by the debate over Iraq. What made this situation so different from past transatlantic differences was that countries, such as France and Germany, were making deliberate efforts to obstruct American security policy. Chancellor Schröder made it clear that he would refuse German participation in a conflict even if a UN mandate was secured. Iraq's 12,000-page report on its weapon stockpiles, submitted in December 2002, was judged to be incomplete by the US and Britain, whilst Hans Blix, the chief UN arms inspector, issued a report in the following January stating that Iraq had not provided a full and frank account of its programmes.[63] The US asserted that Iraq was in contravention of

UNSCR 1441, as well as all previous Security Council Resolutions since the first Gulf War, and that this justified the use of force. President Chirac, on the other hand, repudiated this claim and argued that 1441 was never designed to provide the authorisation for the use of force against Iraq. France went on to frustrate a last-minute attempt by the British ambassador to the UN, Jeremy Greenstock, to obtain a second UNSCR that would have explicitly authorised force. President Chirac made clear he would veto any resolution.

When it came, in March 2003, the conflict was unexpectedly swift and decisive, thereby highlighting the weakness of the Iraqi government and the military superiority of the US.[64] Nevertheless, in spite of the rapid victory it was soon evident that there had been insufficient planning for the aftermath of the conflict and the reconstruction effort. The US declared a formal end to hostilities in May, but then found itself caught up in a vicious insurgency conflict that caused high numbers of casualties and exposed the fragility of the American control over the country. The chronic insecurity made it extremely difficult to improve the quality of life for the inhabitants, such as providing adequate quantities of clean water, supplying electricity and restoring the education system. Attacks on pipelines have frustrated the renovation of the oil industry. An additional factor that has detracted from the American-led occupation has been the scandal of the abuse meted out to Iraqi detainees at the Abu Ghraib prison.[65]

The most significant de-legitimising factor has proved to be the inability to find any weapons of mass destruction in Iraq.[66] This was ostensibly the reason for going to war. It appears that the efforts by UN weapons inspectors during the 1990s had been effective in dismantling both Iraq's stockpiles of chemical and biological weapons and its nascent nuclear weapons programme.[67] Admittedly, most intelligence agencies in the western world were of the opinion that some Iraqi WMD programmes existed before the war.[68] But it was apparent that the imminence of the threat had been exaggerated in Washington and London in order to make the case for war. The justifications for the war began to mutate from WMD to the failure of sanctions, the long-term threat Iraq had presented to its neighbours and the abuse of human rights under the murderous government of Saddam Hussein.

The post-war insurgency continued to place coalition forces in Iraq under pressure, and the US administration raised the issue of whether NATO could play a bigger role in post-conflict stabilisation. However, countries such as France and Germany felt their opposition to the war had been vindicated by events. They opposed an overt NATO mission, arguing that it would legitimise the US-UK action and risk drawing the Alliance into a role and an area of the world for which it was unsuited. The most that could be agreed was to give NATO responsibility for training some elements of the Iraqi security forces through the establishment of a permanent centre at Al-Rustamiyah.[69]

It is an irony that the US went to war against Saddam at least partly based on the justification that it was fighting terror, yet the conflict served to fracture much of the support for the US as architect of the War on Terror. Many important figures in the US have expressed this view. For instance, Brent Scowcroft, the former National Security Adviser to George Bush Snr, warned before the war that 'an attack on Iraq at this time would seriously jeopardize, if not destroy, the global counter-terrorist campaign we have undertaken'.[70] The Counter Terrorism Coordinator Richard Clarke described the invasion of Iraq as 'a completely unnecessary tangent'.[71] Senator John Kerry, in his attempt to obtain the presidency, argued that the US had neglected its priorities by switching attention from Afghanistan and bin Laden to Iraq. Similarly, another contender in the Democratic primaries, General Wesley Clark, argued that the US should have maintained its focus on Al-Qaeda and its associated networks.[72]

The Iraq conflict has been described as representing the 'Perfect Storm' between the Atlantic allies. It was the confluence of a variety of factors. One was personalities: an American administration that had decided upon war from an early stage and European leaders such as Chirac and Schröder who were prepared to exploit anti-Americanism for reasons of domestic political popularity. A second was the contrasting approaches of Europe and America towards how to deal with states of concern and the risks of stimulating greater terrorist violence in the world. As force against Iraq became the likely outcome, the views of the Pentagon began to dominate and those of the State Department – more sympathetic to the views of allies – were drowned out. A third factor was the issue of legitimacy in foreign policy actions and the pretext for the use of force. A fourth was the different attitudes towards the role of international organisations: the US Defense Secretary was accused of treating 'NATO and Europe as a toolbox' from which America could pick and choose.[73] What was clear from the experience was that the transatlantic relationship had reached a nadir and there was a very real danger that permanent damage had been inflicted.[74]

Post-Iraq developments

The action taken by the US in Iraq has not resolved the issue of state sponsorship of terrorism or the proliferation of WMD. There remain countries that are a source of concern both to the United States and to Europe. It has been unlikely in the aftermath of the war against Iraq that the US would want to orchestrate a crisis with such countries, at least not in the short term. With a troop presence numbering around 200,000 in Iraq, and at least that number committed to rotational deployments to the region, it would be hard for the US to use force against another country. Had the post-war situation in Iraq turned out differently then there might have been greater freedom for manoeuvre but as it is, the US has been forced to recognise its own limits.

These practical constraints have not stopped the Bush administration from enjoying the sense of uncertainty that has been sown in the minds of enemies, such as Syria and Iran, by its actions in Iraq. For example, in the latter stages of the conflict against Saddam Hussein, Washington made several bellicose remarks regarding Syria's alleged military support to Iraq as well as its ties to terrorist groups such as Hezbollah sheltering in Lebanon.[75] It has been the policy of the US to cultivate a sense of uncertainty in the minds of its opponents about where it might strike next. The risk inherent in such a policy is that uncertainty can be a double-edged sword. Record questions what lessons states opposed to the US may draw from 'Operation Iraqi Freedom'. Rather than deterring states from seeking to acquire WMD, it could foster the argument that only the possession of such capabilities could dissuade the US from initiating hostilities.[76]

The US has been content to let the EU take the lead in recent dealings with Iran.[77] Although the overthrow of the Taliban marked a short-lived confluence of interest between Washington and Tehran, the relationship quickly returned to hostility.[78] Both the Europeans and the Americans have shared the suspicion that Iran has been pursuing a clandestine nuclear weapons capability under the guise of its civil nuclear programme, based around a Russian-built reactor at Bushehr.[79] The enrichment of uranium at Esfahan has appeared to be far in excess of what Iran requires for the production of civil nuclear power.[80] Despite the fact that Iran signed an additional protocol to its nuclear safeguards agreement with the International Atomic Energy Agency in December 2003, both sides of the Atlantic have pressured the country to prove that its intentions are benign.[81]

Three sorts of options have been available.[82] The first has been to seek to prevent Iran from acquiring the technologies necessary to create WMD. The US and Europe have favoured this option but have sometimes disagreed over tactics. The second option has been to trust Iran's protestations of innocence. This carries the risk that it might be harder to get Tehran to relinquish nuclear technology once it has acquired a bomb-making capability. Neither the US nor Europeans have been willing to accept the word of the government in Tehran that it has no ambition of acquiring nuclear weapons. The third option has been to embrace the prospect of a multipolar nuclear world and to consider strategies for managing such an eventuality.

The foreign ministers of the UK, France and Germany ('E3') have offered Iran numerous inducements to cooperate. These have included trade benefits and possible admission to the World Trade Organization. An appeal was made to Iran from the G-8 summit at Evian in 2003. The US has allowed the E3 to take the lead but has been pressing for International Atomic Energy Agency action and referral to the UN Security Council. By standing aloof, the US has presented a background threat that the E3 have been able to exploit. They have been able to point to the risk of referring the matter to the UN Security Council if a deal is not forthcoming, leading inexorably to American involvement.

In December of 2003 Iran announced it would allow inspections of its nuclear facilities. In November of the following year it formally suspended its enrichment of uranium in response to pressure from the E3.[83] But the equivocal nature of Iran's statements and the deeply held suspicion that it has failed to disclose the full extent of its nuclear ambitions has led the US to press for the imposition of sanctions. The situation was clouded further by the Iranian presidential elections in June 2005 that resulted in the election of a hardliner, Mahmoud Ahmadinejad. At the time of writing the implications of these developments are uncertain.[84] It may be that Iran has calculated, based on the experience of Iraq in 2003, that possession of nuclear weapons is the only guarantee of its safety in the face of both American power and its proximity to Israel.[85] This issue is seen by many analysts as having the potential to cause increasing transatlantic discord.[86]

Whilst the future of western relations with Iran appear shrouded in danger, another former sponsor of terrorism, Libya, has emerged as a relative success story. Its sponsorship of terrorism declined after the 1980s, and the government of Qhaddafi made it clear for some time that it wanted to be rehabilitated in the eyes of the international community. This was partly the result of the pressure of sanctions, which the EU joined in 1992, targeted at Libya's economy and particularly its petrochemical industry. Economic isolation had damaged Libya and made it eager to restore its tarnished image. Moreover, the US-led war against Iraq caused disquiet in Libya, for it was apparent that America was willing to use force to unseat its enemies. It would be incorrect, however, to attribute Tripoli's change of policy to the war: its re-orientation was discernible many years before.[87]

In December 2003 Libya announced it would rid itself of all banned weapons and would allow intrusive inspections of all its weapon sites. A deal to provide compensation for the families of the Lockerbie victims was agreed in April 2004, and this unlocked US and British opposition to the rehabilitation of the country. Sanctions against Libya were duly suspended and Prime Minister Tony Blair even journeyed to visit Qhaddafi in the desert. The Libyan example demonstrated that the European approach towards states of concern – namely dialogue, pressure and inducements – could be made to work over a long period.

The case of North Korea has been less successful than Libya and has aroused more tension between the US and Europe. The US has dominated approaches towards North Korea and achieved the signing of the US-North Korean Agreed Framework in October 1994.[88] As part of this agreement, America undertook to assist in guaranteeing the energy needs of North Korea, by providing two proliferation-resistant light water nuclear reactors and heavy fuel oil. In return, North Korea committed itself to the dismantling of its nascent nuclear weapons programme and the opening of its facilities to safeguard inspections.[89] The US approached the EU for support in financing this agreement, which became formalised in the Korean Energy Development Organization.

In October 2002 suspicions about North Korea's nuclear weapons programme were confirmed when its government admitted to the existence of a covert programme and announced its withdrawal from the Non-Proliferation Treaty.[90] This was followed in the spring of the following year by North Korea's confirmation that it possessed nuclear weapons and had deployed them.[91] The Bush administration has insisted on dealing with North Korea through a six-nation group including China, Russia, Japan and South Korea. The EU has sought occasionally to undertake its own diplomatic initiative, and has been more predisposed towards finding a compromise with the government in Pyongyang.[92] The Europeans have less political investment in the region than the US and see no evidence that the North Koreans are linked to terrorist groups.

Since the crisis in transatlantic relations over the Iraqi conflict, there has been an attempt by both sides to mend political fences. However, there remain fundamental differences in approach towards countries such as Iran and North Korea. If a crisis with one of these states were to develop, then there is a potential for the relationship between the US and Europe to return to the deep freeze.

Conclusion

Under the Bush administration America has chosen to fight a particular type of War on Terror that has reflected its own strengths. Its strategy has emphasised the potential and actual use of military power. This power has been directed against those states that the US has identified as either harbouring its enemies or building weapons capabilities that could place American security at risk. In the exercise of this power, the administration has sought to avoid any constraints upon its freedom of action and has preferred to work with *ad hoc* coalitions of states that support its strategies, rather than working through established multilateral frameworks. The war against Iraq was the apogee of this policy: America used force against a country that was an acknowledged thorn in its side but was patently not a core consideration in the War on Terrorism. The US demonstrated, by attacking Iraq, that it was using the justification of its War on Terror to eradicate unrelated security concerns.

Wall argues that the key difference between the Europeans and the Americans is not about the use of force in international relations.[93] Rather, it is a more fundamental consideration about the rule of law. He argues that 9/11 enabled the Bush administration to put aside the traditional constraints on the willingness of the American public to see its armed services being used in foreign adventures. In addition, the unique strength of the US allowed it to disregard the legal constraints on which the international order has been built. For example, the US has turned its back on the International Criminal Court and it has flouted the 1949 UN Convention Against Torture.[94] The EU, in contrast, adheres to a model of international relations that is predicated on law because it is, after all, a law-based institution. Several European countries opposed the US-led use of force against Iraq because they believed the necessary authority, and therefore legitimacy, for the use of force had not been obtained.

The dominant role played by the US in international relations has meant that the Europeans have found it necessary to react to American policies. However, European governments have tended to advocate different policy priorities. Whilst agreeing about the necessity of countering international terrorism, Europeans have resisted placing issues of non-proliferation and states of concern simply in the same basket as terrorism. They have differentiated amongst these issues in a way that the Bush administration has not. Where the Europeans have been at a disadvantage has been that they have shared no common position. Instead there has been a splintering of European perspectives in which the UK has represented one end of the spectrum and France the other.

The trend towards transatlantic security cooperation against international terrorism has been undermined by tensions in external security. The crisis over Iraq shows how the US and Europe were not working and planning together effectively, at least not in multilateral fora. But now Europe has become alarmed by the untrammelled power of the US and its willingness to exercise that strength. Europe no longer seems to have a privileged relationship with this unilateral America. The Bush administration has either expected its allies to follow its policies or it has resolved to act alone. In essence, the benign hegemon, in which the Europeans had hitherto invested their confidence, has become a chimera.

This is not to rule out the possibility that renewed cooperation may be created in this sphere of the US-European relationship. The US is so much stronger than any other power in the international system that European states may yet realign their policies in accordance with American wishes. There remains little prospect that a countervailing European pole of power will emerge to balance the United States. If cooperation is to emerge then it will take longer to mature because of the entrenched differences between the two sides. The searing experiences generated by the war against Iraq will not quickly disappear. But the approach of the Bush administration should not be seen as the definitive statement of US-European relations. A future administration, after Bush, may have very different priorities.

6   Globalising counter-terrorism

Introduction

International terrorism can only be countered effectively by using a range of instruments as part of a broad-based cooperative effort from a community of states. In order to arrange criminal prosecutions across several jurisdictions, to extradite individuals suspected of terrorist offences, and to prevent money from reaching terrorist organisations, there need to be established relationships, built on trust, within the wider international community. Similarly, when western states seek intelligence sharing, the closing down of terrorist sanctuaries, or access to the territory of sovereign states by their own military advisers,[1] then linkages have to be built up and patient diplomacy undertaken. Such an international effort 'needs to be organised at a global (level)' to the greatest extent possible.[2]

The transatlantic allies have recognised that they need to enlist the help of the global community if their counter-terrorist strategy is going to be effective. Whilst the US and Europe can enhance the security of their own homelands, nevertheless, they depend on others to create a hostile environment in which terrorism can be contained. In this spirit the American National Strategy for Combating Terrorism declared that 'with our . . . allies we aim to establish a new international norm regarding terrorism requiring non-support, non-tolerance and active opposition to terrorists'.[3] The aim has been to build on the cooperation between the US and Europe to draw other states around the world into similar patterns of behaviour. The norms of a transatlantic model of counter-terrorism are being diffused to the wider international community.

European and US interests are complementary in this regard: all recognise that they will have the greatest impact and legitimacy in the world if they are acting together. It does not mean that their outreach activities need to be conducted together, only that these efforts are coordinated to prevent them overlapping.[4] In fact, a division of labour where the US and Europe focus upon different areas of the world is likely to be the most efficient policy. Each side of the Atlantic has special influence in various parts of the world as a result of either history or contemporary patterns of economic and political activity.

Yet encouraging countries to align themselves with the counter-terrorist policies of the US and Europe is a formidable task. Whilst the objective of the transatlantic allies has been to convince others that it is in their own interests to cooperate, the actual motivation of other countries for complying may vary considerably. Some states may seek to emulate the West, attracted by the cooperation between the US and Europe. This reflects the prevailing order and it is something with which many states will want to be associated. In the case of other countries, the US is the dominant power within the international system and it can offer a range of incentives, as well as the threat of penalties for non-cooperation. Its ability to restrict access to international trade, aid and investment, as well as membership of bodies such as the World Trade Organization, provides a powerful source of influence. At the most extreme end of the spectrum, in relation to countries the US sees as material sponsors of terrorism, there is the underlying threat that the US might use its military power against them.

The US and Europe want third parties to adopt their practices without substantial modification. For the two sides of the Atlantic to adapt their security provisions, in order to make them more acceptable to other states, would risk watering down the agreements and unravelling compromises that were difficult to obtain. The result is that third parties are expected to accept policies over which they had little influence in shaping. This is closer to Young's model of a regime that is imposed externally and over which states have limited power to amend.[5]

The US and Europe have sought to reach out to other countries through a variety of organisational settings.[6] An important part of their efforts have involved concerting their activities within the United Nations to try to generate momentum on counter-terrorism. Other settings have included US and EU activities, the work of NATO, and the G-8.

United Nations

The UN occupies a special place in any attempt to promulgate norms and values amongst the international community because of its comprehensive membership.[7] The widest number of states can be drawn into taking action against a problem such as international terrorism. It also provides a political and legal foundation for any action due to the legitimacy and moral authority vested in the organisation.

Europe and the United States have been active in trying to use the UN as a forum in which to disseminate the norms of counter-terrorism that they have agreed amongst themselves.[8] This has been a long-term objective, but it was given added impetus, along with countering international crime and drug trafficking, after the end of the Cold War when the priorities of the global security agenda changed. The transatlantic allies have sought to gather the maximum number of adherents to their policies through the mechanism of the UN whilst simultaneously down-playing the impression that they are imposing their values upon the international community. They have attempted to draw up broadly based political agreements that states are encouraged to sign and then proceed to 'harden' those agreements into binding laws that are enacted by countries.[9]

Throughout the 1990s the US and Europe have striven to obtain conformity with the twelve major UN Conventions that address various aspects of the threat from terrorism. These Conventions establish international standards and include measures ranging from the protection of international transport and the protection of hazardous materials, to the suppression of bombings and the targeting of terrorist finance.[10] Conventions help to establish minimum standards and throw the spotlight on states deviating from these norms. Countries that sign the Conventions then pass their own domestic legislation to implement the measures. For example, the UN 'Convention for the Suppression of the Financing of Terrorism' provides a framework for cooperation in which each state must then pass national legislation in order to criminalise the raising of funds for terrorism. By April 2004, forty-one states were party to all the Conventions and universal adherence remains the ultimate objective of the transatlantic allies.[11]

Some states within the UN have argued for a single, comprehensive agreement on terrorism rather than the twelve piecemeal Conventions which seek to criminalise particular types of actions. Attempts were made from 1996, led by India and Algeria, to negotiate a 'Comprehensive Convention on International Terrorism' and this idea received renewed support after 9/11.[12] European governments, however, have remained sceptical about the likely success of an overarching agreement. They have preferred to concentrate their efforts on enlarging the number of adherents to the existing agreements.[13]

The UN was also used by the US and the UK in the pursuit of the perpetrators of the destruction of Pan Am flight 103 over Lockerbie in

December 1988. The US and the UK were the most ardent supporters of sanctions and the vilification of the Libyan government whom they accused of masterminding the atrocity. Yet as the Qhaddafi government began to show signs of wanting to turn away from its support for terrorist groups, the two governments demonstrated their flexibility. Despite the fact that numerous US citizens were murdered in the attack, the US acceded to a deal under which two Libyan intelligence officers were tried in a court in the Netherlands under Scottish criminal law. Two US prosecutors were accredited to The Hague.[14] One of the accused was found guilty in January 2001 while the other was acquitted.

Nevertheless, in general the US and Europe have found it difficult to achieve progress on terrorism issues within the UN. A particular obstacle to making the UN a more effective actor was the multitude of perspectives on the subject of terrorism within the General Assembly, not least from states that supported terrorist groups or felt sympathy with those who employed terrorism against forces of occupation. This core problem contributed to a variety of other issues such as the absence of an agreed definition of terrorism or the designation of terrorist groups.[15] Without agreement on the nature of the problem it was difficult for the international community to arrive at shared policies or determine which groups to designate as terrorist in nature.

Even the presence within the UN of a hegemonic power such as the US was insufficient to herd a variety of states into coalescing around a particular policy. The inability of the UN to make progress towards reaching a common definition of terrorism contributed to American disillusion and scepticism of the organisation. In essence the American government was unwilling to allow its freedom of action to be constrained by the UN. The Bush administration entered office with a more critical attitude towards the value of international organisations in general, and was less ideologically predisposed towards concepts of global governance. It leant towards reliance upon American power, and demonstrated its priorities by renouncing the Comprehensive Test Ban Treaty (CTBT), the Anti-Ballistic Missile (ABM) treaty and the International Criminal Court (ICC). In the aftermath of 9/11, this rejection of multilateralism was taken a stage further by America's new-found doctrine of pre-emption, which undermined the UN Article 51 justification of self-defence.[16] The War against Iraq seemed to confirm America's rejection of the central role of the UN Security Council in determining issues of war and peace. Yet the US had to pay a price for its disregard of the UN: it has struggled to legitimise its actions in the eyes of the international community.

Although European governments were aware of the deficiencies of the UN they were opposed to the American policy of sidelining the organisation. The adherence of the EU to the principles of multilateralism and the rule of law meant that they regarded the UN as a vital legitimising agent. UN sanction has been seen by countries such as Germany as an 'essential prerequisite' before taking international action.[17] The example of Kosovo was an exception, forced on European countries by the opposition of Russia and China within the Security Council. Even the Blair government, despite its commitment to following the US lead in the 2003 Iraq war, insisted on seeking a second resolution from the UN, regardless of the poor prospects for success. This European attachment to the UN appears to have more justification since the US has found the post-war situation in Iraq to be so challenging and has failed to find the weapons of mass destruction that the UN had been mandated to uncover.

The events of 9/11 infused the UN with the necessary political will to overhaul its attitude towards countering terrorism. On 28 September 2001 Resolution 1373 was adopted, declaring that terrorism presented a threat to international peace and security.[18] The Resolution focused principally on criminalising the financing of terrorist activities, and mandated governments to adopt national terrorist financing legislation.[19] The Resolution also called on countries to deny safe haven to terrorist organisations. It created a Counter Terrorism Committee (CTC) in order to monitor compliance from the signatories and receive reports about the steps being taken against the threat. There was no denying that this was a substantive step forward in globalising policy on countering terrorism.

The transatlantic allies have continued to put pressure on UN members to agree to new measures that would raise global standards in the fight against terrorism. The UN interfaces with bodies such as the International Civil Aviation Organization (ICAO) and the International Maritime Organization (IMO), and the US and Europe have used these channels to press for the improvement of measures such as in relation to airport security.[20] For example, the US and the EU helped to secure an 'International Port Facility and Vessel Security Code' in the IMO, and this has been married up with the US initiative on Container Security which has been extended all around the world.[21]

US-European Union

It is within the cooperation between the US and the EU that there exists the opportunity to establish policies and norms that can be globalised. These two actors are the most influential and dynamic players in countering international terrorism and, when they work together, they have the means to structure the international agenda.[22] This much was acknowledged at the US-EU Summit in June 2004, when the two sides committed themselves 'to work together . . . to target our external relations actions towards priority developing countries where counter-terrorism capacity or commitment to combating terrorism needs to be enhanced'.[23]

The US and the EU have developed international norms in counter-terrorism practice. Prominent examples include document security, passenger profiling and anti-money laundering. By so doing they have not only strengthened their own security but also encouraged the broader cause of international cooperation. In other spheres of policy, the transatlantic allies have pressed the international community to strengthen border security, enhance legal assistance and prevent political justifications for refusing extradition.[24]

The EU and US have taken steps to work more closely together over nuclear non-proliferation.[25] Since the war in Iraq, the EU has been paying greater attention to non-proliferation by including it as an item in agreements with third countries, through its CFSP, and tying it to other matters such as aid and trade.[26] This has reflected a desire to clarify its own strategy towards WMD proliferation and to move closer to the American position. In the European Security Strategy, non-proliferation was designated as one of the five main priorities with particular attention paid to the threat of terrorists acquiring WMD.[27] The EU produced a document on the subject;[28] it accepted much of the American argument that force might be necessary to prevent states from gaining access to WMD. The difference with the US was that the EU only accepted the principle that force could be employed if it was consistent with international law and had been approved by the United Nations.[29]

Greater EU attention to non-proliferation has muted some of the US criticism that this policy area was always left to them to address. The Cooperative Threat Reduction Program, in which the US allocated over $10 billion to dismantle and dispose of post-Soviet nuclear weapons, was illustrative of this American grievance.[30] The US maintained this programme, without the support of Europe, until 2002, when there was agreement in the G-8 on the so-called 'Global Partnership'. A figure of $10 billion of funding over ten years was pledged from the European side in order to secure all WMD material in the former Soviet Union, in addition to the money already committed by the US.

Second, the EU welcomed the US Proliferation Security Initiative (PSI) that was launched by President Bush in a speech in Poland in May 2003.[31] The PSI seeks to further restrict the ability of terrorists to acquire WMD technology by interdicting the movement of weapons and sensitive materials around the world by air, sea or land.[32] It is primarily an intelligence-driven activity, backed up by military forces and law enforcement agencies. As noted by Bayne, the agreement was eventually watered down into a form in which searches could only be conducted in the ports or coastal waters of a sovereign state, or at sea with the permission of the country under which the boat was flagged.[33] In spite of its dilution, the PSI represents a useful addition to the non-proliferation armoury of the international community, and the EU-US Summit in 2005 pledged to strengthen it further.

International trade is another example where the US and the EU have sought to use their strength to influence the policies of third parties. The US took the lead by imposing trade sanctions on countries it identified as sponsoring terrorism. The EU has been slower to resort to coercion but over the last few years has acknowledged that its power in the area of international trade enables it to put pressure on other countries. Since March 2004 the European Council has committed the Union to include counter-terrorism clauses in all its agreements with third countries.[34] Similarly, discussions on terrorism are now a part of all political dialogues with other countries,[35] and readmission clauses on illegal immigrants have been inserted into external agreements.[36] Both of these measures reflect attempts to harden the EU's counter-terrorism policies and recognise the blurring of the divide between Pillar 2 matters concerning external security and Pillar 3 matters of internal security. Monar has suggested that, in future, the EU may use its agreements with the US on internal security as a model for its relations with third countries. He posits that the EU-US accords on mutual legal assistance and extradition could well be extended to other states around the world.[37]

Nevertheless, this commitment on the part of the US and EU to work together has generated its own set of tensions. The two sides of the Atlantic frequently come to issues with opposing priorities, reflecting differences in their philosophical approaches. This is not a new phenomenon; it was evident in attitudes towards issues in the past. For example, even though the US and Europe agreed that international drug trafficking posed a threat to their societies, over the last twenty years they have disagreed about the appropriate means to counter the problem. Crudely defined, the US emphasised a law enforcement approach, undertook the spraying of crops with chemical herbicides and provided military support to governments, such as Colombia's, to fight armed groups that protected drug-growing regions. In contrast, the European Union gave aid and provided alternative cash crops in order to wean farmers away from drug-producing harvests.[38]

Overseas aid and conflict resolution have been examples where US and European priorities have diverged contemporaneously. In the case of aid, the Europeans have been more sympathetic to the argument that poverty can provide a fertile environment of despair and contribute to the radicalisation of ideas in which terrorism flourishes. Poverty reduction, as a result, has been viewed through their eyes as a preventive tool in countering terrorism. In the words of Peterson, the Europeans have sought to '"drain the swamp" in which terrorism festers, eliminating its root causes'.[39] The EU has been giving consideration to establishing a free trade area in North Africa in order to dampen some of the pressures of high birth rates and low employment. Aid is an instrument through which the EU can wield its 'soft power'. The Union now provides about 55 per cent of the world's official development assistance, and this is generally disbursed, without strings, to all parts of the world.

In a similar vein, Europe has viewed many of the armed struggles around the globe as motivating factors in the persistence of terrorism. Conflicts, such as in Palestine and Kashmir, have been cited by Muslims as fuel for extremism. European countries have regarded conflict prevention, conflict resolution and the promotion of human rights as complementary and necessary measures to eradicate some of the underlying causes of terrorism.[40] For example, British Prime Minister Tony Blair contended that the removal of Saddam Hussein's government in Iraq in 2003 had to be accompanied by concrete steps to resolve the Arab-Israeli conflict. He used his influence over President Bush to make the resolution of this conflict in the Middle East a priority in Washington.

In contrast, the US has tended to regard aid and conflict resolution more sceptically. Aid has been treated as just one amongst a range of foreign policy instruments. The US, since 9/11, has greatly increased its development assistance: USAID's budget in 2001 was $7.8 billion whereas in 2003 it had increased 38 per cent to $12.6 billion.[41] But this aid has been targeted much more narrowly than that of Europe. The US has provided financial assistance to those countries that have been sympathetic to American interests, such as Israel and Egypt, or to countries it regards as being in the forefront of the fight against international terrorism. The principal recipients of aid have been regions where the US fears terrorism flourishes, such as Pakistan, Afghanistan and Iraq.[42]

Despite their aspiration to work together the transatlantic allies have been unable to avoid tensions over their differing attitudes towards various regions of the world. In the Middle East, for example, the US has always been far more influential than the EU and has resented attempts to enhance European influence. This tension was demonstrated at the Sharm-El-Sheikh Summit of March 1996 which was designed to address some of the problems stemming from terrorism. The failure to achieve more substantive progress was partly a reflection of the suspicions that existed between Washington and the EU Troika. The US has focused its efforts on those countries with whom it has built up close relations; those that are seen as potential breeding grounds for Islamic extremists; and those states that occupy important geo-strategic locations. States such as Saudi Arabia and Indonesia have been high on the American list of priorities. The US embraced the government of Pervez Musharaff in Pakistan, despite his seizure of power in a military coup, because he took a lead in opposing religious fundamentalism within his own country. The Bush administration has also made an ally of the authoritarian Uzbek government of Islam Karimov, due to that country's possession of an airbase that enabled US aircraft to conduct raids in Afghanistan.[43] This caused friction between the transatlantic allies because European countries have been much more critical of the poor human rights records of these countries. Whilst the US has been guided by *realpolitik*, European states have feared the damage done to the legitimacy of the Western counter-terrorism campaign by relationships with such illiberal governments.

Tensions between the US and the EU have been exacerbated by the latter's perception that America sometimes tramples on the rights of other countries in the pursuit of its counter-terrorism interests. The issue of American extraterritorial legislation and action has been a consistent complaint from the European side. As far as the United States is concerned, any actions it takes, no matter how controversial in the eyes of its allies, must abide by the Constitution and must not contravene international law. The US has three categories of statutes that relate to issues of extra-territoriality.[44] The first relates to the territorial scope of US legal jurisdiction. The US regards its jurisdiction as extending over its land and maritime sphere; its diplomatic space; military installations; its own airlines and those of other carriers leaving or destined for US territory. The second category of statute relates to issues that concern US goods or nationals, such as the counterfeiting of currency or the murder of its citizens by terrorists overseas. The third category relates to US involvement in international treaties which designate certain crimes as contrary to international law. The key statutes in question are the Crime Control Act of 1984, the Electronic Communications Privacy Act of 1986 and the Anti-Terror and Effective Death Penalty Act of 1996.

The Omnibus Diplomatic Security and Anti-Terror Act enables US authorities to seize an individual and return them to the US for trial. Key cases have informed US practice. One was an intended attack on a Philippines Airlines flight that was to serve as a precursor to attacks on US airlines.[45] The defendant, Ramzi Yousef, was subsequently apprehended on US territory. A more sensitive case was that of Fawaz Yunis, who was involved in the hijacking of a Jordanian aircraft in 1985 in which three Americans were killed. He was returned to the United States after having been lured to a boat in international waters, off the coast of Lebanon.[46]

European detractors of American policy have regarded such episodes as reflections of two unfortunate trends. One is the internationalisation of the US law enforcement posture. Hundreds of its officers are deployed overseas as legal attachés, thereby according the US an influence that no other country can replicate. In addition, the US has the capacity to flood a country with its own specialists when a terrorist event occurs. This has the potential to stir ill-feeling about trampled sovereignty amongst states that find themselves hosts to proactive US law enforcement officers. The second is the predilection of America to throw its weight around in cases where it wants to track down and prosecute suspected terrorists. Europeans suspect that by undermining the principle of mutual respect for the integrity of another country's territory, the US is harming the overall cause of fighting terrorism in the long term. The US has argued, in response, that it exercises great care to avoid upsetting cooperative relations with other countries. It acknowledges that to do otherwise would be counter-productive.

A further source of tension between the US and EU, in relation to human rights has been the matter of 'extraordinary renditions' – the extra-judicial transfer between countries of a person held in detention. The US has been engaged in a policy of exchanging terrorist suspects with other countries around the world. It has long been suspected that the US government has been willing to transport individuals accused of terrorist acts to countries whose interrogation techniques are far more brutal than those permitted in America, in contravention of international law.[47] Moving detainees around overseas prisons enables them to be interrogated over prolonged periods of time and diminishes the accountability of their incarceration. Evidence of this practice was forthcoming on 16 May 2005, when the Egyptian Prime Minister, Ahmed Nazif, told a press conference that more than sixty suspects had been rendered to Egypt by the United States since 9/11.[48] The EU has expressed its concern at this practice, worried that important principles of legitimacy and adherence to the rule of law are being sacrificed on the altar of short-term intelligence considerations.

The EU, building upon the links established by the Barcelona Process, has reached out to the states of the Mahgreb in an attempt to engage them in counter-terrorism cooperation. Several member states, including Spain, France and the United Kingdom, have experienced terrorism at the hands of individuals originating from states such as Algeria and Morocco. In April 2002, the Valencia Action Plan was launched with the aim of helping Mediterranean countries combat terrorism as well as other forms of crime.[49] These efforts have been complemented by NATO's Mediterranean Dialogue and Istanbul Cooperation Initiative. The outreach by NATO to the Mediterranean has been aimed at combating terrorism as well as enhancing stability and deterring nuclear proliferation. The European Council Working Group against Terrorism (COTER) has also argued for cooperation to be built up with such countries, and assistance was provided to Morocco to establish a unit to combat the funding of militant groups.[50] But the EU has succeeded in making only limited progress in this regard and has found many North African states uninterested in their initiatives.

In Central and Eastern Europe (CEE), the transatlantic allies have struggled to work in harmony, principally because the Union has treated the US as a potential competitor for influence. The EU has treated the territory of CEE states as its own backyard and it has resented efforts by America to increase its presence in the area. The strength of the EU position has been its ability to offer membership, and as a result its evolving internal security has become the pervasive model for the whole continent.[51] A particular example has been the opening of the 'International Law Enforcement Academy' (ILEA) in Budapest under the auspices of the US Federal Bureau of Investigation.[52] Ironically, this was conceived in the US as a potential flagship for transatlantic cooperation and it was offered up to the EU for collaboration. The curriculum within ILEA has been adapted to develop techniques in counter-terrorism investigations that can be used by police officers from across CEE countries. But opposition from within some member states prevented the EU from participating fully within ILEA.[53]

The G-8

The G-8 has enjoyed a particular role in taking areas of agreement from within the US-European relationship and raising them to the level of the wider international community. In the words of Kirton and Stefanova, 'the G-8 is often able to generate consensus on a course of action and then transfer it to international organisations, such as the UN'.[54] Three principal issues have been the focus of G-8 attention: the use of illegitimate funds within the global financial system, providing specialist anti-terrorist expertise to other countries, and drawing a broader range of countries into the western system of counter-terrorism cooperation.

Terrorist finance has been a recent preoccupation of G-8 members as they have come to recognise that it is one of the few sources of information that can be used to detect terrorist activity. As the efforts of the G-7/G-8 began to become more coherent, it was appreciated that western countries and their banking systems were no longer the main source of the problem: the real vulnerabilities lay in other corners of the world.[55] It was evident that the challenge was to universalise western regulatory policies across the globe. In 1989 at the Paris Summit, the Financial Action Task Force (FATF) was established to prevent and punish the laundering of money. At the very outset it was decided to include eight other countries that were not G-7 members in order to broaden the base of the initiative. Countries joining FATF had to submit to an internal review and agree to become a part of the existing money laundering provisions, which contributed to the raising of standards.[56] Forty recommendations were outlined in the FATF's initial report, and the aim of increasing international cooperation was accorded the highest priority. Since that time the US and European countries have endorsed the FATF's attempts to draw more states into its activities and diminish the number of jurisdictions that fail to comply with its recommendations. Countries joining this community are provided with advice and support on the setting up of their own national Financial Intelligence Units (FIUs). These are then coordinated through the Egmont Group, an informal grouping of some eighty countries with experts on financial intelligence.[57] Levey notes that by 2004 the number of FIUs had increased to ninety-four, thereby providing an important source of global intelligence on the movement of money that might be used for the purposes of terrorism.[58]

After a review had been undertaken in 1993–4 a decision was taken to maintain the FATF and to give it a small secretariat based in Paris at the headquarters of the Organization for Economic Cooperation and Development (OECD). This contrasted with the informal nature of its parent organisation the G-8. In addition to the creation of a secretariat, a Caribbean Financial Action Task Force was established. This was in recognition of the problems of money laundering that had existed in the Caribbean basin for a long period of time. The Caribbean Financial Action Task Force has served as an important policy regulation mechanism between the governments of the region.[59]

Special attention was paid to the issue of terrorism at the G-8 summit in Lyon in July 1996. President Chirac of France followed up the Lyon summit with a meeting devoted to terrorism the following month in Paris, and this resulted in a series of twenty-five recommendations on fighting terrorism from the 'Counter-Terrorism Experts Group'. These included protection of transportation systems from attack, criminalising the possession of biological agents, sharing research and development on explosive detection methods, investigating suspected front organisations and encouraging countries to implement existing counter-terrorist conventions.[60] The French government later took the lead in negotiating the International Convention for the Suppression of the Financing of Terrorism which was agreed at the UN in 1999, with the support of the US and UK.

Following the 9/11 attacks, the G-8 finance ministers agreed to freeze the funds of terrorist groups and to use this initiative as the basis for encouraging other countries to follow suit. An emergency meeting of the Financial Action Task Force was arranged in Washington at the end of October 2001 and recommended extending the FATF's mandate to include terrorism.[61] Eight recommendations on disrupting terrorist financing were agreed. These included such simple steps as ratifying UN conventions against terrorist financing, confiscating assets and agreeing reporting mechanisms for suspicious transactions. By July 2005, 150 countries had issued orders to freeze the assets of alleged terrorist groups,[62] and approximately $147 million dollars had been frozen, with a further $65 million seized.[63]

Yet there have been frictions between the US and Europe within the G-8 over their approaches to terrorist financing. Several EU countries were reluctant in the past to designate organisations as terrorist in nature, despite pressure from the US, because they were wary of damaging their interests. As a result of the 9/11 attacks the EU agreed to try to create a common list of proscribed organisations with the US.[64] The EU froze initially the accounts of twenty-seven individuals and, after meetings with US State Department officials in April 2002, a further ten organisations were added to its list.[65] According to the Commission, 1.6 million euros had been frozen in over 100 accounts by 2004.[66] Here was evidence that US intelligence and dialogue between the two sides was having a material effect on EU policy positions.[67]

Contradictory attitudes towards the funding of the Palestinian Authority illustrate the tensions between the US and Europe. Whilst the Europeans have provided the bulk of development assistance, the US has regarded the Palestinian cause as tarnished by involvement in terrorism. The Europeans have argued that it is possible to discriminate between the armed and the charitable wings of organisations such as Hamas and Hezbollah. The US has taken a harder line, criticising the Europeans for their naivety, and alleging that money is used both for social purposes and to perpetrate acts of violence. The American government has insisted that funding should be stopped to all organisations that have military off-shoots practising terrorism because money is a fungible commodity.[68] At the US-EU summit in June 2003 President Bush pressured his European counterparts to end all funding to Hamas.[69]

The second major contribution by the G-8 towards globalising counter-terrorism efforts has been its programme of specialist support. This support has reflected a growing awareness on the part of the leading western nations that poor countries often struggle to combat terrorism effectively due to limited resources, technology and knowledge of best practices. The G-8 has aimed to remedy these deficiencies, help to build capacity and sustain the will of countries to resist threats. Assistance has been provided in the form of equipment, training and technical assistance. It has also extended to the drafting of appropriate legislation; to implement international conventions; and to create the domestic framework for seizing terrorist assets and enforcing immigration controls. An additional benefit has been to build links with the law enforcement agencies of countries around the world that can be activated when an issue of common concern arises.

The US was the first of the G-8 countries to initiate an 'Anti-Terror Assistance Program' as early as 1983. It was organised by the State Department and it was viewed as an integral element in US counter-terrorism strategy. It grew in size until over ninety countries were benefiting from US training and equipment. The US was especially concerned with providing technical assistance in the security of airports and borders and advising how the financial systems of countries could be made less susceptible to infiltration from illegitimate sources. US efforts from an early stage were coordinated with America's partners through the mechanism of the G-8. Since 9/11 the US has increased its programme substantially and has provided additional supplements in terms of intelligence sharing and enhanced military training. For example, the US has despatched military training teams to locations as diverse as Yemen, the Philippines and the former Soviet republic of Georgia.

Over the last five years, the other G-8 members have contributed to overseas assistance through the provision of training, the building of institutions, the fostering of cooperation between law enforcement and intelligence agencies and the sharing of technical expertise.[70] This was in recognition that the burden assumed by the US had to be shared more equitably. The Kananaskis summit of 2002 acknowledged the need to build the capacity of less developed countries to counter the terrorist threat, whilst at the subsequent Evian summit, an 'Action Plan on Building Capacity to Combat Terrorism' was adopted.[71]

The last major role played by the G-8 has been to draw Russia into close cooperation with the West. This is not a role unique to the G-8. NATO has contributed to this aim through its 'Partnership Action Plan for Terrorism', of November 2002, and subsequently the creation of the NATO-Russia Council.[72] Similarly, the EU has participated in this process by stepping up its cooperation with Russia and establishing a liaison arrangement with Europol designed to allow the agency access to Russian information on suspects in the fields of terrorism and organised crime.[73] Yet the G-8 has been able to play a special part because, unlike other organisations, it has been able to offer full membership to Russia and thereby grant it a position of equality. As early as the Halifax Summit, in June 1995, Russia was invited to contribute to efforts to combat international terrorism,[74] and by the end of the decade it had been admitted as a full member.

Including Russia in the G-8, however, has brought with it several problems. Although a vital actor in world-wide efforts to combat international terrorism, there has been no disguising the fact that Russia has different ideas to its western neighbours about the nature of the problem. President Putin has been adept at making use of the international environment to justify Russia's repressive policies in the break-away republic of Chechnya.[75] Whilst the US and Europeans have been anxious to associate Russia with their counter-terrorist priorities, they in turn have not escaped association with Russia's own domestic troubles.

Conclusion

Building global counter-terrorism cooperation is, by definition, a slow process. The construction of a transatlantic regime is itself at an early stage of development and, as a result, the building of a global system is only in its infancy. Sophisticated models of transatlantic cooperation, with close cooperation between law enforcement agencies and the sharing of intelligence information, will not be replicated overnight. There is a perpetual risk that outcomes will reflect the lowest common denominator that can be accepted by all parties. Agreements tend to be sub-optimal and need to be strengthened, through a process of negotiation, over time. Ensuring that states proceed to implement the agreements that they sign is even more difficult. Patience and persistence must be the watchwords of those trying to ratchet up the counter-terrorist efforts of the international community.

Nevertheless, there is a growing recognition that this global architecture needs to be constructed to address future threats. International terrorism is a phenomenon that can strike anywhere in the world. Countering the threat from terrorist groups, deterring states from providing support and severing the linkage between state proliferation and terrorist acquisition of WMD, require universal adherence from countries. International norms must be generated even if they take a long time to achieve. These must include a commitment to combat the threat, to report the activities of groups and extradite suspects. In the words of the 9/11 Commission Report, almost all aspects of counterterrorism strategy 'relies on international cooperation'.[76]

The transatlantic allies have a special role to play in the construction of this architecture. Based upon their shared values, they have been forging patterns of cooperation and so they have the most advanced models of cooperation to offer to the international community. The United States, with its global interests, has long recognised the need to provide global leadership and Europe has increasingly come to play its part in the same endeavour. The law enforcement presence of the US overseas, its power to get things done and drag the international community behind its initiatives, has made it a formidable actor with which to collaborate. Transatlantic differences of perspective over how best to combat international terrorism should not be allowed to obstruct progress. Their common interests transcend their differences.

Conclusion

The security regime that developed over five decades of the Cold War has enabled the transatlantic allies to adapt their relationship to deal with new threats. The shared values and trust that had been built up in the field of military security allowed the US and Europe to cooperate against a significant new security danger: international terrorism. In the 1990s this was a nebulous threat, but after the catastrophe of 9/11 it became the West's foremost security concern. International terrorism has presented a very real challenge to that security regime because of its diffuse and unique nature. The two sides of the Atlantic have been forced to re-orientate their patterns of cooperation in order to confront this menace.

This re-orientation process has been made possible by the continuation of transatlantic multilateral organisations that survived the end of the Cold War. These organisations were established originally for different purposes but have served as the vehicles through which new patterns of transatlantic cooperation have been developed. Although US-European efforts to cooperate against international terrorism are still at a relatively early stage of development, organisations have played a central role in that process. They have helped the US and Europe to remain together during a period of unprecedented strains and disagreements and, by so doing, have acted as a testament to the underlying bond of the relationship.

Amongst the three major transatlantic security frameworks, NATO has been the least appropriate to countering the contemporary challenge from international terrorism. Its focus on military security issues has relegated it to a supporting function in the War on Terror, with the result that the Bush administration has downplayed its importance. Nevertheless, the Atlantic Alliance has acted in a vital facilitating role as the lynchpin of transatlantic military relations and the repository for the shared values on which other patterns of transatlantic cooperation have been founded. The G-8 and the US-EU relationship, enjoying greater prominence in counter-terrorism, have benefited from the foundations established by NATO. The G-8 has prospered because of its inherent flexibility, allowing it to undertake initiatives that could not be imitated in any other organisational setting. As for the US-EU relationship, this has evolved into the foremost framework for transatlantic counter-terrorism due to the breadth of the Union's competences.

The fact that the two sides of the Atlantic have suffered from different historical experiences of terrorism has influenced both their perceptions of the threat and their responses. The US and Europe have differed over the nature of the threat from terrorism – ironic, in light of the fact that security threats used to provide the glue that bound them together. The American government has linked the threat from international terrorism to WMD proliferation and states of concern, an understandable fear if one considers the enormous destruction that could be wrought by nuclear terrorism. It was this fear that was manipulated by the Bush administration to justify attacking Iraq. The Europeans, on the other hand, whilst acknowledging the risk of terrorists acquiring WMD, have not shared this American preoccupation.[1] It is important not to oversimplify this divergence: not every European state has disagreed with the US position. Countries such as the UK and Italy have tended to share many US assumptions, whilst France, Germany and Belgium have tended to demur. Meanwhile, because terrorism straddles the traditional divide between external and internal security,[2] the US and Europe have found themselves broadly in agreement regarding internal security threats. This has been an additional source of novelty, as internal security was not hitherto a subject for substantive international cooperation.

Disagreement has also characterised the responses that the US and Europe have advocated to combat terrorism. Both sides have utilised the full panoply of instruments, ranging from law enforcement to the application of military force, but they have differed over relative priorities. The US has adopted a national security approach, consistent with its strategic culture. Through massive increases of funding to defence and the unleashing of its military against Afghanistan and Iraq, the US has relied heavily upon its powers of coercion. The Europeans, true to their own strategic culture, have advocated an approach based upon non-military means.[3] European governments have been unnerved by the ferocity of the American response and the predilection for the employment of force. The unity of the Europeans has fractured over the issue of whether to support the American use of force against states accused of supporting terrorism.

The reality of Europe's situation has been that it is cooperating with a hegemonic power. Even under the Clinton administration, Europe found that differing approaches towards dealing with problems could result in unilateral American actions that were prejudicial to their interests. The imposition of US extra-territorial legislation in the cases of Iran and Libya were early illustrations of these divergences. The problem was exacerbated after 9/11 when the US accorded counter-terrorism its highest priority and sought to mould transatlantic policies around its own authoritative set of ideas. The Bush administration no longer acted as a benign hegemon towards its allies. It exhibited a disregard for international organisations, arguing that they were slow moving, prone to lowest-common-denominator outcomes and potential constraints on US freedom of action.[4] Instead of building a consensus around its policies the administration presented its initiatives to its allies and expected them to follow its lead. There was evidence that the US was no longer willing to be constrained by its alliance relationships, that it wanted to act alone or only with those that shared its priorities. America was determined to use its unparalleled strength to negate perceived threats by the pre-emptive use of force.

Europe has advanced its own model of counter-terrorism: one that emphasises the importance of multilateralism, the use of law enforcement and judicial instruments and the pursuit of policies of constructive engagement with states of concern. The Europeans have been wedded to the value of pursuing counter-terrorism in conjunction with the broadest possible array of countries. This has reflected their own experience of working together through the EU, and their belief in the legitimising power of organisations such as the UN and in the centrality of international law.[5] Their model of counter-terrorism has taken longer to evolve – due partly to the diversity of views amongst EU members,[6] and partly to the need to react to unilateral American initiatives. Hoffman has questioned the conventional wisdom that this European model of counter-terrorism is less effective than that of the United States. He contends that 'although it has become fashionable to dismiss Europe's approach toward terrorism as counterproductive, there is reason to believe that the European way of doing things might yield more effective results in the long run'.[7]

Despite its hegemonical status, two lessons have led the US back towards cooperation with its European allies. The first has been the realisation that it lacks the power to defeat international terrorism alone. The belief that American objectives could be pursued regardless of opposition from the international community, and that multilateral relationships could be ignored, has proved to be counter-productive. Policy-makers in Washington have found themselves unable to make other countries follow their path.[8] The war in Iraq has fuelled international terrorism, America has been unable to enlist support against a vicious insurgency and it has squandered the goodwill bestowed upon it after 9/11. Even the Bush administration has come to recognise that it requires cooperation from its allies and the legitimacy that derives from acting within multilateral frameworks.

In order to build a counter-terrorism culture within the broader international community, the transatlantic allies must first cooperate amongst themselves. US-European patterns of collaboration provide a range of measures and the necessary legitimacy to reach out to the rest of the world. Unilateral American action could never hope to carry the authority that will convince other governments to adopt measures such as combating terrorist financing and implementing UN conventions. It is widely recognised that the US must be seen to cooperate with other countries, and only the Europeans can fulfil the role of effective partners.[9] Indeed, the EU is the closest thing to an equal that the US experiences in the world today.[10] In the words of the former American Ambassador to NATO, 'the US . . . and Europe are natural allies. We are the most like-minded peoples on the planet, sharing a common history, common democratic values and an interconnected economy.'[11]

The second lesson for the US has been that the unique nature of terrorism necessitates cooperation with Europe. Because terrorism is fluid and amorphous, it requires patterns of inter-state cooperation in order for it to be combated successfully. Progress in the War on Terrorism will not come in the form of decisive victories, but the patient accumulation of small steps forward such as arresting key individuals, frustrating terrorist plans, seizing finances and deterring states from sponsoring groups. The US has come to acknowledge that its counter-terrorism offensive is crucially dependent upon the sharing of intelligence information and judicial and law enforcement collaboration with its European allies. In 2004 the US State Department's Deputy Coordinator for Counter Terrorism testified that 'the contributions of European countries in sharing vital information, arresting members of terrorist cells, interdicting terrorist financing and logistics, and assisting in the rebuilding of Afghanistan have been, and continue to be, vital in the war on terrorism'.[12]

The EU has made significant strides forward in the field of internal security, as a result of its JHA activities, and this has made it an actor of increasing significance for the US. By agreeing upon a common definition of terrorism, developing a common arrest warrant that is enforceable throughout the European space, pooling its criminal intelligence information and creating joint investigative teams, the Union has enhanced its capability to fight terrorism. Europe is most attractive to the US when it is speaking and acting with one voice,[13] and international terrorism has encouraged European governments to see their internal security as interdependent. Further steps are being taken towards enhancing intelligence sharing and speeding up the implementation of agreements. Paradoxically, new patterns of transatlantic internal security cooperation have flourished at a time when the external security relationship has been in crisis. The two sides of the Atlantic have established agreements in relation to airline and border security, mutual legal assistance including extradition, biometric identifiers on travel documents and common efforts in ensuring the integrity of financial systems. They are even beginning to consult one another over the launching of security initiatives.

There has been increasing evidence of convergence in transatlantic approaches to counter-terrorism. On the part of the United States, in 2005 there were signs that it was retreating from its propensity to resort to military force. In March of that year Secretary of Defense, Donald Rumsfeld, and Chairman of the Joint Chiefs of Staff, General Richard Myers, endorsed a Pentagon document entitled the 'National Military Strategic Plan for the War on Terrorism' that set new priorities in US policy. The re-think had been prompted by the experience of a growing insurgency in Iraq and a realisation that reliance on the use of force was unlikely to bring an American victory in the struggle against terrorism. General Myers himself made it clear that he did not believe that the adversaries of the US could be defeated by force of arms alone.[14] Rhetoric coming out of the US administration has placed more emphasis upon winning hearts and minds and less upon killing terrorists.

Military reappraisal has found echoes in new political thinking in Washington, at the State Department and the National Security Council. Secretary of State Condoleezza Rice established a ten-member committee, headed by one of her trusted advisers, Philip Zelikow, to make recommendations on the future direction of US strategy. This committee made a point of crossing the Atlantic to talk to European officials, in order to signal a desire to repair the damage to transatlantic relations that had been wrought by the Iraqi war.[15] This desire to mend fences and bring the two sides of the Atlantic together was evident at the highest level after President Bush's re-election when he and his Secretary of State made a high-profile visit to Brussels in February 2005. The President visited both the European Union and NATO headquarters and spoke of their importance in cementing US-European relations.[16] In addition, the US has begun to pay greater attention to assisting other nations in combating the threats that they face, to target the supporters of terrorist organisations and reduce the ideological support for extremism.

Convergence with the US has been evident in European policies. The European Security Strategy demonstrated the influence of American thinking on continental attitudes towards nuclear proliferation, WMD and states of concern. This was an important signal, as divergences over foreign policy matters have tended to be the source of the greatest friction in transatlantic relations. It was also an important source of reassurance to the US that a stronger European identity would not be forged in opposition to America. Europe continued to work with the US over matters of internal security even when the relationship had reached its nadir over Iraq. For example, revulsion over the revelations concerning Abu Ghraib prison did not result in a breakdown in EU relations with the US. This has reflected a recognition on the part of European states that they must engage with the US in order to be able to exert influence over its policies. Constraining American policy remains an important objective for the Europeans.

In the words of Asmus and Pollack, the future challenge for the US and Europe is whether they can overcome their differences and 'coalesce around a new strategic purpose and paradigm to guide future cooperation across the Atlantic'.[17] For this to happen, the US needs to consult its allies more systematically and demonstrate its willingness to be influenced by them. Whilst the US has taken the threat from catastrophic terrorism very seriously, it must be willing to modify its policies after listening to the views of its allies. It is not enough for policy to be justified only in terms of what is in the interests of the US: if it is to lead the international community, the American government must demonstrate that its policies have broader appeal. For its part, Europe must harness its energies and seek to work with the United States more systematically. It should be prepared to shoulder an equal burden and not leave foreign policy issues for Washington to resolve. A failure to confront their respective challenges risks transatlantic relations atrophying or resulting in periodic clashes. Neither outcome would be in the interests of Europe or the United States.

Notes

Introduction

1 Joffe, J. (1984) 'Europe's American Pacifier', *Foreign Affairs*, 54, 1, pp. 64–82.
2 Schwartz, D. (1983) *NATO's Nuclear Dilemmas*, Brookings Institution Press, Washington DC.
3 Stromseth, J. (1988) *The Origins of Flexible Response: NATO's Debate over Strategy in the 1960s*, Macmillan, Basingstoke.
4 Quoted in Lundestad, G. (2003) *The United States and Western Europe Since 1945*, Oxford University Press, Oxford, p. 163.
5 De Porte (1979) *Europe Between the Superpowers: The Enduring Balance*, Yale University Press, New Haven CT and London.
6 Fursdon, E. (1980) *The European Defence Community: A History*, Macmillan, Basingstoke.
7 Winand, P. (1993) *Eisenhower, Kennedy and the United States of Europe*, St Martin's Press, New York.
8 Cromwell, W. C. (1992) *The United States and the European Pillar: The Strained Alliance*, Macmillan Press, London, p. 197.
9 Weidenfeld, W. (1997) 'America and Europe: Is the Break Inevitable?', *Washington Quarterly*, 20, 3, summer. See also Hoffmann, S. (2003) 'US-European Relations: Past and Future', *International Affairs*, 79, 5, October.
10 Baker, J. (1989) 'A New Europe, A New Atlanticism: Architecture for a New Europe', speech by the US Secretary of State to the Berlin Press Club, 12 December.
11 Daalder, I. (2003) 'The End of Atlanticism', *Survival*, 45, 2, summer, p. 149.
12 Mahncke, D., Rees, W. and Thompson, W. (2004) *Redefining Transatlantic Security Relations: The Challenge of Change*, Manchester University Press, Manchester. See also Walker, J. (1991) 'Keeping America in Europe', *Foreign Policy*, 83, summer; and Nelson, M. (1993) 'Transatlantic Travails', *Foreign Policy*, fall; and Dassu, M. and Menotti, R. (2005) 'Europe and America in the Age of Bush', *Survival*, 47, 1, spring, p. 106.
13 Gompert, D. and Larabee, S. (eds) (1997) *America and Europe*, Cambridge University Press, Cambridge.
14 Menon, A. (2000) *France, NATO and the Limits of Independence 1981–97*, Macmillan, Basingstoke.

15 Yost, D. (1998) *NATO Transformed: The Alliance's New Roles in International Security*, US Institute of Peace Press, Washington DC.
16 Ruhle, M. (2003) 'NATO after Prague', *Parameters*, summer.
17 In 1990 the Schengen Implementing Agreement was signed. As part of the Treaty of Amsterdam, the Schengen Agreement was incorporated into the EU. Thirteen states were party to the Agreement at the time and the UK and Ireland retained the right to opt in.
18 Politi, A. (1997) 'European Security: The New Transnational Risks', *Chaillot Papers 29*, Institute for Security Studies Western European Union, Paris, October, pp. 14–15.
19 The language of a 'war' on terrorism is not unique to the Bush administration. For example, the Nixon administration declared war on illegal drugs.
20 Politi, A. (1997) *op. cit.* pp. 9–10.
21 Code of Federal Regulations 28: Section 0.85, United States of America.
22 US National Strategy for Combating Terrorism (2003) The White House, Washington DC, February.
23 European Council (2002) 'Council Framework Decision of 13 June 2002 on Combating Terrorism', Brussels.

Chapter 1

1 Mayer, P., Rittberger, V. and Zurn, M. (1997) 'Regime Theory: State of the Art and Perspectives', in Rittberger, V. (ed.) *Regime Theory and International Relations*, Clarendon Press, Oxford, p. 393.
2 Keohane, R. and Nye, J. (1977) *Power and Interdependence: World Politics in Transition*, Little, Brown, Boston MA, p. 65.
3 Stein (1983) in Krasner, S. (ed.) *International Regimes*, Cornell University Press, Ithaca NY and London, section 3.
4 Keohane, R. (1984) *After Hegemony: Cooperation and Discord in the World Political Economy*, Princeton University Press, Princeton NJ.
5 Young, O. (1983) in Krasner, S. (ed.) *op. cit.* section 2.
6 See Olson, M. (1977) *The Logic of Collective Action: Public Goods and the Theory of Groups*, Harvard University Press, Cambridge MA, on collective action; and Hardin, G. and Baden, J. (eds) (1977) *Managing the Commons*, W. H. Freeman, San Francisco, on the 'tragedy of the commons'.
7 Mayer, P., Rittberger, V. and Zurn, M. (1997) in Rittberger, V. (ed.) *op. cit.* p. 393.
8 Mayer, P., Rittberger, V. and Zurn, M. (1997) in Rittberger, V. (ed.) *ibid.*
9 Young, O. (1983) in Krasner, S. (ed.) *op. cit.* section 2, pp. 94–5.
10 Haas, E. (1980) 'Why Collaborate? Issue Linkage and International Regimes', *World Politics*, 32, April, p. 358.
11 Muller, H. (1997) 'The Internationalization of Principles, Norms, and Rules by Governments', in Rittberger, V. (ed.) *op. cit.*
12 Strange, S. (1994) *States and Markets*, 2nd edn, Pinter, London.
13 Krasner, S. (ed.) (1983) *op. cit.* p. 6.
14 Ikenberry, G. J. (2001) *After Victory: Institutions, Strategic Restraint and the Rebuilding of Order After Major Wars*, Princeton University Press, Princeton NJ, p. 16.
15 Krasner, S. (ed.) (1983) *op. cit.* p. 2.

16 Young, O. (1980) 'International Regimes: Problems of Concept Foundation', *World Politics*, 32, April, pp. 88–9; and Keohane, R. (1997) 'The Analysis of International Regimes', in Rittberger, V. (ed.) *op. cit.* p. 26.
17 Jonsson, C. (1997) 'Cognitive Factors in Explaining Regime Dynamics', in Rittberger, V. (ed.) *ibid.*
18 Krasner, S. (ed.) (1983) *op. cit.* p. 2.
19 Haas, P. (1997) 'Epistemic Communities and the Dynamics of International Environmental Cooperation', in Rittberger, V. (ed.) *op. cit.* p. 172. See Hasenclever, A., Mayer, P. and Rittberger, V., *Theories of International Regimes*, Cambridge University Press, Cambridge, for their three schools of cognitive theorists, p. 137.
20 Mayer, P., Rittberger, V. and Zurn, M. (1997) in Rittberger, V. (ed.) *op. cit.* p. 393.
21 Mayer, P., Rittberger, V. and Zurn, M. (1997) in Rittberger, V. (ed.) *ibid.* p. 394.
22 Haas, E. (1980) *op. cit.* p. 358.
23 Risse-Kappen, T. (1995) *Cooperation Among Democracies: The European Influence on US Foreign Policy*, Princeton University Press, Princeton NJ.
24 Keohane, R. (1984) *op. cit.* p. 63.
25 Keohane, R. and Nye, J. (1977) *op. cit.* p. 44.
26 Hasenclever, A., Mayer, P. and Rittberger, V. (1997) *op. cit.* p. 103.
27 Haas, E. (1980) *op. cit.* p. 396.
28 Gilpin, R. (1987) *The Political Economy of International Relations*, Princeton University Press, Princeton NJ.
29 Ikenberry, G. J. (2001) *op. cit.* p. 11.
30 Schwok, R. (2001) ch. 12 in Philippart, E. and Winand, P. (eds) *Ever Closer Partnership: Policy-making in US-EU Relations*, PIE Peter Lang, Brussels, p. 383.
31 Risse-Kappen, T. (1995) *op. cit.*
32 See Holsti, K., Siverson, R. and George, A. (eds) (1980) *Changes in the International System*, Westview, Boulder CO.
33 Keohane, R. (1984) *op. cit.* p. 46.
34 Young, O. and Osherenko, G. (1997) 'Testing Theories of Regime Formation: Findings from a Large Collaborative Research Project', in Rittberger, V. (ed.) *op. cit.* p. 239.
35 Ikenberry, G. J. (2001) *op. cit.* p. 29.
36 Young, O. (ed.) (1975) *Bargaining: Theories of Negotiation*, University of Illinois Press; and Young, O. (1968) *The Politics of Force: Bargaining During International Crises*, Princeton University Press, Princeton NJ.
37 Lansford, T. (2002) *All for One: Terrorism, NATO and the United States*, Ashgate, Aldershot.
38 Jervis, S. (1982) 'Security Regimes', *International Organization*, 36, 2, spring, p. 359.
39 Doyle, M. (1995) 'On the Democratic Peace', *International Security*, 19, 4; and Doyle, M. (1997) *Ways of War and Peace: Realism, Liberalism and Socialism*, W. W. Norton and Co., New York.
40 Ikenberry, G. J. (2000) 'Strengthening the Atlantic Political Order', *The International Spectator*, 35, 3, July–September, p. 60.
41 Deutsch, K. (1957) *Political Community and the North Atlantic Area: International Organisation in the Light of Historical Experience*, Princeton University Press, Princeton NJ.
42 Risse-Kappen, T. (1995) *op. cit.* p. 222.

43 Lepgold, J. (1990) *The Declining Hegemon. The United States and European Defense, 1960–1990*, Greenwood Press, New York, p. 37.
44 Mead, R. (2004) 'Troubled Partnership: What's Next for the US and Europe?', Brookings and Hoover Institutions Briefing, Brookings Institution, Washington DC, 10 November, http://www.Brookings.edu/dybdocroot/comm./events/20041110.pdf
45 Lundestad, G. (1998) *'Empire' by Integration: The United States and European Integration 1945–1997*, Oxford University Press, Oxford; and Cox, R. (1987) *Production, Power and World Order*, Columbia University Press, New York.
46 Ikenberry, G. J. (2001) *op. cit.* p. 35.
47 Krasner has observed that regimes tend to emerge after major upheavals or wars, as new rules and ways of cooperating are put in place. Krasner, S. (ed.) (1983) *op. cit.* p. 357.
48 Mearsheimer, J. (1990) 'Back to the Future: Instability in Europe after the Cold War', *International Security*, 15, 1, summer.
49 Clark, I. (1997) *Globalization and Fragmentation: International Relations in the Twentieth Century*, Oxford University Press, Oxford.
50 Keohane, R. (1984) *op. cit.* p. 107.
51 Jervis, S. (1982) *op. cit.* pp. 365–7.
52 Keohane, R. (1983) in Krasner, S. (ed.) *op. cit.* p. 150.
53 Ignatieff, M. (2000) *Virtual War: Kosovo and Beyond*, Henry Holt, New York.
54 Haas defines epistemic communities as 'networks of knowledge-based communities with an authoritative claim to policy relevant knowledge within their domain of expertise'. Haas, P. (1997) 'Epistemic Communities and the Dynamics of International Environmental Cooperation', in Rittberger, V. (ed.) *op. cit.* p. 179.
55 Young, O. (1983) in Krasner, S. (ed.) *op. cit.* section 2.
56 Young, O. (1980) *op. cit.* p. 349.
57 Nadelmann, E. (1993) *Cops Across Borders: The Internationalization of US Criminal Law Enforcement*, Pennsylvania State University Press, University Park PA.
58 Rittberger, V. (1997) 'Research on International Regimes in Germany', in Rittberger, V. (ed.) *op. cit.* p. 19.
59 Young, O. (1983) in Krasner, S. (ed.) *op. cit.* section 2.
60 Young, O. (1982) 'Regime Dynamics: The Rise and Fall of International Regimes', *International Organization*, 36, 2, spring, p. 284.
61 Keohane, R. (1997) 'The Analysis of International Regimes', in Rittberger, V. (ed.) *op. cit.*

Chapter 2

1 Clarke, R., McCaffrey, B. and Nelson, R. (2004) *NATO's Role in Confronting International Terrorism*, Policy Paper, June, The Atlantic Council, Washington DC.
2 Clarke, R. (2004) *Against All Enemies: Inside America's War on Terror*, Free Press, New York.
3 Aaron, D., Beauchesne, A., Burwell, F., Nelson, C. R., Riley, K. J. and Zimmer, B. (2004) *The Post 9/11 Partnership: Transatlantic Cooperation*

Against Terrorism, Policy Paper, December, The Atlantic Council, Washington DC, p. ix.

4 Keohane, R. (1984) *After Hegemony: Cooperation and Discord in the World Political Economy*, Princeton University Press, Princeton NJ, p. 12.

5 Haas, P. (1997) 'Epistemic Communities and the Dynamics of International Environmental Cooperation', in Rittberger, V. (ed.) *Regime Theory and International Relations*, Clarendon Press, Oxford.

6 In 1997, for example, Senator John Kerry, who was later to run as the Democratic Presidential nominee in 2004, labelled the fight against organised crime as America's 'new war'. See Kerry, J. (1997) *The New War: The Web of Crime that Threatens America's Security*, Simon and Schuster, New York, pp. 26–8.

7 International Crime Control Strategy (1998) The White House, Washington DC.

8 Caulkins, J., Kleinman, M. and Reuter, P. (2003) 'Lessons of the "War" on Drugs for the "War" on Terrorism', in Howitt, A. and Pangi, R. (eds) *Countering Terrorism: Dimensions of Preparedness*, MIT Press, Cambridge MA.

9 Winer, J. (1997) 'Crime and Cooperation: An American Concern', in Gedwin, J. (ed.) *European Integration and American Interests*, AEI Press, Washington DC, pp. 180–1.

10 Interview conducted by the author (2001) US Department of Justice, May, Washington DC.

11 McDonald, W. (2002) 'International Law Enforcement Cooperation and Conflict: McDonaldization and Implosion Before and After September 11th', unpublished paper, Georgetown University, Washington DC.

12 Nadelmann, E. (1993) *Cops Across Borders: The Internationalization of US Criminal Law Enforcement*, Pennsylvania State University Press, University Park PA.

13 Interview conducted by the author (2001) Office for International Affairs, US Department of Justice, May, Washington DC.

14 Interview conducted by the author (2001) US Embassy to the UK, June, London.

15 The US Department of Homeland Security decided to send an attaché to the US Mission to the EU in Brussels in the early part of 2005. Interview conducted by the author (2005) US Mission to the EU, February, Brussels.

16 Gennaro, G. de (1997) Testimony of Giovanni de Gennaro, Italian National Police, to Hearing before the Committee on International Relations, US House of Representatives, October, 105th Congress, US Government Printing Office, Washington DC, p. 13.

17 Jamieson, A. (1995) 'The Transnational Dimension of Italian Organised Crime', *Transnational Organised Crime*, 1, 2, summer, pp. 156–57.

18 Freeh, L. (1997) Testimony of Louis Freeh, Director of the FBI to Hearing before the Committee on International Relations, US House of Representatives, October, 105th Congress, US Government Printing Office, Washington DC, p. 6.

19 Stevenson, J. (2004) 'Counter-terrorism: Containment and Beyond', *Adelphi Paper 367*, International Institute for Strategic Studies, London, p. 55.

20 Since 9/11 the UK has introduced a variety of counter-terrorism measures. These have included plans for anti-terror courts to sit without juries; to permit wiretap evidence in some trials and to introduce identity cards.

Webster, P. (2004) 'Blunkett Takes Aim at Crime to Outflank the Tories', *The Times*, 22 November, p. 4.

21 Clarke, R., McCaffrey, B. and Nelson, R. (2004) *op. cit.* Annex A: 'The French Approach to Terrorism'. See also Shapiro, J. and Suzan, B. (2003) 'The French Experience of Counter-terrorism', *Survival*, 45, 1, spring.

22 Cettina, N. (2003) 'The French Approach: Vigour and Vigilance', in Leeuwen, M. van (ed.) *Confronting Terrorism: European Experiences, Threat Perceptions and Policies*, Kluwer Law International, The Hague.

23 Priest, D. (2005) 'Alliance Base: US-sponsored, French-led Counter-Terrorism Centre in Europe', *Washington Post*, 3 July.

24 Interview conducted by the author (2004) Office for International Narcotics and Law Enforcement, US Department of State, September, Washington DC.

25 Chalk, P. (1996) *West European Terrorism and Counter-Terrorism: The Evolving Dynamic*, Macmillan, Basingstoke, p. 67.

26 US Department of State (1997) *Patterns of Global Terrorism 1996–7*, US Government Printing Office, Washington DC.

27 Mitsilegas, V., Monar, J. and Rees, W. (2003) *The European Union and Internal Security: Guardian of the People?*, Palgrave Macmillan, Basingstoke, pp. 10–15.

28 *Economist, The* (1999) 'Europe's Borders: A Single Market in Crime', 16 October, p. 28.

29 The Council of Europe has played an important role as a generator of international policies that have been taken up subsequently by the EC/EU. For example, the 2001 Convention on Cybercrime was a Council of Europe document. I am indebted to a Senior Counselor from the Department of Justice for this point. Interview conducted by the author (2005) US Mission to the EU, February, Brussels.

30 Occhipinti, J. (2003) *The Politics of EU Police Cooperation: Toward a European FBI?*, Lynne Reinner, Boulder CO, p. 227.

31 Politi, A. (1997) 'European Security: The New Transnational Risks', *Chaillot Papers 29*, October, Institute for Security Studies Western European Union, Paris, p. 48.

32 Vries, G. de (2004) Introductory speech by Gijs de Vries to the seminar hosted by the EU presidency on the Prevention of the Financing of Terrorism, 22 September, Brussels.

33 The Director General of JHA once complained that 'we devote an inordinate . . . amount of time to devising legal solutions to issues which straddle pillars'. Faull, J. (2005) Director General of Justice and Home Affairs, Evidence before EU Committee, House of Lords, in 'After Madrid: the EU's Response to Terrorism', EU Committee, 5th Report of Session 2004–5, Paper 53, HMSO, London, p. 95.

34 Boer, M. den (2003) 'The EU Counter-Terrorism Wave: Window of Opportunity or Profound Policy Transformation?', in Leeuwen, M. van (ed.) *op. cit.* p. 198.

35 Calleo, D. (2004) 'The Broken West', *Survival*, 46, 3, autumn, p. 34.

36 US Ambassador S. Eizenstat quoted in Winand, P. (2001) 'The US Mission to the EU in "Brussels DC": The European Commission Delegation in Washington DC and the New Transatlantic Agenda', in Philippart, E. and Winand, P. (eds) *Ever Closer Partnership: Policy-making in US-EU Relations*, PIE Peter Lang, Brussels, p. 121. In 2005 this problem was being

addressed by a series of so-called 'confidence building measures' initiated by the US Embassy to the EU. This brought law enforcement officers, judicial officers and members of the Executive and Congress over to the EU to be shown how it works. There will be reciprocal visits on the EU side to look at the workings of the US government. Interview conducted by the author (2005) US Mission to the EU, February, Brussels.

37   Dubois, D. (2002) 'The Attacks of 11 September: EU-US Cooperation Against Terrorism in the Field of Justice and Home Affairs', *European Foreign Affairs Review*, 7, 3, autumn, p. 325.
38   Interview conducted by the author (2001) Office for European Union Affairs, US Department of State, May, Washington DC.
39   See Peers, S. (2000) *EU Justice and Home Affairs*, Longman, Harlow.
40   Chalk, P. (1996) *op. cit.* p. 133.
41   Boer, M. den and Monar, J. (2002) 'Keynote Article: 11 September and the Challenge of Global Terrorism to the EU as a Security Actor', *Journal of Common Market Studies Annual Review*, 40, p. 20.
42   Monar, J. (2000) 'An "Area of Freedom, Justice and Security?" Progress and Deficits in Justice and Home Affairs', in Lynch, P., Neuwahl, N. and Rees, W. (eds) *Reforming the European Union: From Maastricht to Amsterdam*, Longman, Harlow.
43   Article 29, Title VI, Treaty on European Union.
44   Presidency Conclusions, European Council, 17–18 June 2004, Brussels, I: paragraph 7 and subsequently European Council (2004) 'The Hague Programme: Strengthening Freedom, Security and Justice in the European Union', 4–5 November.
45   Lebl, L. (2005) 'Security beyond Borders', *Policy Review Online*, no.130, Stanford, http://www.policyreview.org/apr05/lebl.html
46   Boer, M. den (2003) 'The EU Counter-Terrorism Wave: Window of Opportunity or Profound Policy Transformation?', in Leeuwen, M. van (ed.) *op. cit.* p. 185.
47   *Bulletin Quotidien Europe* (2004) 'Adoption on Friday of New Five Year Programme for Justice and Home Affairs', No. 8821, 5 November, Agence Presse, p. 10.
48   *Bulletin Quotidien Europe* (2004) 'Dutch Proposals for Future of Freedom, Security and Justice Policy to Be Debated Thursday and Friday', No. 8796, 30 September, Agence Presse, p. 15.
49   Baker, J. (1989) 'A New Europe and a New Atlanticism', address by James Baker, Secretary of State, before the Berlin Press Club, Berlin, 12 December, *American Foreign Policy, Current Documents*, 1989, Department of State, Washington DC, 1990, pp. 299–305; and Zoellick, R. (1990) 'The New Europe in a New Age: Insular, Itinerant or International? Prospects for an Alliance of Values', address by Robert Zoellick, Counselor of the State Department, before the American-European Community Association International's Conference on 'US/EC Relations and Europe's New Architecture', Annapolis MD, 21 September, *US Department of State Despatch*.
50   See Gardiner, A. (1997) *A New Era in US-EU Relations? The Clinton Administration and the New Transatlantic Agenda*, Avebury, Aldershot.
51   Philippart, E. and Winand, P. (eds) (2001) *op. cit.* p. 48.

52 Christopher, W. (1995) 'Charting a Transatlantic Agenda for the 21st Century', address by Warren Christopher, US Secretary of State, at Casa de America, Spain, 2 June.

53 Interview conducted by the author (2000) US Mission to the EU, September, Brussels.

54 Gardiner, A. (1997) *op. cit.* See also Krenzler, H. and Schomaker, A. (1996) 'A New Transatlantic Agenda', *European Foreign Affairs Review*, 1, 1, July; and Monar, J. (ed.) (1998) *The New Transatlantic Agenda and the Future of EU-US Relations*, Kluwer Law International, London and The Hague.

55 Philippart, E. and Winand, P. (2001) 'From "Equal Partnership" to the "New Transatlantic Agenda": Enduring Features and Successive Forms of the US-EU Relationship', in Philippart, E. and Winand, P. (eds) *op. cit.* p. 51.

56 Interview conducted by the author (2001) Office for European Union Affairs, US Department of State, May, Washington DC.

57 North Atlantic Council (2004) Istanbul Summit Communiqué issued by Heads of State, Istanbul 28 June, NATO Integrated Data Service.

58 Daalder, I. and Goldgeier, J. (2001) 'Putting Europe First', *Survival*, 43, 1, spring, p. 80.

59 Robertson, G. Lord, NATO Secretary General (2001) 'International Security and Law Enforcement – A Look Ahead', Law Enforcement and National Security Global Forum, Edinburgh International Conference Centre, UK, 19 June.

60 North Atlantic Council (1991) 'The NATO Strategic Concept', November, Rome, NATO Integrated Data Service, natodoc@HQ.NATO.INT.

61 North Atlantic Council (1999) 'The NATO Strategic Concept', April, Washington, NATO Integrated Data Service, natodoc@HQ.NATO.INT.

62 Lugar, R. (2002) 'Redefining NATO's Mission: Preventing WMD Terrorism', *Washington Quarterly*, 25, 3, summer. See also Forster, A. and Wallace, W. (2001) 'What is NATO for?', *Survival*, 43, 4, December; and Gordon, P. (2002) 'Re-forging the Atlantic Alliance', *The National Interest*, fall.

63 Barry, C. (1996) 'NATO's Combined Joint Task Forces in Theory and Practice', *Survival*, 38, spring; and Bolton, J. (2000) 'The End of NATO?', *The World Today*, 56, 6, June, pp. 13–14.

64 Gnesotto, N. (2002–3) 'Reacting to America', *Survival*, 44, 4, winter, p. 100.

65 Lansford, T. (2002) *All for One: Terrorism, NATO and the United States*, Ashgate, Aldershot, p. 65.

66 North Atlantic Council (2002) The Prague Summit, Prague. See also Asmus, R. (2003) 'Rebuilding the Atlantic Alliance', *Foreign Affairs*, 82, 5, September-October; and Kamp, K-H. (1999) 'A Global Role for NATO?', *Washington Quarterly*, winter; and Talbott, S. (2002) 'From Prague to Baghdad', *Foreign Affairs*, 81, 6, November-December.

67 The idea for restructuring the Alliance was not new as the proposal for a third NATO command for Out of Area missions was discussed in Thomson, J. (1997) 'New NATO Structures', in Gompert, D. and Larabee, S. (eds) *America and Europe*, Cambridge University Press, Cambridge.

68 See Rynning, S. (2005) 'A New Military Ethos: NATO's Response Force', *Journal of Transatlantic Studies*, 3, 1, spring.

69 Interview conducted by the author (2004) RAND, September, Washington DC.

70 Bensahel, N. (2003) 'The Counterterror Coalitions: Cooperation with Europe, NATO, and the European Union', *RAND Project Air Force*, Arlington VA, pp. 24–5.

71 Howorth, J. (2003–4) 'France, Britain and the Euro-Atlantic Crisis', *Survival*, 45, 4, winter, p. 180.

72 Grant, C. (2002) 'The Eleventh of September and Beyond: The Impact on the European Union', in Freedman, L. (ed.) *Superterrorism: Policy Responses*, Blackwell, Oxford, p. 136. See also Binnendijk, H. and Kugler, R. (2002) 'Transforming Europe's Forces', *Survival*, 43, 3, autumn; and Cornish, P. and Edwards, G. (2001) 'Beyond the EU/NATO Dichotomy: The Beginnings of a European Strategic Culture', *International Affairs*, 77, 3, July.

73 Clarke, R., McCaffrey, B. and Nelson, R. (2004) *op. cit.*

74 North Atlantic Council (2004) Istanbul Summit Communiqué issued by heads of state, Istanbul, 28 June, NATO Integrated Data Service, natodoc@HQ.NATO.INT.

75 The EU is in the process of creating thirteen 'battle groups', of 1,500 troops, for rapid deployment.

76 The need for the Europeans to improve their military capabilities across the board is matched by their need to develop specialised capabilities for countering terrorism such as Chemical, Biological, Nuclear and Radiological (CBNR) that was the subject of the Prague Capabilities Commitment.

77 NATO International Military Staff (2003) 'NATO's Military Concept for Defence Against Terrorism', NATO Headquarters, 15 December, Brussels, http://www.nato.int/ims/docu/terrorism.htm

78 Bensahel, N. (2003) *op. cit.* p. 25.

79 Clarke, R., McCaffrey, B. and Nelson, R. (2004) *op. cit.*

80 North Atlantic Council (2004) Istanbul Summit Communiqué issued by heads of state, *op. cit.*

81 Russia was admitted to the forum in 1992 and this was formalised into membership in 1998.

82 Kirton, J. and Stefanova, R. (eds) (2003) *The G-8, the United Nations and Conflict Prevention*, Ashgate, Aldershot.

83 Penttila, R. (2003) 'The Role of the G8 in International Peace and Security', *Adelphi Paper 355*, International Institute for Strategic Studies, London, p. 47.

84 Badey, T. (1998) 'US Anti-terrorism Policy: The Clinton Administration', *Contemporary Security Policy*, 19, 2, August, p. 60.

85 Wrench, P. (1998) 'The G8 and Transnational Organised Crime', in Cullen, P. and Gilmore, W. (eds) 'Crime Sans Frontières: International and European Legal Approaches', *Hume Papers on Public Policy*, 6, 1 and 2, Edinburgh University Press, Edinburgh. See also *Bulletin Quotidien Europe* (29/6/1996) 'The Lyon Summit Decides to Hold a Meeting on the Fight against Terrorism in July', No. 6760, Agence Presse.

86 Bayne, N. (2005) *Staying Together: The G8 Summit Confronts the 21st Century*, Ashgate, Aldershot, p. 177.

87 'G-8 Foreign Ministers' Progress Report on the Fight against Terrorism', Whistler, 12 June 2002, Appendix L, in Kirton, J. and Stefanova, R. (eds) (2003) *op. cit.*

88 After the end of the Cold War, the US took the lead in controlling the spread of nuclear technology from the former Soviet Union. See Davis, Z.

(1994) 'US Counterproliferation Doctrine: Issues for Congress', *Congressional Research Service Report for Congress*, 21 September, Library of Congress, Washington DC.

89 Financial Action Task Force (2001) 'Financial Action Task Force on Money Laundering: Special Recommendations on Terrorist Financing', 31 October, Washington DC.

90 Penttila, R. (2003) *op. cit.* p. 49.

91 Asmus, R. (2005) 'Rethinking the EU: Why Washington Needs to Support European Integration', *Survival*, 47, 3, autumn, p. 93.

Chapter 3

1 Haas, P. (1992) 'Epistemic Communities and International Policy Coordination', in Haas, P. (ed.) 'Knowledge, Power and International Policy Coordination', *International Organization*, 46, 1, p. 29.

2 Hoffman, B. (1998) *Inside Terrorism*, Columbia University Press, New York; Lesser, I., Hoffman, B., Arquilla, J., Ronfeldt, D. and Zanini, M. (1999) *Countering the New Terrorism*, MR-989-AF, RAND, Santa Monica; Homer-Dixon, T. (2002) 'The Rise of Complex Terrorism', *Foreign Policy*, 128, January-February; and Roy, O., Hoffman, B., Paz, R., Simon, S. and Benjamin, D. (2000) 'America and the New Terrorism: An Exchange', *Survival*, summer, 42, 2, pp. 156–72.

3 Tenet, G. (2001) Statement of CIA Director George Tenet before Senate Select Committee on Intelligence, 7 February, quoted in Prados, J. (2002) (ed.) *America Confronts Terrorism: Understanding the Danger and How to Think about It*, Ivan Dee, Chicago, pp. 21–7. See also Probst, P. (1996) 'Remarks of Peter Probst, Assistant Secretary for Terrorism Intelligence, Office of the Secretary of Defense', report prepared for the Permanent Select Committee on Intelligence, US House of Representatives, by the Congressional Research Service, July, US Government Printing Office, Washington DC.

4 Raufer, X. (2000) 'New World Disorder, New Terrorisms: New Threats for Europe and the Western World', in Taylor, M and Horgan, J. (eds) *The Future of Terrorism*, Frank Cass, London, pp. 30–1.

5 Freedman, L. (ed.) (2002) *Superterrorism: Policy Responses*, Blackwell, Oxford; and Sprinzak, E. (1998) 'The Great Super-terrorism Scare', *Foreign Policy*, 112, fall.

6 Asmus, R. and Pollack, M. (2002) 'The New Transatlantic Project', *Policy Review Online*, no. 115, Stanford, http://www.policyreview.org/OCT02/asmus.html

7 Muller, H. (2003) 'Terrorism, Proliferation: A European Threat Assessment', *Chaillot Paper No. 58*, European Union Institute for Security Studies, Paris, March, p. 26.

8 Benjamin, D. and Simon, S. (2002) *The Age of Sacred Terror*, Random House, New York.

9 Evidence given by the Federal Bureau of Investigation to a Senate Committee in 1999, cited by Cordesman, A. (2002) *Terrorism, Asymmetric Warfare, and Weapons of Mass Destruction. Defending the US Homeland*, Praeger, Westport CT, pp. 54–5.

10 Laqeur, W. (2002) 'Left, Right and Beyond: The Changing Face of Terror', in Hoge, J. and Rose, G. (eds) *How Did This Happen? Terrorism and the New War*, Public Affairs, New York.

11 Pillar, P. (2001) *Terrorism and US Foreign Policy*, Brookings Institution Press, Washington DC, pp. 54–5.

12 Simon, S. and Benjamin, D. (2000) 'America and the New Terrorism', *Survival*, 42, 1, spring, p. 70.

13 Manningham-Buller, E. (2003) 'Global Terrorism: Are We Meeting the Challenge?', James Smart Memorial Lecture 2003, City of London Police Headquarters, 16 October, http://www.homeoffice.gov.uk/docs2/james_smart_lecture2003.html

14 Many of the 9/11 hijackers were from affluent backgrounds and had enjoyed good educations and employment.

15 The 9/11 Commission Report: *Final Report of the National Commission on Terrorist Attacks upon the United States* (2004), W. W. Norton, New York, p. 363.

16 Chalk, P. (1996) *West European Terrorism and Counter-Terrorism: The Evolving Dynamic*, Macmillan, Basingstoke, p. 66.

17 Chalk, P. (1996) *ibid.* p. 118.

18 Shearman, P. and Sussex, M. (2004) 'America and Europe after 9/11', in Shearman, P. and Sussex, M. (eds) *European Security after 9/11*, Ashgate, Aldershot, p. 59.

19 Quoted in Riddell, P. (2003) *Hug them Close: Blair, Clinton, Bush and the 'Special Relationship'*, Politico's, London, p. 15.

20 Boer, M. den, (2003) 'The EU Counter-Terrorism Wave: Window of Opportunity or Profound Policy Transformation?' in Leeuwen, M. van (ed.) *Confronting Terrorism: European Experiences, Threat Perceptions and Policies*, Kluwer Law International, The Hague, p. 191. Germany's Office for the Protection of the Constitution regards Islamic extremism as the foremost threat to Germany's internal security. See Pope, W. (2004) Principal Deputy Coordinator for Counter Terrorism, US Department of State, Statement before the Sub Committee on Europe and on International Terrorism, Non-Proliferation and Human Rights, US House of Representatives, Washington DC, 14 September.

21 Delpech, T. (2002) 'International Terrorism and Europe', *Chaillot Paper No. 56*, European Union Institute for Security Studies, Paris, December, pp. 16–20. See also Hoffman, B. (1999) 'Is Europe Soft on Terrorism?', *Foreign Policy*, 115, summer.

22 Bremner, C. (2004) 'Stoned to Death . . . Why Europe is Starting to Lose Its Faith in Islam', *The Times*, 4 December, p. 55; and *Economist, The* (2004) 'Big Dominique and His Struggle against the Islamists', 18 December, pp. 57–8.

23 Laqeur, W. (2004) 'The Terrorism to Come', *Policy Review Online*, Hoover Institution, http://www.policyreview.org/aug04/laqeur.html

24 Roy, O. (2003) 'EuroIslam: The Jihad Within', *The National Interest*, 71, spring, p. 64.

25 *Economist, The* (2004) 'Charlemagne: A Civil War on Terrorism', 27 November, p. 50.

26 It is noteworthy in this regard that the EU has entered recently into a dialogue with the US in an attempt to learn from America's historical success in assimilating minorities. This suggests that European countries

are much more aware of this problem than before. Interview conducted by the author (2005) US Mission to the EU, February, Brussels.

27 Fukuyama, F. (2004) speaking at 'Troubled Partnership: What's Next for the US and Europe?', Brookings and Hoover Institutions Briefing, Brookings Institution, Washington DC, 10 November, http://www.Brookings.edu/dybdocroot/comm./events/20041110.pdf

28 Stevenson, J. (2004) 'Counter-terrorism: Containment and Beyond', *Adelphi Paper 367*, International Institute for Strategic Studies, London, p. 27.

29 *Economist, The* (2004) 'Islamic Terrorism in Europe', 13 November, p. 43.

30 Akerboom, E. (2004) 'Counter-Terrorism in the Netherlands', General Intelligence and Security Service of the Netherlands, http://wwwaivd.nl/ See also *Economist, The* (2004) 'After Van Gogh', 13 November, pp. 43–4.

31 Chalk, P. (1996) *op. cit.* p. 28.

32 Hewitt, C. (2003) *Understanding Terrorism in America: From the Klan to Al Qaeda*, Routledge, London, p. 18.

33 See Counter Terrorism Assessment and Warning Unit (1999) 'Terrorism in the United States 1998', National Security Division, Federal Bureau of Investigation, US Department of Justice, US Government Printing Office, Washington DC.

34 Prados, J. (ed.) (2002) *op. cit.* p. 3.

35 Quoted in Naftali, T. (2005) *Blind Spot: The Secret History of American Counter Terrorism*, Basic Books, New York, p. 228.

36 United States State Department (1999) *Patterns of Global Terrorism 1999*, US Government Printing Office, Washington DC.

37 I am indebted to N. Wyllie for this point.

38 Cited by Nye, J. (2001) 'Government's Challenge: Getting Serious About Terrorism', in Hoge, J. and Rose, G. (eds) *op. cit.* p. 199.

39 'Countering the Changing Threat of International Terrorism' (2000) Report of the National Commission on Terrorism, 105th Congress, 2nd Session, Doc 106–250, US Government Printing Office, Washington DC.

40 Clarke, R. (2004) *Against All Enemies: Inside America's War on Terror*, Free Press, New York.

41 Simon, S. and Benjamin, D. (2000) *op. cit.* p. 60; and Badey, T. (1998) 'US Anti-terrorism Policy: The Clinton Administration', *Contemporary Security Policy*, 19, 2, August, pp. 55–65.

42 Bush, G. (2001) 'Radio Address of the President to the Nation', http://www.whitehouse.gov/news/releases/2001

43 Tellis, A. (2004) 'Assessing America's War on Terrorism: Confronting Insurgency, Cementing Primacy', National Bureau of Asian Research Analysis in cooperation with Carnegie Endowment for International Peace, 15, 4, December, http://www.carnegieendowment.org/files/NBRAnalysis-Tellis_December2004.pdf, pp. 65–6.

44 Zelikow, P. (2003) 'The Transformation of National Security', *The National Interest*, 71, spring.

45 Cordesman, A. (2002) *op. cit.* p. 2.

46 Lake, A. (1994) 'Confronting Backlash States', *Foreign Affairs*, 73, 2, March/April.

47 Perl, R. (2001) *Terrorism, the Future and US Foreign Policy*, Congressional Research Service Report, Library of Congress, Washington DC, 13 September.

48 US National Strategy for Combating Terrorism (2003) The White House, Washington DC, February.
49 Bush, G. (2001) Address by President George Bush to a Joint Session of Congress, 20 September.
50 Haas, R. (ed.) (1999) *Transatlantic Tensions: The United States, Europe and Problem Countries*, Brookings Institution Press, Washington DC, p. 4.
51 Muller, H. (2003) *op. cit.*
52 Hoffman, B. (1998) *op. cit.* p. 68.
53 Freedman, L. (2002) 'The Coming War on Terrorism', in Freedman, L. (ed.) *op. cit.* See also Walt, S. (2001–2) 'Beyond Bin Laden', *International Security*, 26, 3, winter, p. 57.
54 'A Secure Europe in a Better World – European Security Strategy' (2003) European Council, Brussels, 12 December. The Strategy was first presented as a draft by Javier Solana to the European Council at Thessaloniki in June 2003.
55 Cooper, R. (2003) *The Breaking of Nations: Order and Chaos in the Twenty First Century*, Atlantic Books, London. Robert Cooper was a British diplomat but went on to serve as Director General for External and Politico-Military Affairs at the European Council.
56 US National Security Strategy (2003) The White House, Washington DC, June; and US National Strategy for Combating Terrorism (2003) *op. cit.*
57 Litwak, R. (2002) 'The New Calculus of Pre-emption', *Survival*, 44, 4, winter, p. 55.
58 Clinton, W. (1996) Speech of US President William Clinton to the United Nations General Assembly, 24 September. For academic perspectives see Betts, R. (1998) 'The New Threats of Mass Destruction', *Foreign Affairs*, January-February; and Kamp, K-H. (1998) 'WMD Terrorism: An Exchange', *Survival*, 40, 4, winter 1998–9.
59 Freedman, L. (ed.) (2002) *op. cit.*; and Muller, H. (2003) *op. cit.* p. 28.
60 President Bush (2001) State of the Union speech to Joint Session of Congress, 29 January.
61 US National Strategy to Combat Weapons of Mass Destruction (2003) The White House, Washington DC.
62 Falkenrath, R., Newman, R. and Thayer, B. (1998) *America's Achilles' Heel: Nuclear, Biological, and Chemical Terrorism and Covert Attack*, MIT Press, Cambridge MA, p. 27.
63 Muller, H. (2003) *op. cit.*
64 Record, J. (2003) *Bounding the Global War on Terrorism*, Strategic Studies Institute, Carlisle Barracks, Pennsylvania, December, pp. 16–17, http://www.carlisle.army.mil/ssi/pdfiles/PUB207.pdf
65 Hussain, Z. (2004) 'Scientist Pardoned for Selling Nuclear Secrets', *The Times*, 6 February, p. 18; and Maddox, B. (2004) 'On the Trail of Nuclear Supply and Demand', *The Times*, 13 February, p. 23. See also Bowen, W. and Kidd, J. (2004) 'The Iranian Nuclear Challenge', *International Affairs*, 80, 2, p. 262; and *Economist, The* (2004) 'A World Wide Web of Nuclear Danger', special report: 'Proliferation', 28 February, p. 25.
66 Koblentz, G. (2003) 'Biological Terrorism: Understanding the Threat and America's Response', in Howitt, A. and Pangi, R. (eds) *Countering Terrorism: Dimensions of Preparedness*, MIT Press, Cambridge MA, p. 101.

Notes 163

67 *Economist, The* (2005) 'Imagining Something Much Worse than London', 16 July, pp. 40–1.
68 Koblentz, G. (2003) *op. cit.* p. 124.
69 Nye, J. (2001) in Hoge, J. and Rose, G. (eds) *op. cit.* p. 201.
70 Walsh, J. (2003) 'Nuclear Terrorism: Risks, Consequences and Response', in Howitt, A. and Pangi, R. (eds) *op. cit.* p. 184.
71 *Economist, The* (2002) 'Special Report: The War on Terror. Weapons of Mass Dislocation', 15 June, p. 26.
72 *Bulletin Quotidien Europe* (2/12/2004) 'Counterterrorist Strategies at Thursday's Council', No. 8839, Agence Presse, p. 11.
73 Marotta, E. (1999) 'Europol's Role in Anti-Terrorism Policy', *Terrorism and Political Violence*, 11, p. 15.
74 Simon, S. and Benjamin, D. (2000) *op. cit.* p. 60.
75 *Bulletin Quotidien Europe* (17/12/2004) 'EU/European Council / Terrorism', No. 8850, Agence Presse, p. 7. See also Frattini, F. (2005) 'The Fight Against Terrorism', Speech/05/474 to Mykolas Romeris University, Vilnius, 2 September.
76 Record, J. (2003) *op. cit.* p. 1.
77 Johnston, A. (1995) 'Thinking about Strategic Culture', *International Security*, 19, 4, spring, pp. 33–45. See also Snyder, J. (1977) *The Soviet Strategic Culture: Implications for Nuclear Options*, RAND, Santa Monica.
78 Toje, A. (2005) 'The 2003 European Union Security Strategy: A Critical Appraisal', *European Foreign Affairs Review*, 10, p. 122.
79 This description was coined by the former French foreign minister Hubert Vedrine.
80 Spear, J. (2003) 'The Emergence of a European "Strategic Personality"', *Arms Control Today*, November.
81 The EU was given the power only to 'request' the Western European Union to act on its behalf. See Rees, W. (1998) *The Western European Union at the Crossroads: Between Trans-Atlantic Solidarity and European Integration*, Westview Press, Boulder CO.
82 Longhurst, K. (2004) *Germany and the Use of Force: The Evolution of German Security Policy 1990–2003*, Manchester University Press, Manchester, p. 7.
83 Freedman, L. (2004) 'Can the EU Develop an Effective Military Doctrine?', in Everts, S., Freedman, L., Grant, C., Heisbourg, F., Keohane, D. and O'Hanlon, M., *A European Way of War*, Centre for European Reform, London, May, p. 15.
84 Heisbourg, F. (2004) in S. Everts *et al.*, *ibid.* p. 31. Calls for a *Livre blanc* have been championed also by the European Union Institute for Security Studies in Paris.
85 Everts, S. (2001) *Unilateral America, Lightweight Europe? Managing Divergence in Transatlantic Foreign Policy*, Centre for European Reform, London, February.
86 Kagan, R. (2003) *Paradise and Power: America and Europe in the New World Order*, Atlantic Books, London, p. 32.
87 Kagan, R. (2003) *ibid.* p. 3.
88 Cooper, R. (2003) *op. cit.*
89 Archik, K. (2004) *Europe and Counterterrorism: Strengthening Police and Judicial Cooperation*, Congressional Research Service Report, Library of Congress, Washington DC, 23 August, p. 22.

90 Litwak, R. (2002) 'The New Calculus of Pre-emption', *Survival*, 44, 4, winter, p. 58.
91 This thinking is not new. President Clinton launched the Defense Counter-proliferation Initiative in December 1993, which the Europeans opposed because it discussed the possibility of using force pre-emptively. See Litwak, R. (1999) *op. cit.*
92 Bush, G. (2002) 'President George W. Bush Delivers Graduation Speech at West Point', the White House, Washington DC, 1 June.
93 See Heisbourg, F. (2003) 'A Work In Progress: The Bush Doctrine and Its Consequences', *Washington Quarterly*, 26, 2; and Freedman, L. (2003) 'Prevention not Pre-emption', *Washington Quarterly*, spring.
94 *Bulletin Quotidien Europe* (13/11/2004) 'NATO Secretary General urges EU to Take the Same Attitude to Terrorism and Iraq as the US', No. 8826, Agence Presse, p. 8. See also Hassner, P. (2002) 'The US: The Empire of Force or the Force of Empire?', *Chaillot Paper 54*, European Union Institute for Security Studies, Paris, September.
95 Duke, S. (2004) 'The European Security Strategy in a Comparative Framework: Does it Make for Secure Alliances in a Better World?', *European Foreign Affairs Review*, 9, p. 464.
96 Peterson argues the two documents are in 'considerable harmony'. Peterson, J. (2004) 'America as a European Power: The End of Empire by Integration?', *International Affairs*, 80, 4, July.
97 Sir Stephen Wall, a former British ambassador to the EU, accused the US of abandoning the rule of law towards its conflict with Iraq in 2003. Wall, S. (2004) 'The UK, the EU and the United States: Bridge, or Just Troubled Water?', speech at Chatham House, 8 November, http://www.riia.org
98 Manners, I. (2002) 'Normative Power Europe? A Contradiction in Terms?', *Journal of Common Market Studies*, 40, 2.
99 Nye, J. (2003) 'The Decline of America's Soft Power: Why Washington Should Worry', *Foreign Affairs*, 83, 3, May-June.
100 Malvesti noted that in 2,400 attacks on US personnel or interests in the period 1983–98, the US had responded with military force on only three occasions. Malvesti, M. (2001) 'Explaining the United States' Decision to Strike Back at Terrorists', *Terrorism and Political Violence*, 13, 2, summer, p. 86.
101 US National Strategy for Combating Terrorism (2003) The White House, Washington DC, February, p. 1.
102 Muller, H. (2003) *op. cit.* p. 44.
103 The 9/11 Commission Report (2004) *op. cit.* pp. 363–4.
104 Perl, R. (2003) 'US Anti-Terrorism Strategy', speech to the Konrad Adenauer Foundation, Berlin, 30 June, http://www.usembassy.org.uk/terror512.html
105 The Strategy for Homeland Defense and Civil Support (2005) US Department of Defense, June; and the US National Strategy for Homeland Security (2002) The White House, Washington DC, July.
106 Chertoff, M. (2005) 'Statement of Secretary Michael Chertoff, US Department of Homeland Security, before the US Senate Committee on Commerce, Science and Transportation, 19 July, Washington DC'. See also, *Economist, The* (2005) 'Imagining Something Much Worse than London', *op.cit.* pp. 40–1.

107 Carter, A. (2003) 'The Architecture of Government in the Face of Terrorism', in Howitt, A. and Pangi, R. (eds) *op. cit.* p. 27.

108 Flynn, S. (2004) *America the Vulnerable: How Our Government is Failing to Protect Us from Terrorism*, HarperCollins, New York, p. 2.

109 *Economist, The* (2001) 'America the Unready', 22 December, pp. 49–50; and *Economist, The* (2002) 'Washington's Mega-merger', 23 November, pp. 51–2.

110 Asmus, R. (2003) 'Rebuilding the Atlantic Alliance', *Foreign Affairs*, September/October, p. 27.

111 Stevenson, J. (2003) 'How Europe and America Defend Themselves', *Foreign Affairs*, 82, 2, March-April, p. 78.

112 House of Lords (2005) 'After Madrid: the EU's Response to Terrorism', EU Committee, 5th Report of Session 2004–5, Paper 53, HMSO, London.

113 Stevenson, J. (2004) *op. cit.* p. 32.

114 Vries, G. de (2004) EU Counter-Terrorism Coordinator Statement before the Committee on International Relations, US House of Representatives, Washington DC, 14 September.

115 A senior US administration official briefing the press for the June 2003 US-EU Summit in Washington declared: 'we are struck by a convergence of European and American thinking about the nature of security threats in the 21st century and the nature of a combined, transatlantic US-European response'. 'US Officials Brief on June 25 US-EU Summit', *Washington File*, US Embassy in London, http://www.usembassy.org.uk/euro232.html

Chapter 4

1 Stevenson, J. (2003) 'How Europe and America Defend Themselves', *Foreign Affairs*, 82, 2, March-April, p. 84.

2 'Conclusions and Plan of Action of the Extraordinary European Council meeting on 21 September 2001' (2001) European Council, Brussels, 21 September.

3 *Bulletin Quotidien Europe* (21/9/2001) 'Terrorism', No. 8052, Agence Presse, p. 5.

4 European Council (2001) 'Informal European Council of Ghent', 19 October, Ghent.

5 The Police Chiefs Operational Task Force comprises the leaders of police forces within the EU. It has traditionally shared information on subjects ranging from organised crime to drug trafficking but, since 9/11 and particularly the Madrid bomb attacks, its focus has switched to counter-terrorism.

6 Boer, M. den and Monar, J. (2002) 'Keynote Article: 11 September and the Challenge of Global Terrorism to the EU as a Security Actor', *Journal of Common Market Studies Annual Review*, 40, p. 14.

7 Justice and Home Affairs Council (2001) 'Conclusions Adopted by the Council', SN 3926, Brussels, 20 September.

8 Anderson, M. (1995) 'The Merging of Internal and External Security', in Anderson, M., den Boer, M., Cullen, P., Gilmore, W., Raab, C. and Walker, N. *Policing the European Union*, Clarendon Press, Oxford, p. 172.

9 Naylor, R. (1995), 'From Cold War to Crime War: The Search for a New "National Security" Threat', *Transnational Organized Crime*, 1, 4, winter, p. 39.

10 McDonald, W. (2002) 'International Law Enforcement Cooperation and Conflict: McDonaldization and Implosion before and after September 11th', unpublished paper, Georgetown University, Washington DC, p. 16.

11 Aaron, D., Beauchesne, A., Burwell, F., Nelson, C. R., Riley, K. J. and Zimmer, B. (2004) 'The Post 9/11 Partnership: Transatlantic Cooperation Against Terrorism', Policy Paper, The Atlantic Council, Washington DC, December, p. x, http://www.acus.org/docs/0412-Post_9–11_Partnership_Transatlantic_Cooperation_Against-Terrorism.pdf

12 UK Home Office, 'Terrorism Legislation', http://www.homeoffice.gov.uk/terrorism/govprotect/legislation/index.html

13 In the case of the radical Egyptian cleric Abu Hamza, for instance, it has been suggested that the US possessed telephone and email intercepts on him that the UK was unable to use in its own legal process. See *Economist, The* (2004) 'A Long Stretch', 5 June, p. 28. It is notable that since the 7 July 2005 terrorist attacks in London, UK Home Secretary Charles Clarke has pressed his EU counterparts for an agreement by which telecommunications companies would have to keep records of mobile phone use for up to a year.

14 Schnabel, R. (2001) 'US Ambassador to the EU on Terrorism, Transatlantic Cooperation', *Washington File*, 13 December, http://www.usembassy.org.uk/euro167.html

15 'EU-US Declaration on Combating Terrorism' (2004) Dromoland Castle, Ireland, 26 June 2004 in Press Release, Council of the EU, 10760/04, Brussels.

16 This is not universal. Some countries, such as the Netherlands, have developed mechanisms so that intelligence information can be made available to the police. See Akerboom, E. (2004) 'Counter-Terrorism in the Netherlands', General Intelligence and Security Service of the Netherlands, http://www.aivd.nl/

17 FISA was a 1978 statute that created a court in Washington to consider applications for surveillance to gather intelligence information on foreigners suspected of acting in ways prejudicial to US national security. Material that had been gained under FISA was designated 'Secret' and was not made available for law enforcement purposes.

18 Interview conducted by the author (2004) Counter Terrorism Section, Criminal Division, US Department of Justice, September, Washington DC.

19 'Report from the Field: The USA PATRIOT Act at Work' (2004) Department of Justice, Washington DC, July, p. 5.

20 A past adviser to the Department of Homeland Security, Richard Falkenrath, called for the EU to follow the US lead in removing the barrier between intelligence gathered for national security and for police prosecutions. See Vries, G. de (2005) 'Gijs de Vries on Terrorism, Islam and Democracy', interview to EurActiv.com, 4 March.

21 Occhipinti, J. (2003) *The Politics of EU Police Cooperation: Toward a European FBI?*, Lynne Reinner, Boulder CO, pp. 58–9.

22 Marotta, E. (1999) 'Europol's Role in Anti-Terrorism Policy', *Terrorism and Political Violence*, 11, p. 17.

23 A 'Council Framework Decision on Joint Investigation Team' was agreed on 28 November 2001. See Dubois, D. (2002) 'The Attacks of 11 September: EU-US Cooperation Against Terrorism in the Field of Justice and Home Affairs', *European Foreign Affairs Review*, 7, 3, autumn. One reason why the US has been so interested in the Joint Investigation Teams concept is because it mirrors the way the US has chosen to coordinate different law enforcement agencies in counter-terrorist operations in so-called 'Joint Terrorism Task Forces'.

24 *Bulletin Quotidien Europe* (24/7/2004) No. 8754, Agence Presse, p. 12.

25 For a discussion of the architecture of Europol's data storage systems see Segell, G. (2004) 'Intelligence Agency Relations between the European Union and the US', *International Journal of Intelligence and Counter Intelligence*, 17, 1, spring, pp. 83–4.

26 Before leaving office the Director of Europol, Jürgen Storbeck, addressed the Council and complained about the lack of resources available to the organisation as a whole.

27 Interview conducted by the author (2004) US Mission to the EU, September, Brussels.

28 *Bulletin Quotidien Europe* (21/9/2004) 'EU/Terrorism: Europeans and Americans Want to Work together', No. 8789, Agence Presse, p. 10.

29 Dubois, D. (2002) *op. cit.* p. 328.

30 *Bulletin Quotidien Europe* (20/3/2004) No. 8670, Agence Presse, p. 5.

31 Two Europol officers are stationed in the Washington office. They have experienced a tripling of the information shared with their US counterparts over the course of their first year in operation.

32 Interview conducted by the author (2004) Europol Liaison Unit, Offices of the European Commission, September, Washington DC.

33 New members have been expected to implement the JHA *acquis* in full. Some new accession states have been found to be ahead of the pre-existing members but the majority are far behind and doubts have been raised about their ability to fulfil their commitments.

34 Interview conducted by the author (2001) Office for European Union Affairs, US Department of State, May, Washington DC.

35 Review of the Framework for Relations between the European Union and the United States, Independent Study Commissioned by Directorate General External Relations C1, European Commission, Final Report, p. 47.

36 Interview conducted by the author (2004) Counter Terrorism Section, US Department of Justice, September, Washington DC.

37 Pope, W. (2004) Principal Deputy Coordinator for Counter Terrorism, US Department of State, Statement before the Sub Committee on Europe and on International Terrorism, Non-Proliferation and Human Rights, US House of Representatives, Washington DC, 14 September.

38 Interview conducted by the author (2004) Counter Terrorism Section, Criminal Division, US Department of Justice, September, Washington DC.

39 Stevenson, J. (2004) 'Counter-terrorism: Containment and Beyond', *Adelphi Paper 367*, International Institute for Strategic Studies, London, p. 84. See also Chalk, P. (1996) *West European Terrorism and Counter-Terrorism: The Evolving Dynamic*, Macmillan, Basingstoke, pp. 100–1 for details of pre-existing legislation on terrorism in the major West European countries.

40 European Parliament (2001) 'Report on the Role of the EU in Combating Terrorism', Committee on Citizens Freedoms and Rights, Justice and Home Affairs (2001/2016 INI), A5 0273/2001 Final, Rapporteur Graham Watson, 12 July, p. 15. See also The Cabinet Office (2002) 'The United Kingdom and the Campaign Against International Terrorism. Progress Report', London, 9 September, para. 39, http://www.cabinetoffice.gov.uk/publications/reports/sept11/coi-0809.pdf

41 Cofer Black, J. (2004) Testimony by Ambassador Cofer Black, Coordinator for Counter Terrorism, Department of State before the Senate Foreign Relations Subcommittee on Europe, US Senate, Washington DC, 31 March.

42 Archik, K. (2004) 'Europe and Counterterrorism: Strengthening Police and Judicial Cooperation', *Congressional Research Service Report*, Library of Congress, Washington DC, 23 August, p. 19.

43 'Law Lords Leave Terror Laws in Tatters' (2004) *The Times*, 17 December, pp. 1 and 6. See also *Economist, The* (2005) 'Practice What You Preach', 29 January, p. 12.

44 Doyle, C. (2002) 'The USA PATRIOT Act: A Sketch', *Congressional Research Service Report for Congress*, Library of Congress, Washington DC, 18 April.

45 Bovard, J. (2003) *Terrorism and Tyranny. Trampling Freedom, Justice and Peace to Rid the World of Evil*, Palgrave Macmillan, New York, ch. 4. In defence of the Patriot Act, the 9/11 Commission argued that many of its most controversial aspects have 'sunset' clauses necessitating their renewal after the end of 2005. See *The 9/11 Commission Report: Final Report of the National Commission on Terrorist Attacks upon the United States* (2004) W. W. Norton, New York, p. 394.

46 Council of the European Union (2002) 'Council Framework Decision of 13 June 2002 on Combating Terrorism', Brussels. See also *Official Journal of the European Communities*, L 22 June 2002, p. 3.

47 European Commission (2004) 'EU Counter Terrorism Efforts in JHA Field', press release, Mem0/04/59, 12 March, Brussels, http://europa/eu.int/rapid/start/cgi/guesten.ksh?p-action.gettxt = gtanddoc = MEMO/04/5

48 Archik, K. (2004) *op. cit.* p. 13.

49 'Decision on a European Arrest Warrant from the Commission' (2001) COM 522 and then *Official Journal of the European Communities* (2002) L 190 18 July, p. 1. The European Arrest Warrant was designed to replace the two conventions of 1995 and 1996 which were themselves derived from a Council of Europe convention of 1957.

50 Vries, G. de (2004) EU Counter-Terrorism Coordinator Statement before the Committee on International Relations, US House of Representatives, Washington DC, 14 September.

51 Dubois, D. (2002) *op. cit.* p. 328.

52 Occhipinti, J. (2003) *op. cit.* p. 127.

53 European Council (2002) 'Decision on Setting Up Eurojust with a View to Reinforcing the Fight against Serious Crime', 28 February, Brussels.

54 Interview conducted by the author (2005) Criminal Division, European Council, February, Brussels.

55 Mitsilegas, V. (2003) 'The New EU-USA Cooperation on Extradition, Mutual Legal Assistance and the Exchange of Police Data', *European Foreign Affairs Review*, 8, 4, winter, pp. 523–4.

56 Interview conducted by the author (2004) International Narcotics and Law Enforcement Office, US Department of State, September, Washington DC.

57 Interview conducted by the author (2001) Office for International Affairs, US Department of Justice, May, Washington DC.

58 *Bulletin Quotidien Europe* (24/7/2004) *op. cit.* p. 11. By May 2005 all states had implemented the European Arrest Warrant, although Germany may have to reassess its own legislation because of a successful legal challenge to the EAW.

59 A good example of the intelligence cooperation between the US and France was the arrest of an Algerian, Ahmed Ressam, intent on causing an explosion at Los Angeles airport during the millennium celebrations. Ressam was duly convicted in April 2001.

60 Interview conducted by the author (2004) Office of Counter Terrorism, US Department of State, September, Washington DC.

61 Clarke, R., McCaffrey, B. and Nelson, R. (2004) 'NATO's Role in Confronting International Terrorism', Policy Paper, The Atlantic Council, Washington DC, June.

62 Clarke, R. (2004) *Against All Enemies: Inside America's War on Terror*, Free Press, New York, p. 14.

63 *The 9/11 Commission Report* (2004) *op. cit.* p. 417.

64 Aldrich, R. (2004) 'Transatlantic Intelligence and Security Cooperation', *International Affairs*, 80, 4, July.

65 Boer, M. den (2003) 'The EU Counter-Terrorism Wave: Window of Opportunity or Profound Policy Transformation?', in Leeuwen, M. van (ed.) *Confronting Terrorism: European Experiences, Threat Perceptions and Policies*, Kluwer Law International, The Hague, p. 203.

66 Occhipinti, J. (2003) *op. cit.* p. 153. A report by the UK House of Lords endorses the view that there has been a selective sharing of information by some EU states with Europol, and goes on to suggest that information from Europol and the Schengen Information System should be pooled with Interpol. House of Lords (2005) 'After Madrid: The EU's Response to Terrorism', EU Committee, 5th Report of Session 2004–5, Paper 53, HMSO, London, pp. 32–3.

67 *Bulletin Quotidien Europe* (16/3/2004) No. 8666, Agence Presse, p. 4.

68 Presidency Conclusions (2004) European Council, Brussels, 17–18 June, I: para. 14.

69 House of Lords (2005) *op. cit.* p. 25.

70 *Bulletin Quotidien Europe* (22/9/2004) 'EU/Terrorism: Interview with Gijs de Vries', No. 8790, Agence Presse, p. 6.

71 Muller-Wille advocates an expansion of the SitCen and improved mechanisms by which nationally derived intelligence can be fed into the EU system. Muller-Wille, B. (2004) 'For Our Eyes Only? Shaping an Intelligence Community within the EU', *Occasional Paper No. 50*, EU Institute for Security Studies, January, http://www.iss-eu.org

72 There were proposals that the US should establish a new intelligence service dedicated to countering terrorism. RAND undertook a study to determine what lessons the US could draw from intelligence agencies in the UK (MI5), France (Directorate of Territorial Security – DST), Canada and Australia. It found that none of these countries gave their intelligence agencies enforcement powers, instead relying on law enforcement agencies to carry out arrests. They also focused more heavily on human rather than

technical intelligence sources. See Chalk, P. and Rosenau, W. (2004) 'Confronting the Enemy Within: Security Intelligence, the Police and Counterterrorism in Four Democracies', Research Brief, RAND, http://www.rand.org

73 Mueller, R. (2004) Testimony of the Director of the FBI to the Select Committee on Intelligence, US Senate, Washington DC, 24 February.

74 Interview conducted by the author (2000) US Mission to the EU, September, Brussels.

75 EU Directive 95/46/EC of 1995.

76 Cofer Black, J. (2004) Testimony by Ambassador Cofer Black, Coordinator for Counter Terrorism, Department of State before the Senate Foreign Relations Subcommittee on Europe, US Senate, Washington DC, 31 March.

77 Mitsilegas, V. (2003) *op. cit.* p. 517.

78 Aaron, D. *et al.* (2004) *op. cit.* p. 4.

79 Interview conducted by the author (2005) Relex C1, European Commission, February, Brussels.

80 Bort, E. (2000) 'Illegal Migration and Cross-Border Crime: Challenges at the Eastern Frontier of the European Union', European University Institute, Working Paper 2000/9, Florence, p. 3.

81 Mitsilegas, V., Monar, J. and Rees, W. (2003) *The European Union and Internal Security: Guardian of the People?*, Palgrave Macmillan, Basingstoke, pp. 33–4.

82 A similar issue exists over the linking of the Visa Information System (VIS) with 'Eurodac', which is a database of fingerprints for asylum seekers. Eurodac enables immigration officials to check the fingerprints of an asylum seeker against records held in other EU countries. But there remain limitations over the way in which information obtained for immigration purposes can be shared with other law enforcement authorities, thereby limiting its utility in the fight against terrorism.

83 Occhipinti, J. (2003) *op. cit.* p. 61.

84 Frattini, F. (2005) 'The Hague Programme: A Partnership for the European Renewal in the Field of Freedom, Security and Justice', Speech/05/441 to the Centre for European Policy Studies, 14 July, Brussels.

85 House of Lords (2005) *op. cit.*

86 *Bulletin Quotidien Europe* (1/10/2004) 'Debate on Information Exchange between Member States', No. 8797, Agence Presse, p. 14. See also *Bulletin Quotidien Europe* (11/5/2005) 'Commission's Detailed Programme for Freedom, Security and Justice Programme over Next Five Years', No. 8944, Agence Presse, p. 7.

87 Interview conducted by the author (2005) Criminal Division, European Council, February, Brussels.

88 *Bulletin Quotidien Europe* (3/12/2004) 'Progress on Information Exchange on Police Records', No. 8840, Agence Presse, p. 8.

89 Center for Strategic and International Studies (2004) 'Transatlantic Dialogue on Terrorism', Washington DC, August, http://www.csis.org/index.php?option = com_csisprojandtask = viewandid = 368.

90 Interview conducted by the author (2001) European Commission offices, May, Washington DC; and Grant, C. (2002) 'The Eleventh of September and Beyond: The Impact on the European Union', in Freedman, L. (ed.) (2002) *Superterrorism: Policy Responses*, Blackwell, Oxford, p. 148.

91   Guild, E. (2003) 'International Terrorism and EU Immigration, Asylum and Borders Policy: The Unexpected Victims of 11 September 2001', *European Foreign Affairs Review*, 8, 3, autumn, p. 338.

92   *The 9/11 Commission Report* (2004) *op. cit.* p. 384.

93   Lebl, L. (2005) 'Security beyond Borders', *Policy Review Online*, no.130, April, http://www.policyreview.org/apr05/lebl.html

94   *Bulletin Quotidien Europe* (20/5/2005) 'EU Steps Up Pressure to Extend "Visa Waiver Programme" to All Member States', No. 8950, Agence Presse, p. 8.

95   'Conclusions and Plan of Action of the Extraordinary European Council meeting on 21 September 2001' (2001) European Council, Brussels, 21 September.

96   Interview conducted by the author (2004) Department of Homeland Security, October, Washington DC.

97   *Bulletin Quotidien Europe* (20/3/2004) No. 8670, Agence Presse, p. 4.

98   Interview conducted by the author (2005) US Embassy to the EU, February, Brussels.

99   Interview conducted by the author (2004) Department of Homeland Security, October, Washington DC.

100 *Bulletin Quotidien Europe* (23/4/2004) No. 8691, Agence Presse, p. 9. The US also operates a system known as the 'Customs-Trade Partnership Against Terrorism' (C-TPAT) by which cargo manifests have to be submitted twenty-four hours before they are loaded on to a vessel bound for the US. See Flynn, S. (2004) *America the Vulnerable: How our Government is Failing to Protect us from Terrorism*, HarperCollins, New York, p. 106.

101 *Bulletin Quotidien Europe* (17/9/2004) 'EU-US Troika Focuses on Protection of Biometric Data', No. 8787, Agence Presse, p. 10.

102 *Bulletin Quotidien Europe* (27/10/2004) 'Political Agreement on Biometric Passports', No. 8815, Agence Presse, p. 9.

103 Interview conducted by the author (2004) European Commission offices, September, Washington DC.

104 US Department of State (2004) 'US, EU Discuss Transportation, Border Security', 28 April, http://www.USInfo.state.gov

105 *Bulletin Quotidien Europe* (24 and 25/6/2002) 'Money Laundering/ Terrorism', No. 8240, Agence Presse.

106 Dam, K. (2002) 'The Financial Front of the War on Terrorism – The Next Phase', speech by Kenneth Dam, Deputy Secretary of the Treasury to the Council on Foreign Relations, 6 June, New York, in *Washington File*, US Embassy to the UK, London, http://www.usembassy.org.uk/

107 Pillar, P. (2001) *Terrorism and US Foreign Policy*, Brookings Institution Press, Washington DC, p. 94. This view is contested by those who argue that the real cost to terrorists is not in conducting operations but in maintaining their networks. See Levey, S. (2004) 'Funding Terror Becoming Costlier, Riskier, US Official Says', testimony of Stuart Levey, Under Secretary for Terrorism and Financial Intelligence, US Department of the Treasury, before the Senate Committee on Banking and Urban Affairs, 29 September, *Washington File*, 13 July, US Embassy to the UK, London, http://www.usembassy.org.uk/

108 *Bulletin Quotidien Europe* (12/10/2001) 'EU Money Laundering', No. 8068, Agence Presse.

109 Winer, J. and Roule, T. (2002) 'Fighting Terrorist Finance', *Survival*, 44, 3, autumn, p. 88.
110 Hawalas are informal systems for transferring money that depend on trust or family ties.
111 Interview conducted by the author (2004) Office of Counter Terrorism, US Department of State, September, Washington DC.
112 *Bulletin Quotidien Europe* (24/7/2004) No. 8754, Agence Presse, p. 7.
113 *Bulletin Quotidien Europe* (8/6/2004) No. 8720, Agence Presse, p. 10.
114 Archik, K. (2004) *op. cit.* p. 9.
115 Interview conducted by the author (2005) US Embassy to the EU, February, Brussels.
116 *Economist, The* (2002) 'Special Report: Civil Liberties. For Whom the Liberty Bell Tolls', 31 August, p. 19.
117 *Bulletin Quotidien Europe* (13/3/2004) No. 8665, Agence Presse, p. 4.
118 *Bulletin Quotidien Europe* (25/3/2004) 'European Council, "Declaration on Combating Terrorism" ', Europe Documents, No. 2366, Brussels, Agence Presse. The position of Mr de Vries does not carry enforcement powers and he resides within the Council Secretariat rather than the Commission. See also House of Lords (2005) *op. cit.* p. 26.
119 *Bulletin Quotidien Europe* (1/10/2004) 'EU/JHA/US: Highly Consensual Meeting Thursday between Europeans and Americans', No. 8797, Agence Presse, p. 13.

Chapter 5

1 Rose, G. (1999) 'The United States and Libya', in Haass, R. (ed.) *Transatlantic Tensions: The US, Europe, and Problem Countries*, Brookings Institution Press, Washington DC, pp. 143–4.
2 See annual editions of the publication by the United States Department of State, *Patterns of Global Terrorism*, US Government Printing Office, Washington DC.
3 Yaphe, J. (2001) 'Iraq: The Exception to the Rule', *Washington Quarterly*, 24, 1, winter, p. 126.
4 Simon, S. and Benjamin, D. (2000) 'America and the New Terrorism', *Survival*, 42, 1, spring, pp. 65–6.
5 Tenet, G. (2001) 'Worldwide Threat 2001: National Security in a Changing World', statement by the Director of the Central Intelligence Agency, before the Senate Select Committee on Intelligence, 7 February, *Washington File*, US Embassy in London, http://www.usembassy.org.uk/euro232.html
6 Sheehan, M. (1999) 'Extremist Movements and their Threat to the US', statement of Ambassador Sheehan, Coordinator for Counter Terrorism, Department of State, to Hearing Subcommittee on Near Eastern and South Asian Affairs, 106th Congress, 1st Session, 2 November.
7 Pillar, P. (2001) *Terrorism and US Foreign Policy*, Brookings Institution Press, Washington DC.
8 United States vs Bin Ladin (2004) Southern District of New York for conspiracy to bomb US Embassies in Africa, US Department of Justice, March.
9 Litwak, R. (1999) *Rogue States and US Foreign Policy: Containment after the Cold War*, Woodrow Wilson Center Press, Washington DC.

10 Timmerman, K. (1995) 'Trading with Iran: Clinton Needs to Club Europe', *Wall Street Journal*, 5 April.
11 Kemp, G. (1999) 'The Challenge of Iran for US and European Policy', in Haass, R. (ed.), (1999) *op.cit.*
12 *Ibid.* p. 55.
13 Gordon, P. (1999) ' "Rogue States" and Transatlantic Relations', in Burwell, F. and Daalder, I. (eds) *The US and Europe in the Global Arena*, Macmillan, Basingstoke, p. 116.
14 European Commission (2005) Review of the Framework for Relations between the European Union and the United States, Independent Study Commissioned by Directorate General External Relations C1, European Commission, Final Report, p. 23.
15 Interview conducted by the author (2000) European Commission, Brussels, November.
16 Kemp, G. (2001) 'Iran: Can the US Do a Deal?', *Washington Quarterly*, winter, p. 111.
17 Lansford argues that the Article V declaration was little more than a symbolic gesture. See Lansford, T. (2002) *All for One: Terrorism, NATO and the United States*, Ashgate, Aldershot, p. 72.
18 Daalder, I. and Lindsay, J. (2003) *America Unbound: The Bush Revolution in Foreign Policy*, Brookings Institution Press, Washington DC, p. 85.
19 Presidential Statement (2001) 'Address to the Nation Announcing Strikes against Al Qaeda Training Camps and Taliban Military Installations', the White House, 7 October, Washington DC.
20 Oswald, F. (2004) 'German Security after 9/11', in Shearman, P. and Sussex, M. (eds) *European Security after 9/11*, Ashgate, Aldershot, p. 92.
21 European Council, (2001) 'Conclusions and Plan of Action of the Extraordinary European Council meeting on 21 September 2001', 21 September, Brussels.
22 Duke, S. (2002) 'CESDP and the European Response to 11 September: Identifying the Weakest Link', *European Foreign Affairs Review* 7, 2, summer, p. 158.
23 Grant, C. (2002) 'The Eleventh of September and Beyond: The Impact on the European Union', in Freedman, L. (ed.) (2002) *Superterrorism: Policy Responses*, Blackwell, Oxford, p. 139.
24 Aaron, D., Beauchesne, A., Burwell, F., Nelson, C. R., Riley, K. J. and Zimmer, B. (2004) 'The Post 9/11 Partnership: Transatlantic Cooperation Against Terrorism', Policy Paper, The Atlantic Council, Washington DC, December, http://www.acus.org/docs/0412-Post_9–11_Partnership_Transatlantic_Cooperation_Against-Terrorism.pdf (p. 12). See also Howorth, J. (2003) 'France, Britain and the Euro-Atlantic Crisis', *Survival*, 45, 4, winter, p. 177.
25 Foreign and Commonwealth Office (2003) 'UK International Priorities', http://www.fco.gov.uk
26 Dunne, T. (2004) ' "When the Shooting Starts": Atlanticism in British Security Strategy', *International Affairs*, 80, 5, October, p. 894.
27 Quoted in Lansford, T. (2005) 'Introduction: US Security Policy and the New Europe', in T. Lansford and B. Tashev (eds) *Old Europe, New Europe: Renegotiating Transatlantic Security in the Post 9/11 Era*, Ashgate, Aldershot, p. xix; and Daalder, I. and Lindsay, J. (2003) *op. cit.* p. 104.

28   For details see Mahncke, D., Rees, W. and Thompson, W. (2004) *Redefining Transatlantic Security Relations: The Challenge of Change*, Manchester University Press, Manchester, pp. 176–7.

29   Serfaty, S. (2003) 'Renewing the Transatlantic Partnership', Center for Strategic and International Studies Briefing Paper, Washington DC, May, p. 10.

30   Gordon, P., Indyk, M. and O'Hanlon, M. (2002) 'Getting Serious about Iraq', *Survival*, 44, 3, autumn, pp. 11–15.

31   Burns, N. (2004) 'NATO and the Transatlantic Relationship', remarks by Nicholas Burns, US Permanent Representative to NATO to the Bundeswehr Forum, 8 November, Berlin, http://nato.usmission.gov/ambassador/2004/2004 Nov08_Burns_Berlin.htm

32   Davison, R. (2004) 'French Security after 9/11: Franco-American Discord', in Shearman, P. and Sussex, M. *op. cit.* p. 74.

33   Elsea, J. (2001) 'Terrorism and the Law of War: Trying Terrorists as War Criminals before Military Commissions', *Congressional Research Service Report for Congress*, Washington DC, 11 December.

34   Vries, G. de (2004) EU Counter-Terrorism Coordinator Statement before the Committee on International Relations, US House of Representatives, Washington DC, 14 September. On Abu Ghraib see, *Economist, The* (2005) 'Just a Few Bad Apples?', 22 January, pp. 47–8.

35   Pollack, K. (2002) 'Next Stop Baghdad', *Foreign Affairs*, 81, 2, March–April, p. 38.

36   Daalder, I. and Lindsay, J. (2003) *op. cit.*

37   Bush, G. (2002) President George W. Bush, State of the Union Address to both Houses of Congress, January, Washington DC. *Washington File*, Office of International Information Programs, US Department of State, http://usinfo.state.gov

38   US National Strategy for Combating Terrorism (2003) The White House, Washington DC, February, p. 21.

39   Mann, J. (2004) *Rise of the Vulcans: The History of Bush's War Cabinet*, Penguin, New York.

40   Clarke, R. (2004) *Against All Enemies: Inside America's War on Terror*, Free Press, New York, pp. 26 and 30.

41   Bluth, C. (2004) 'The British Road to War: Blair, Bush and the Decision to Invade Iraq', *International Affairs*, 80, 5, October, p. 875.

42   Perl, R. (2004a) 'Terrorism and National Security: Issues and Trends', *Congressional Research Service Report for Congress*, Washington DC, 23 September, p. 2.

43   Text of President Clinton's Remarks to the Joint Chiefs of Staff, *New York Times*, 18/2/1998, p. A9, quoted in Litwak, R. (1999) *op. cit.* p. xiii.

44   *The 9/11 Commission Report: Final Report of the National Commission on Terrorist Attacks upon the United States* (2004) W. W. Norton, New York, pp. 334–6.

45   Quoted in Daalder, I. and Lindsay, J. (2003) *op. cit.* pp. 123–4.

46   The article by Condoleezza Rice, prior to her becoming National Security Adviser, was evidence of this thinking. Rice, C. (2000) 'Promoting the National Interest', *Foreign Affairs*, 79, 1, January–February.

47   US National Strategy for Combating Terrorism (2003) *op. cit.* p. 2.

48   Calleo argues that the approach of the Bush administration was a logical continuation of a strand of post-Cold War thinking in the US that

yearned for a unipolar world. See Calleo, D. (2004) 'The Broken West', *Survival*, 46, 3, autumn, pp. 31–3.

49 European Parliament (2002) 'Report on the Commission Communication to the Council on Reinforcing the Transatlantic Relationship', Committee on Foreign Affairs, Human Rights, Common Security and Defence Policy, Focusing on Strategy and Delivering Results, Rapporteur Elles, J. A5–0148/2002, 25 April, p. 8.

50 Wallace, W. (2002) 'American Hegemony: European Dilemmas', in Freedman, L. (ed.) *op. cit.* p. 112.

51 Nelson, D. 'Transatlantic Transmutations', *Washington Quarterly*, autumn 2002, p. 60.

52 Haass, R. (2002) 'Charting a New Course in the Transatlantic Relationship', speech to the Centre for European Reform, London, 10 June, http://www.state.gov/s/p/rem/10968.htm

53 Briefing by Secretary of Defense Donald Rumsfeld and Chairman of the Joint Chiefs of Staff Richard Myers, US Department of Defense, press briefing, 23 January 2003.

54 Yaphe, J. (2001) *op. cit.* p. 133.

55 Strauss, M. (2002) 'Attacking Iraq', *Foreign Policy*, March-April, pp. 14–17.

56 Prados, A. and Katzman, K. (2001) 'Iraq-US Confrontation', *Congressional Research Service Report for Congress*, US Government Printing Office, Washington DC, 4 April, p. 17.

57 *Economist, The* (2001) 'Can Sanctions Be Smarter?', Special Report: America, Iraq and Iran, 26 May, pp. 29–31.

58 In a very public display of disagreement the German Foreign Minister Joschka Fisher told American Defense Secretary Donald Rumsfeld at the annual Munich Conference on security, that the German government was not convinced by the arguments of the US over Iraq.

59 Boer, M. den and Monar, J. (2002) 'Keynote Article: 11 September and the Challenge of Global Terrorism to the EU as a Security Actor', *Journal of Common Market Studies Annual Review*, 40, p. 13.

60 Riddell, P. (2003) *Hug them Close: Blair, Clinton, Bush and the 'Special Relationship'*, Politico's, London, p. 58.

61 Hill, C. (2004) 'Renationalizing or Regrouping? EU Foreign Policy since 11 September 2001', *Journal of Common Market Studies*, 42, 1, p. 152.

62 Muller, H. (2003) 'Terrorism, Proliferation: A European Threat Assessment', *Chaillot Paper No. 58*, European Union Institute for Security Studies, Paris, March, pp. 89–92.

63 Blix, H. (2003) 'An Update on Inspection', report by Hans Blix, Executive Chairman of UNMOVIC to the Security Council of the UN, 27 January, http://www.un.org/Depts/unmovic/Bx27.htm See also, *Economist, The* (2002) 'Inspecting, Squeezing, Threatening', 7 December, pp. 65–6.

64 Cheney, R. (2003) 'Cheney Says Ending the Links between Terrorists and Rogue States Is Vital', Remarks by the Vice-President to the Heritage Foundation on 1 May, *Washington File*, 2 May.

65 Omar, R. (2005) *Revolution Day: The Real Story of the Battle for Iraq*, Penguin, London, p. 259.

66 *Economist, The* (2003) 'Casus or Casuistry? Special Report: Weapons of Mass Destruction', 31 May, pp. 22–3.

67 See Aldrich, R. (2005) 'Whitehall and the Iraq War: The UK's Four Intelligence Enquiries', *Irish Studies in International Affairs*, 16.

68 This was the opinion of the influential report on Iraq's weapons programmes by the independent International Institute for Strategic Studies. See International Institute for Strategic Studies (2002) 'Iraq's Weapons of Mass Destruction. A Net Assessment', London, 9 September, http://www.iiss.org/conferencepage.php?confID = 3andPHPSESSID = b6029ee3ac61b86acab407fd9cc69d10

69 Burns, N. (2004) 'NATO and the Transatlantic Relationship', remarks by Nicholas Burns, US Permanent Representative to NATO to the Bundeswehr Forum, 8 November, Berlin, http://nato.usmission.gov/ambassador/2004/2004 Nov08_Burns_Berlin.htm

70 Daalder, I. and Lindsay, J. (2003) *op. cit.* p. 137.

71 Clarke, R. (2004) *op. cit.* p. ix.

72 Clark, W. (2003) *Winning Modern Wars: Iraq, Terrorism and the American Empire*, New York, Public Affairs.

73 Asmus, R. (2003) 'Rebuilding the Atlantic Alliance', *Foreign Affairs*, 82, 5, September–October, p. 28.

74 Pond, E. (2003) *The Near Death of the Transatlantic Alliance*, Brookings Institution Press, Washington DC.

75 Green, A. (2003) 'Why Syria is america's Next Target', *Guardian Unlimited*, 17 April, http://www.guardian.co.uk/comment/story/0,3604, 938326,00.html

76 Record, J. (2003) 'Bounding the Global War on Terrorism', Strategic Studies Institute, Carlisle Barracks, Pennsylvania, December, p. 30, http://www.carlisle.army.mil/ssi/pdfiles/PUB207.pdf

77 Chubin, S. (1998) 'Engaging Iran', *Survival*, autumn; Kemp, G. (2001) 'Iran: Can the US Do a Deal?', *Washington Quarterly*, winter; and Grand, C. (2000) 'The EU and the Non-proliferation of Nuclear Weapons', *Chaillot Paper No. 37*, Institute for Security Studies Western European Union, Paris, January.

78 Bahgat, G. (2003) 'Iran, the United States and the War on Terrorism', *Studies in Conflict and Terrorism*, 26, p. 94.

79 Goldman, S., Katzman, K. and Shuey, R. (1998) 'Russian Missile Technology and Nuclear Reactor Transfers to Iran', *Congressional Research Service Report for Congress*, Washington DC, 14 December.

80 *Bulletin Quotidien Europe* (19/8/2005) 'EU Calls on Iran to Change Its Mind about Its Unilateral Rejection of EU-3 Proposals', No. 9008, Agence Presse, p. 2.

81 Bowen, W. and Kidd, J. (2004) 'The Iranian Nuclear Challenge', *International Affairs*, 80, 2, p. 257.

82 Daalder, I. and Goldgeier, J. (2001) 'Putting Europe First', *Survival*, 43, 1, spring, p. 87.

83 *Economist, The* (2004) 'The Nuclear Route', 13 November, p. 13; and Evans, M. (2004) 'Iran Bows to UN Threat over Nuclear Programme', *The Times*, 23 November, p. 37.

84 Maddox, B. (2005) 'Europe Loses Bargaining Chip in Negotiations', *The Times*, 27 June, p. 28; and Naval, R. (2005) 'Hardliner Turns Back on US but Will Pursue Nuclear Aim', *The Times*, 27 June, p. 28.

85 Pollack, K. and Takeyh, R. (2005) 'Taking on Tehran', *Foreign Affairs*, March–April, p. 24.

86 European Commission (2005) Review of the Framework for Relations between the European Union and the United States, Independent Study

Commissioned by Directorate General External Relations C1, European Commission, Final Report. In contrast, a US intelligence review in August 2005 estimated that Iran is more than ten years away from developing a nuclear weapon. See Linzer, D. (2005) 'Review Finds Iran Far from Nuclear Bomb: Estimate of Progress Contrasts with Administration Statements', *Washington Post*, 2 August. I am grateful to Richard Aldrich for this reference.

87 Gordon, P. (2004) 'American Choices in the "War on Terror" ', review essays, *Survival*, 46, 1, spring, p. 149.

88 Prior to the 1994 agreement the US had considered the option of preventive military strikes against North Korea's nuclear facilities. See Litwak, R. (2002) 'The New Calculus of Pre-emption', *Survival*, 44, 4, winter, p. 64.

89 Samore, G. (2003) 'The Korean Nuclear Crisis', *Survival*, 45, 1, spring, pp. 9–11.

90 Cha, V. (2003) 'Engaging North Korea Credibly', *Survival*, 42, 2, summer, p. 145.

91 *Economist, The* (2003) 'When Bluff Turns Deadly', 'Special Report: North Korea', 3 May, pp. 29–31.

92 *Economist, The* (2005) 'When the Party Has to Stop', 12 February, p. 57.

93 Wall, S. (2004) 'The UK, the EU and the United States: Bridge, or Just Troubled Water?', speech at Chatham House, 8 November, http://www.riia.org/

94 *Economist, The* (2005) 'The Insidious Wiles of Foreign Influence', 11 June, p. 45.

Chapter 6

1 Miko, F. (2004) 'Removing Terrorist Sanctuaries: The 9/11 Commission Recommendations and US Policy', *Congressional Research Service Report for Congress*, Washington DC, 10 August, p. 3.

2 House of Lords (2005) 'After Madrid: the EU's Response to Terrorism', EU Committee, 5th Report of Session 2004–5, Paper 53, HMSO, London, p. 30.

3 US National Strategy for Combating Terrorism (2003) The White House, Washington DC, February, p. 24.

4 Frellesen, T. (2001) 'Processes and Procedures in EU-US Foreign Policy Cooperation: From the Transatlantic Declaration to the New Transatlantic Agenda', in Philippart, E. and Winand, P. (eds) (2001) *Ever Closer Partnership: Policy-making in US-EU Relations*, PIE Peter Lang, Brussels, p. 341.

5 Young, O. (1980) 'International Regimes: Problems of Concept Foundation', *World Politics*, 32, April.

6 One of these organisations is Interpol, composed of 182 members and located in Lyon. The sharing of some police information through Interpol has been established for some time. The weaknesses of Interpol are three-fold. First, it suffers from a reputation for leaking sensitive information. Second, the police services of some of its member states are judged to be of a low quality, making states reluctant to make information available to Interpol as a whole. Finally, it only developed a competence for dealing with terrorism matters in 1984.

7 Oudraat, C. de Jonge (2003) 'Combating Terrorism', *Washington Quarterly*, 26, 4, autumn, p. 174.

8 European Council (2004) Presidency Conclusions, Brussels, 17–18 June, I: para. 18.

9 Savona, E. (1998) 'The Organisational Framework of European Crime in the Globalisation Process', *Transcrime Working Paper No. 20*, February; and Politi, A. (1997) 'European Security: The New Transnational Risks', *Chaillot Papers 29*, Institute for Security Studies Western European Union, Paris, October, p. 51.

10 The twelve conventions are the following: (1) Convention on Offences and Certain Other Acts Committed On Board Aircraft (1963 Tokyo Convention); (2) Convention for the Suppression of Unlawful Seizure of Aircraft (1970 Hague Convention); (3) Convention for the Suppression of Unlawful Acts Against the Safety of Civil Aircraft (1971 Montreal Convention); (4) Convention on the Prevention and Punishment of Crimes Against Internationally Protected Persons (1973); (5) International Convention Against the Taking of Hostages (1979); (6) Convention on the Physical Protection of Nuclear Material (1980); (7) Protocol for the Suppression of Unlawful Acts of Violence at Airports (1988); (8) Convention for the Suppression of Unlawful Acts Against the Safety of Maritime Navigation (1988); (9) Protocol for the Suppression of Unlawful Acts Against the Safety of Fixed Platforms Located on the Continental Shelf (1988); (10) Convention on the Marking of Plastic Explosives for the Purposes of Detection (1991); (11) International Convention for the Suppression of Terrorist Bombings (1997); (12) International Convention for the Suppression of the Financing of Terrorism (1999).

11 'EU-US Declaration on Combating Terrorism' (2004) Dromoland Castle, Ireland, 26 June, press release, Council of the EU, 10760/04, Brussels.

12 European Council (2001) 'Conclusions and Plan of Action of the Extraordinary European Council meeting on 21 September 2001', 21 September, Brussels.

13 Ginkel, B. van (2003) 'The United Nations: Towards a Comprehensive Convention on Combating Terrorism', in Leeuwen, M. van (ed.) (2003) *Confronting Terrorism: European Experiences, Threat Perceptions and Policies*, Kluwer Law International, The Hague, p. 219.

14 Interview conducted by the author (2004) Counter Terrorism Section, Criminal Division, US Department of Justice, September, Washington DC.

15 The UN 60th anniversary summit, held in September 2005, failed to reach agreement on a single definition of terrorism. See Maddox, B. (2005) 'UN Faces Its Biggest Challenge in Wars against Poverty and Terror', *The Times*, 15 September, p. 40; and *Economist, The* (2005) 'Can Its Credibility Be Repaired? Special Report: The United Nations', 10–16 September, p. 30.

16 Oudraat, C. de Jonge (2003) *op. cit.* p. 164.

17 Kagan, R. (2004) 'America's Crisis of Legitimacy', *Foreign Affairs*, 83, 2, March–April, p. 82.

18 Dubois, D. (2002) 'The Attacks of 11 September: EU-US Cooperation Against Terrorism in the Field of Justice and Home Affairs', *European Foreign Affairs Review*, 7, 3, autumn, p. 322.

19 Wechsler, W. and Wolosky, L. (2004) 'Update on the Global Campaign against Terrorist Financing: Second Report of an Independent Task Force

on Terrorist Financing', sponsored by the Council on Foreign Relations, 15 June, New York, http://www.cfr.org

20 Aaron, D., Beauchesne, A., Burwell, F., Nelson, C. R., Riley, K. J. and Zimmer, B. (2004) 'The Post 9/11 Partnership: Transatlantic Cooperation against Terrorism', Policy Paper, The Atlantic Council, Washington DC, December, p. x, http://www.acus.org/docs/0412-Post_9–11_Partnership_ Transatlantic_Cooperation_Against-Terrorism.pdf

21 Vries, G. de (2004) EU Counter-Terrorism Coordinator, Statement before the Committee on International Relations, US House of Representatives, Washington DC, 14 September.

22 Asmus, R. (2005) 'Rethinking the EU: Why Washington Needs to Support European Integration', *Survival*, 47, 3, autumn, p. 99.

23 Pope, W. (2004) Principal Deputy Coordinator for Counter Terrorism, US Department of State, Statement before the Subcommittee on Europe and on International Terrorism, Non-Proliferation and Human Rights, US House of Representatives, Washington DC, 14 September.

24 'G-8 Recommendations on Counter-terrorism, G-8 Foreign Ministers' Meeting', Whistler, 12 June 2002, appendix P in Kirton, J. and Stefanova, R. (eds) (2003) *The G-8, the United Nations and Conflict Prevention*, Ashgate, Aldershot, pp. 276–7.

25 'European Union and United States Joint Program of Work on the Non-proliferation of Weapons of Mass Destruction' (2005) EU-US Summit, June.

26 Spear, J. (2003) 'The Emergence of a European "Strategic Personality" and the Implications for the Transatlantic Relationship', *Arms Control Today*, 33, 9, November, p. 16.

27 In spite of this greater attention to non-proliferation the EU was unable to prevent the 2005 Non-Proliferation Treaty Review Conference passing without achieving any progress on new measures.

28 European Council (2003) 'Basic Principles for an EU Strategy against Proliferation of Weapons of Mass Destruction', December, Brussels.

29 Pullinger, S. and Quille, G. (2003) 'The EU: Tackling the Threat from Weapons of Mass Destruction', Saferworld and the International Security Information Service, Policy Paper, Brussels.

30 *Economist, The* (2003) 'Loose Nukes', by special invitation Allison, G, 29 November, pp. 23–25.

31 Interview conducted by the author (2005) European Commission, Relex C1, February; and Stevenson, J. (2004) 'Counter-terrorism: Containment and Beyond', *Adelphi Paper 367*, International Institute for Strategic Studies, London, p. 34.

32 This measure was designed to complement some of the existing agreements pertaining to the control of nuclear materials, such as the Nuclear Suppliers Group, the Australia Group and the Zangger Committee.

33 Bayne, N. (2005) *Staying Together: The G8 Summit Confronts the 21st Century*, Ashgate, Aldershot, p. 180.

34 Cofer Black, J. (2004) Testimony by Ambassador Cofer Black, Coordinator for Counter Terrorism, Department of State before the Senate Foreign Relations Subcommittee on Europe, US Senate, Washington DC, 31 March.

35 *Bulletin Quotidien Europe* (19/7/2005) 'Counter Terrorism Must Be the Key Element in Political Dialogue with Third Countries, Council Says', No. 8993, Agence Presse, p. 5.

36 Smith, K. (2003) *European Union Foreign Policy in a Changing World*, Polity Press, Oxford, p. 178.

37 Monar, J. (2004) 'The EU as an International Actor in the Domain of Justice and Home Affairs', *European Foreign Affairs Review*, 9, 3, autumn, p. 409.

38 Friman, H. (1996) *NarcoDiplomacy: Exporting the US War on Drugs*, Cornell University Press, Ithaca NY.

39 Peterson, J. (2004) 'America as a European Power: The End of Empire by Integration?', *International Affairs*, 80, 4, July, p. 615.

40 European Council (2002) Presidency Conclusions, 21–2 June, Seville.

41 US Agency for International Development, 'Summary of FY 2005 Budget Request', quoted in the Center for Strategic and International Studies (2004) 'Transatlantic Dialogue on Terrorism', Washington DC, August, http://www.csis.org/index.php?option = com_csisprojandtask = viewandid = 368. 'The Transatlantic Dialogue on Terrorism', CSIS, August 2004.

42 Perl, R. (2002) 'Terrorism and United States Foreign Policy', remarks by Raphael Perl, Congressional Research Service to the German Council on Foreign relations, 2 July, Berlin, *Washington File*, US Embassy in London, http://www.usembassy.org.uk/terror428.html

43 BBC News (2005) 'Profile: Islam Karimov', 17 May, http://news.bbc.co.uk/1/hi/world/asia-pacific/4554997.stm

44 Interview conducted by the author (2004) Department of Justice, Washington DC, September.

45 Tucker, D. (1998) 'Responding to Terrorism', *Washington Quarterly*, 21, 1, winter, p. 107.

46 Clarke, R. (2004) *Against All Enemies: Inside America's War on Terror*, Free Press, New York, p. 143.

47 Naftali, T. (2005) *Blind Spot: The Secret History of American Counter Terrorism*, Basic Books, New York, p. 238.

48 See Rees, W. and Aldrich, R. (2005) 'Contending Cultures of Counterterrorism: Transatlantic Divergence or Convergence?', *International Affairs*, 81, 5. For a detailed discussion of the practice of renditions see Garcia, M. (2005) 'Renditions: Constraints Imposed by Laws on Torture', *Congressional Research Service Report for Congress*, Library of Congress, Washington DC, 28 April.

49 Smith, K. (2003) *European Union Foreign Policy in a Changing World*, Polity Press, Oxford, p. 184.

50 *Bulletin Quotidien Europe* (16/10/2004) 'EU/Justice/Police', No. 8808, Agence Presse, p. 10.

51 Ten states joined the EU in May 2004. Money has been given to CEE countries to prepare them for accession and they in turn have been expected to prove that they can absorb and implement the EU's *acquis communitaire* in full to avoid them becoming a weak link in its internal security arrangements. A further 1 billion euros have been earmarked to assist new CEE members in developing their internal security from accession to 2006, including money for the management of borders. See Vries, G. de (2004) EU Counter-Terrorism Coordinator, Statement before the Committee on International Relations, US House of Representatives, Washington DC, 14 September. Thus the EU has seen no reason to share its influence over these countries with the US. Interview conducted by the

author (2001) International Narcotics and Law Enforcement, US Department of State, May, Washington DC.

52 Gelbard, R. (1995) Testimony of Robert Gelbard, Assistant Secretary of State for International Narcotics and Law Enforcement, Before the House of Representatives Committee on International Relations, 7 December, *Atlantic Outlook*, 91, 15 December, p. 2.

53 Interview conducted by the author (2004) Representative of US Training Academy, Quantico, Virginia.

54 Kirton, J. and Stefanova, R. (2003) 'Introduction: The G-8's role in Global Conflict Prevention', in Kirton, J. and Stefanova, R. (eds) *op. cit.* p. 12.

55 For a detailed assessment of various regions of the world see Winer, J. and Roule, T. (2002) 'Fighting Terrorist Finance', *Survival*, 44, 3, autumn.

56 Interview conducted by the author (2001) Counter-Money Laundering Section, US Department of Justice, May, Washington DC.

57 Vries, G. de (2004) Evidence before the House of Lords Committee (2005) 'After Madrid: The EU's Response to Terrorism', EU Committee, 5th Report of Session 2004–5, Paper 53, HMSO, London, p. 66.

58 Levey, S. (2004) 'Funding Terror Becoming Costlier, Riskier, US Official Says', testimony of Stuart Levey, Under Secretary for Terrorism and Financial Intelligence, US Department of the Treasury, before the Senate Committee on Banking and Urban Affairs, 29 September, *Washington File*, 13 July, US Embassy to the UK, London, http://www.usembassy.org.uk/terror428.html

59 Interview conducted by the author (2001) Counter-Money Laundering Section, US Department of Justice, May, Washington DC.

60 White House Fact Sheet (1996) 'Comprehensive Strategy to Fight Terrorism', *Official Text*, US Information Service, US Embassy, London, 5 August, http://www.usembassy.org.uk/

61 Financial Action Task Force (2001) 'Financial Action Task Force on Money Laundering. Special Recommendations on Terrorist Financing', 31 October, Washington DC. See also the recommendations from the European finance ministers in *Bulletin Quotidien Europe* (22/9/2001) 'Finance Ministers Put Forward Concrete Initiatives for Combating Financial Crimes Committed by Terrorists', No. 8054, Agence Presse, special edition, Brussels.

62 Bayne, N. (2005) *op. cit.* p. 178.

63 Wayne, E. (2005) 'Evidence of E. Anthony Wayne, Assistant Secretary of State for Economic and Business Affairs', to the Senate Committee on Banking, Housing and Urban Affairs, Washington, 13 July, *Washington File*, US Embassy to the UK, London, http://www.usembassy.org.uk/

64 Dubois, D. (2002) *op. cit.* p. 323.

65 *Bulletin Quotidien Europe* (5/5/2004) No. 8699, Agence Presse, p. 12.

66 *Bulletin Quotidien Europe* (19/3/2004) No. 8669, Agence Presse, p. 4.

67 Archik, K. (2004) 'Europe and Counterterrorism: Strengthening Police and Judicial Cooperation', *Congressional Research Service Report for Congress*, Washington DC, 23 August, pp. 3 and 17.

68 Pope, W. (2004) *op. cit.*

69 Wechsler, W. and Wolosky, L. (2004) *op. cit.*

70 'G-8 Foreign Ministers' Progress Report on the Fight against Terrorism', Whistler, 12 June 2002, Appendix L, in Kirton, J. and Stefanova, R. (eds) (2003) *op. cit.* pp. 258–9.

71 'G-8 Leaders Announce Action Plan to Fight Global Terrorism' (2003) *Washington File*, 2 June, US Embassy to the UK, London, http://www.usembassy.org.uk/terror428.html
72 NATO-Russia Council (2004) Action Plan on Terrorism, 9 December, NATO Integrated Data Service, natodoc@HQ.NATO.INT.
73 Interview conducted by the author (2001) European Commission offices, May, Washington DC.
74 Kash, D. (1998) 'An International Legislative Approach to 21st-Century Terrorism', in Kushner, H. (ed.) *The Future of Terrorism: Violence in the New Millennium*, Sage, London, p. 166.
75 Walt, S. (2001–2) 'Beyond Bin Laden', *International Security*, 26, 3, winter, p. 61. See also 'Bush, Putin Pledge a United Front against Terrorism' (2002), press conference at G-8, 27 June, Kananaskis, Canada, US Department of State Information Programs, http://usinfo.state.Gov/topical/econ/group8/02062702.htm
76 *The 9/11 Commission Report, Final Report of the National Commission on Terrorist Attacks upon the United States* (2004) W. W. Norton, New York, p. 379.

Conclusion

1 Kagan, R. (2004) 'America's Crisis of Legitimacy', *Foreign Affairs*, 83, 2, March–April, p. 69.
2 Boer, M. den (2003) 'The EU Counter-Terrorism Wave: Window of Opportunity or Profound Policy Transformation?', in Leeuwen, M. van (ed.) *Confronting Terrorism: European Experiences, Threat Perceptions and Policies*, Kluwer Law International, The Hague, p. 185.
3 Smith, K. (2003) *European Union Foreign Policy in a Changing World*, Polity Press, Oxford, p. 176.
4 Nye, J. (2003) 'US Power and Strategy after Iraq', *Foreign Affairs*, 82, 4, July–August, pp. 63–4.
5 Daalder, I. (2004) speaking at 'Troubled Partnership: What's Next for the US and Europe?', Brookings and Hoover Institutions Briefing, Brookings Institution, 10 November, Washington DC, http://www.Brookings.edu/dybdocroot/comm./events/20041110.pdf
6 Dassu, M. and Menotti, R. (2005) 'Europe and America in the Age of Bush', *Survival*, 47, 1, spring, p. 107.
7 Hoffman, B. (1999) 'Is Europe Soft on Terrorism?', *Foreign Policy*, 115, summer, p. 63.
8 Kagan, R. (2004) *op. cit.* p. 72.
9 Aaron, D., Beauchesne, A., Burwell, F., Nelson, C. R., Riley, K. J. and Zimmer, B. (2004) 'The Post 9/11 Partnership: Transatlantic Cooperation against Terrorism', The Atlantic Council, Washington DC, December, http://www.acus.org/docs/0412-Post_9-11_Partnership_Transatlantic_Cooperation_Against-Terrorism.pdf
10 Nye, J. (2002) *The Paradox of American Power: Why the World's Only Superpower Can't Go it Alone*, Oxford University Press, New York, p. 29; and Moravcsik, A. (2003) 'Striking a New Transatlantic Bargain', *Foreign Affairs*, 82, 4, July–August, p. 74.

11 Burns, N. (2004) 'NATO and the Transatlantic Relationship', remarks by Nicholas Burns, US Permanent Representative to NATO, to the Bundeswehr Forum, 8 November, Berlin, http://nato.usmission.gov/ambassador/2004/2004Nov08_Burns_Berlin.htm

12 Pope, W. (2004) Principal Deputy Coordinator for Counter terrorism, US Department of State, Statement before the Sub Committee on Europe and on International Terrorism, Non-Proliferation and Human Rights, US House of Representatives, Washington DC, 14 September.

13 Daalder, I. and Goldgeier, J. (2001) 'Putting Europe First', *Survival*, 43, 1, spring, p. 88.

14 Robinson, L. (2005) 'Plan of Attack: The Pentagon Has a Secret New Strategy for Taking On Terrorists – and Taking Them Down', *US News and World Report*, 1 August.

15 Dinmore, G. (2005) 'US Shifts Anti-terror Policy', *Financial Times*, 31 July.

16 *Economist, The* (2005) 'Mr Bush Goes to Belgium', 19 February, pp. 9–10; and *Economist, The* (2005) 'Into the Lion's Den', 26 February, pp. 39–40.

17 Asmus, R. and Pollack, M. (2002) 'The New Transatlantic Project', *Policy Review Online*, no. 115, Stanford, http://www.policyreview.org/OCT02/asmus.html

Bibliography

Books

Anderson, M., den Boer, M., Cullen, P., Gilmore, W., Raab, C. & Walker, N. (1995) *Policing the European Union*, Clarendon Press, Oxford.

Bayne, N. (2005) *Staying Together. The G8 Summit Confronts the 21st Century*, Ashgate, Aldershot.

Benjamin, D. and Simon, S. (2002) *The Age of Sacred Terror*, Random House, New York.

Bovard, J. (2003) *Terrorism and Tyranny. Trampling Freedom, Justice and Peace to Rid the World of Evil*, Palgrave Macmillan, New York.

Burwell, F. and Daalder, I. (eds) (1999) *The US and Europe in the Global Arena*, Macmillan, Basingstoke.

Chalk, P. (1996) *West European Terrorism and Counter-Terrorism: The Evolving Dynamic*, Macmillan, Basingstoke.

Chalk, P. (2000) *Non-Military Security and Global Order: The Impact of Extremism, Violence and Chaos on National and International Security*, Macmillan, Basingstoke.

Clark, I. (1997) *Globalization and Fragmentation: International Relations in the Twentieth Century*, Oxford University Press, Oxford.

Clark, W. (2003) *Winning Modern Wars: Iraq, Terrorism and the American Empire*, New York, Public Affairs.

Clarke, R. (2004) *Against All Enemies: Inside America's War on Terror*, Free Press, New York.

Cooper, R. (2003) *The Breaking of Nations: Order and Chaos in the Twenty First Century*, Atlantic Books, London.

Cox, R. (1987) *Production, Power and World Order*, Columbia University Press, New York.

Cromwell, W. C. (1992) *The United States and the European Pillar: The Strained Alliance*, Macmillan Press, London.

Daalder, I. and Lindsay, J. (2003) *America Unbound: The Bush Revolution in Foreign Policy*, Brookings Institution Press, Washington DC.

De Porte (1979) *Europe Between the Superpowers. The Enduring Balance*, Yale University Press, New Haven and London.

Deutsch, K. (1957) *Political Community and the North Atlantic Area: International Organisation in the Light of Historical Experience*, Princeton University Press, New Jersey.

Doyle, M. (1997) *Ways of War and Peace: Realism, Liberalism and Socialism*, W.W. Norton and Co., New York.

Falkenrath, R., Newman, R. and Thayer, B. (1998) *America's Achilles' Heel. Nuclear, Biological, and Chemical Terrorism and Covert Attack*, The Massachusetts Institute of Technology Press, Cambridge, Mass.

Flynn, S. (2004) *America the Vulnerable: How our Government is Failing to Protect us from Terrorism*, HarperCollins, New York.

Freedman, L. (ed.) (2002) *Superterrorism: Policy Responses*, Blackwell Publishing, Oxford.

Friman, H. (1996) *NarcoDiplomacy: Exporting the US War on Drugs*, Cornell University Press, Ithaca.

Fursdon, E. (1980) *The European Defence Community: A History*, Macmillan, Basingstoke.

Gantz, N. and Roper, J. (eds) (1993) *Towards a New Partnership: US-European Relations in the Post-Cold War Era*, RAND Corporation and the Institute for Security Studies Western European Union, Paris.

Gardiner, A. (1997) *A New Era in US-EU Relations? The Clinton Administration and the New Transatlantic Agenda*, Avebury, Aldershot.

Gedwin, J. (ed.) (1997) *European Integration and American Interests*, AEI Press, Washington DC.

Gompert, D. and Larabee, S. (eds) (1997) *America and Europe: A Partnership for a new Era*, RAND and Cambridge University Press.

Haass, R. (ed.) (1999) *Transatlantic Tensions: The US, Europe, and Problem Countries*, The Brookings Institution, Washington DC.

Hardin, G. and Baden, J. (eds) (1977) *Managing the Commons*, W.H. Freeman, San Francisco.

Harmon, C. (2000) *Terrorism Today*, Frank Cass, London.

Hasenclever, A., Mayer, P. and Rittberger, V. (1997) *Theories of International Regimes*, Cambridge University Press, Cambridge.

Hewitt, C. (2003) *Understanding Terrorism in America: From the Klan to Al Qaeda*, Routledge, London.

Heymann, P. (1998) *Terrorism and America. A Commonsense Strategy for a Democratic Society*, The Massachusetts Institute of Technology Press, Cambridge, Mass.

Hoffman, B. (1998) *Inside Terrorism*, Columbia University Press, New York.

Hoge, J. and Rose, G. (eds) (2001) *How Did This Happen? Terrorism and the New War*, Public Affairs, New York.

Howitt, A. and Pangi, R. (eds) (2003) *Countering Terrorism: Dimensions of Preparedness*, Massachussetts Institute of Technology Press, Cambridge, Mass.

Ikenberry, G. J. (2001) *After Victory: Institutions, Strategic Restraint and the Rebuilding of Order After Major Wars*, Princeton University Press, Princeton.

Kagan, R. (2003) *Paradise and Power: America and Europe in the New World Order*, Atlantic Books, London.

Kampfner, J. (2003) *Blair's Wars*, Free Press, London.

Keohane, R. (1984) *After Hegemony: Cooperation and Discord in the World Political Economy*, Princeton University Press, New Jersey.

Keohane, R. and Nye, J. (1977) *Power and Interdependence*, Little, Brown, Boston.

Kirton, J. and Stefanova, R. (eds) (2003) *The G-8, the United Nations and Conflict Prevention*, Ashgate, Aldershot.

Krasner, S. (ed.) (1983) *International Regimes*, Cornell University Press, Ithaca and London.

Kushner, H. (ed.) (1998) *The Future of Terrorism: Violence in the New Millennium*, Sage, London.

Lansford, T. (2002) *All for One: Terrorism, NATO and the United States*, Ashgate, Aldershot.

Lansford, T. and Blagovest, T. (eds) (2005) *Old Europe, New Europe: Renegotiating Transatlantic Security in the Post 9/11 Era*, Ashgate, Aldershot.

Leeuwen, M. van (ed.) (2003) *Confronting Terrorism: European Experiences, Threat Perceptions and Policies*, Kluwer Law International, The Hague.

Lepgold, J. (1990) *The Declining Hegemon. The United States and European Defense, 1960–1990*, Greenwood Press, New York.

Litwak, R. (1999) *Rogue States and US Foreign Policy. Containment after the Cold War*, Woodrow Wilson Center Press, Washington DC.

Longhurst, K. (2004) *Germany and the Use of Force. The Evolution of German Security Policy 1990–2003*, Manchester University Press, Manchester.

Lundestad, G. (1998) *Empire by Integration: the US and European Integration 1945–1997*, Oxford University Press, Oxford.

Lundestad, G. (2003) *The United States and Western Europe Since 1945*, Oxford University Press, Oxford.

Lynch, P., Neuwahl, N. and Rees, W. (eds) (2000) *Reforming the European Union: From Maastricht to Amsterdam*, Longman, Essex.

Mahncke, D., Rees, W. and Thompson, W. (2004) *Redefining Transatlantic Security Relations: The Challenge of Change*, Manchester University Press, Manchester.

Mann, J. (2004) *Rise of the Vulcans: The History of Bush's War Cabinet*, Penguin, New York.

McGoldrick, D. (2004) *From '9–11' to the Iraq War 2003: International Law in an Age of Complexity*, Hart Publishing, Portland, Oregon.

Mitsilegas, V., Monar, J. and Rees, W. (2003) *The European Union and Internal Security: Guardian of the People?* Palgrave Macmillan, Basingstoke.

Menon, A. (2000) *France, NATO and the Limits of Independence 1981–97*, Macmillan, Basingstoke.

Monar, J. (ed.) (1998) *The New Transatlantic Agenda and the Future of EU-US Relations*, Kluwer Law International, London and The Hague.

Nadelmann, E. (1993) *Cops Across Borders: The Internationalization of US Criminal Law Enforcement*, Pennsylvania State University Press, University Park.

Naftali, T. (2005) *Blind Spot: The Secret History of American Counter Terrorism*, Basic Books, New York.

Nye, J. (1992) *Bound to Lead: The Changing Nature of American Power*, Basic Books, New York.

Nye, J. (2002) *The Paradox of American Power: Why the World's Only Superpower Can't Go it Alone*, Oxford University Press, New York.

Occhipinti, J. (2003) *The Politics of EU Police Cooperation: Toward a European FBI?* Lynne Reinner, Boulder, Co.

Omar, R. (2005) *Revolution Day: The Real Story of the Battle for Iraq*, Penguin, London.

Oye, K. (1986) *Cooperation under Anarchy*, Princeton University Press, New Jersey.

Peers, S. (2000) *EU Justice and Home Affairs*, Longman, Harlow.

Peterson, J. and Pollack, M. (eds) (2003) *Europe, America, Bush. Transatlantic Relations in the Twenty-First Century*, Routledge, London.

Philippart, E. and Winand, P. (eds) (2001) *Ever Closer Partnership: Policymaking in US-EU Relations*, PIE Peter Lang, Brussels.

Pillar, P. (2001) *Terrorism and US Foreign Policy*, Brookings Institution Press, Washington DC.

Pond, E. (2003) *The Near Death of the Transatlantic Alliance*, Brookings Institution Press, Washington DC.

Prados, J. (ed.) (2002) *America Confronts Terrorism: Understanding the Danger and How to Think About It*, Ivan Dee, Chicago.

Reinares, F. (ed.) (2000) *European Democracies against Terrorism. Governmental Policies and Intergovernmental Cooperation*, Onati International Institute for the Sociology of Law, Ashgate, Aldershot.

Riddell, P. (2003) *Hug them Close: Blair, Clinton, Bush and the 'Special Relationship'*, Politico's, London.

Risse-Kappen, T. (1995) *Cooperation Among Democracies: The European Influence on US Foreign Policy*, Princeton University Press, Princeton NJ.

Rittberger, V. (ed.) (1997) *Regime Theory and International Relations*, Clarendon Press, Oxford.

Rosenau, J. and Czempiel, E. (eds) (1992) *Governance without Government: Order and Change in World Politics*, Cambridge University Press, Cambridge.

Salmon, T. and Shepherd, A. (2003) *Toward a European Army: A Military Power in the Making*, Lynne Reinner, Boulder, Co.

Schwartz, D. (1983) *NATO's Nuclear Dilemmas*, Brookings Institution, Washington DC.

Shearman, P. and Sussex, M. (eds) (2004) *European Security after 9/11*, Ashgate, Aldershot.

Singer, M. and Wildavsky, A. (1993) *The Real World Order. Zones of Peace, Zones of Turmoil*, Chatham House Publishers, New Jersey.

Smith, K. (2003) *European Union Foreign Policy in a Changing World*, Polity, Oxford.

Stromseth, J. (1988) *The Origins of Flexible Response: NATO's Debate over Strategy in the 1960s*, Macmillan, Basingstoke.

Tanter, R. (1999) *Rogue Regimes: Terrorism and Proliferation*, St Martin's Griffin, London.

Taylor, M. and Horgan, J. (eds) (2000) *The Future of Terrorism*, Frank Cass, London.

Walt, S. (1987) *The Origins of Alliances*, Cornell University Press, Ithaca and London.

Winand, P. (1993) *Eisenhower, Kennedy and the United States of Europe*, St Martin's Press, New York.

Woodward, B. (2002) *Bush at War*, Simon and Schuster, New York.

Yost, D. (1998) *NATO Transformed. The Alliance's New Roles in International Security*, US Institute of Peace Press, Washington DC.

Articles and Book Chapters

Aldrich, R. (2004) 'Transatlantic Intelligence and Security Cooperation', *International Affairs*, 80, 4, July, pp. 731–753.

Aldrich, R. (2005) 'Whitehall and the Iraq War: The UK's Four Intelligence Enquiries', *Irish Studies in International Affairs*, 16, pp. 1–16.

Asmus, R. (2003) 'Rebuilding the Atlantic Alliance', *Foreign Affairs*, 82, 5, September–October, pp. 20–32.

Asmus, R. (2005) 'Rethinking the EU: Why Washington Needs to Support European Integration', *Survival*, 47, 3, Autumn, pp. 93–102.

Asmus, R. and Pollack, M. (2002) 'The New Transatlantic Project', *Policy Review Online*, No. 115, Stanford, *http://www.policyreview.org/OCT02/asmus.html*. (Accessed 17/5/2003)

Badey, T. (1998) 'US Anti-terrorism Policy: The Clinton Administration', *Contemporary Security Policy*, 19, 2, August, pp. 50–70.

Bahgat, G. (2003) 'Iran, the United States and the War on Terrorism', *Studies in Conflict and Terrorism*, 26, pp. 93–104.

Bahgat, G. (2003) 'The United States, Iraq and Weapons of Mass Destruction', *Defence and Security Analysis*, 19, 1, pp. 5–14.

Bailes, A. (2005) 'The European Security Strategy: An Evolutionary History', *Stockholm International Peace Research Institute Paper 10*, February, *http://www.sipri.org* (Accessed 11/4/2005)

Barry, C. (1996) 'NATO's Combined Joint Task Forces in theory and practice', *Survival*, 38, 1, Spring, pp. 81–97.

Betts, R. (1998) 'The new threat of mass destruction', *Foreign Affairs*, 77, 1, January–February, pp. 26–41.

Binnendijk, H. and Kugler, R. (2002) 'Transforming Europe's Forces', *Survival*, 43, 3, Autumn, pp. 117–132.

Bluth, C. (2004) 'The British Road to War: Blair, Bush and the Decision to Invade Iraq', *International Affairs*, 80, 5, October, pp. 871–892.

Boer, M. den (2003) 'The EU Counter-Terrorism Wave: Window of Opportunity or Profound Policy Transformation?' in Leeuwen, M. van (ed.) *Confronting Terrorism: European Experiences, Threat Perceptions and Policies*, Kluwer Law International, The Hague.

Boer, M. den and Monar, J. (2002) 'Keynote Article: 11 September and the Challenge of Global Terrorism to the EU as a Security Actor', *Journal of Common Market Studies Annual Review*, 40, pp. 11–28.

Bolton, J. (2000) 'The end of NATO?' *The World Today*, 56, 6, June, pp. 12–14.

Bowen, W. and Kidd, J. (2004) 'The Iranian Nuclear Challenge', *International Affairs*, 80, 2, pp. 257–276.

Calleo, D. (2004) 'The Broken West', *Survival*, 46, 3, Autumn, pp. 29–38.

Cha, V. (2003) 'Engaging North Korea Credibly', *Survival*, 42, 2, Summer, pp. 136–155.

Chubin, S. and Green, J. (1998) 'Engaging Iran: A US Strategy', *Survival*, 40, 3, Autumn, pp. 153–169.

Daalder, I. (2003) 'The End of Atlanticism', *Survival*, 45, 2, Summer, pp. 147–166.

Daalder, I. and Goldgeier, J. (2001) 'Putting Europe First', *Survival*, 43, 1, Spring, pp. 71–92.

Dassu, M. and Menotti, R. (2005) 'Europe and America in the Age of Bush', *Survival*, 47, 1, Spring, pp. 105–122.

Davison, R. (2004) 'French Security after 9/11: Franco-American Discord', in Shearman, P. and Sussex, M. (2004) (eds) *European Security after 9/11*, Ashgate, Aldershot.

Delpech, T. (2002) 'International Terrorism and Europe', *Chaillot Paper 56*, European Union Institute for Security Studies, Paris, December.

Doyle, M. (1995) 'On the Democratic Peace', *International Security*, 19, 4, pp. 180–184.

Drozdiak,W. (2005) 'The North Atlantic Drift', *Foreign Affairs*, 84, 1, January–February, pp. 88–100.

Dubois, D. (2002) 'The Attacks of 11 September: EU-US Cooperation Against Terrorism in the Field of Justice and Home Affairs', *European Foreign Affairs Review*, 7, 3, Autumn, pp. 317–335.

Duke, S. (2002) 'CESDP and the European Response to 11 September: Identifying the Weakest Link', *European Foreign Affairs Review* 7, 2, Summer, pp. 153–169.

Duke, S. (2004) 'The European Security Strategy in a Comparative Framework: Does it make for Secure Alliances in a Better World?' *European Foreign Affairs Review*, 9, pp. 459–481.

Dunne, T. (2004) ' "When the Shooting Starts": Atlanticism in British Security Strategy', *International Affairs*, 80, 5, October, pp. 893–909.

Edwards, G. and Cornish, P. (2001) 'Beyond the EU/NATO Dichotomy: The Beginnings of a European Strategic Culture', *International Affairs*, 77, 3, July, pp. 587–604.

Forster, A. and Wallace, W. (2001) 'What is NATO for?' *Survival*, 43, 4, December, pp. 107–122.

Freedman, L. (2003) 'Prevention, not pre-emption', *The Washington Quarterly*, 26, 2, Spring, pp. 105–114.

Frellesen, T. (2001) 'Processes and Procedures in EU-US Foreign Policy Cooperation: From the Transatlantic Declaration to the New Transatlantic Agenda', in Philippart, E. and Winand, P. (2001) (eds) *Ever Closer Partnership: Policy-making in US-EU Relations*, PIE Peter Lang, Brussels.

Ginkel, B. van (2003) 'The United Nations: Towards a Comprehensive Convention on Combating Terrorism', in Leeuwen, M. Van (ed.) *Confronting Terrorism: European Experiences, Threat Perceptions and Policies*, Kluwer Law International, The Hague.

Gnesotto, N. (2002) 'Reacting to America', *Survival*, 44, 4, Winter, pp. 99–106.

Gordon, G. (2003) 'Bridging the Atlantic Divide', *Foreign Affairs*, 82, 1, January–February, pp. 70–83.

Gordon, P. (2002) 'Reforging the Atlantic Alliance', *The National Interest*, Fall.

Gordon, P. (2004) 'American Choices in the "War on Terror"', Review Essays, *Survival*, 46, 1, Spring, pp. 145–155.

Gordon, P., Indyk, M. and O'Hanlon, M. (2002) 'Getting serious about Iraq', *Survival*, 44, 3, Autumn, pp. 9–22.

Grand, C. (2000) 'The EU and the Non-proliferation of Nuclear Weapons', *Chaillot Paper 37*, Institute for Security Studies Western European Union, Paris, January.

Grant, C. (2002) 'The Eleventh of September and Beyond: The Impact on the European Union', in Freedman, L. (ed.) (2002) *Superterrorism: Policy Responses*, Blackwell Publishing, Oxford.

Guild, E. (2003) 'International Terrorism and EU Immigration, Asylum and Borders Policy: The Unexpected Victims of 11 September 2001', *European Foreign Affairs Review*, 8, 3, Autumn, pp. 331–346.

Haas, E. (1975) 'On Systems and International Regimes', *World Politics*, 27, January, pp. 147–174.

Haas, E. (1980) 'Why Collaborate? Issue Linkage and International Regimes', *World Politics*, 32, April, pp. 357–405.

Haas, P. (1992) 'Epistemic Communities and International Policy Coordination', *International Organization*, 46, 1, Winter, pp. 1–35.

Haas, P. (1992) 'Epistemic Communities and International Policy Coordination', in Haas, P. (ed.) 'Knowledge, Power and International Policy Coordination', *International Organization*, 46, 1, pp. 1–35.

Hassner, P. (2002) 'The US: The empire of force or the force of empire?' *Chaillot Paper 55*, European Union Institute for Security Studies, Paris, September.

Heisbourg, F. (2003) 'A work in progress: The Bush doctrine and its consequences', *The Washington Quarterly*, 26, 2, pp. 75–88.

Hill, C. (2004) 'Renationalizing or Regrouping? EU Foreign Policy since 11 September 2001', *Journal of Common Market Studies*, 42, 1, pp. 143–163.

Hoffman, B. (1999) 'Is Europe Soft on Terrorism?' *Foreign Policy*, 115, Summer, pp. 62–77.

Hoffmann, S. (2003) 'US-European Relations: Past and Future', *International Affairs*, 79, 5, October, pp. 1029–1036.

Homer-Dixon, T. (2002) 'The rise of complex terrorism', 128, *Foreign Policy*, January–February, pp. 52–62.

Howorth, J. (2003) 'France, Britain and the Euro-Atlantic Crisis', *Survival*, 45, 4, Winter, pp. 173–192.

Ikenberry, G. J. (2000) 'Strengthening the Atlantic Political Order', *The International Spectator*, 35, 3, July–September, pp. 57–68.

Ikenberry, G. J. (2004) 'Illusions of Empire: Defining the New American Order', *Foreign Affairs*, 83, 2, March–April, pp. 144–154.

Jamieson, A. (1995) 'The Transnational Dimension of Italian Organised Crime', *Transnational Organised Crime*, 1, 2, Summer, pp. 156–157.

Jervis, R. (1982) 'Security Regimes', *International Organisation*, 36, 2, Spring, pp. 357–378.

Joffe, J. (1984) 'Europe's American pacifier', *Foreign Affairs*, 54, 1, pp. 64–82.

Johnston, A. (1995) 'Thinking about Strategic Culture', *International Security*, 19, 4, Spring, pp. 32–64.

Jordan, A. and Ku, J. (1998) 'Coping with North Korea', *The Washington Quarterly*, 21, 1, Winter, pp. 33–46.

Kagan, R. (2004) 'America's Crisis of Legitimacy', *Foreign Affairs*, 83, 2, March–April, pp. 65–87.

Kamp, K-H. (1998) 'WMD terrorism: An exchange', *Survival*, 40, 4, Winter, pp. 168–83.

Kamp, K-H. (1999) 'A global role for NATO?' *The Washington Quarterly*, 22, 1, Winter, pp. 7–13.

Kash, D. (1998) 'An International Legislative Approach to 21st Century Terrorism', in Kushner, H. (ed.) *The Future of Terrorism: Violence in the New Millennium*, Sage, London.

Kemp, G. (2001) 'Iran: Can the US do a deal?' *The Washington Quarterly*, 24, 1, Winter, pp. 109–124.

Kramer, S. (2003) 'Blair's Britain after Iraq', *Foreign Affairs*, 82, 4, July–August, pp. 90–104.

Krenzler, H. and Schomaker, A. (1996) 'A new transatlantic agenda', *European Foreign Affairs Review*, 1, 1, July, pp. 9–28.

Lake, A. (1994) 'Confronting Backlash States', *Foreign Affairs*, 73, 2, March–April.

Lansford, T. (2005) 'Introduction: US security policy and the new Europe', in Lansford, T. and Blagovest, T. (eds) *Old Europe, New Europe: Renegotiating Transatlantic Security in the Post 9/11 Era*, Ashgate, Aldershot.

Laqeur, W. (2004) 'The Terrorism to Come', *Policy Review Online*, Hoover Institution, *http://www.policyreview.org/aug04/laqeur.html* (Accessed 13/12/2004)

Lebl, L. (2005) 'Security beyond Borders', *Policy Review Online*, No.130, *http://www.policyreview.org/apr05/lebl.html* (Accessed 15/07/2005)

Litwak, R. (2002) 'The new calculus of pre-emption', *Survival*, 44, 4, Winter, pp. 53–80.

Lugar, R. (2002) 'Redefining NATO's Mission: Preventing WMD Terrorism', *The Washington Quarterly*, 25, 3, Summer, pp. 7–13.

Malvesti, M. (2001) 'Explaining the United States' Decision to Strike Back at Terrorists', *Terrorism and Political Violence*, 13, 2, Summer, pp. 85–106.

Manners, I. (2002) 'Normative Power Europe? A Contradiction in Terms?' *Journal of Common Market Studies*, 40, 2, pp. 234–258.

Marotta, E. (1999) 'Europol's Role in Anti-Terrorism Policy', *Terrorism and Political Violence*, 11, pp. 15–18.

Mearsheimer, J. (1990) 'Back to the future: Instability in Europe after the Cold War', *International Security*, 15, 1, Summer, pp. 5–56.

Miles, J. (2002) 'Waiting out North Korea', *Survival*, 44, 2, Summer, pp. 37–50.

Mitsilegas, V. (2003) 'The New EU-USA Cooperation on Extradition, Mutual Legal Assistance and the Exchange of Police Data', *European Foreign Affairs Review*, 8, 4, Winter, pp. 515–536.

Monar, J. (2000) 'An "Area of Freedom, Justice and Security?" Progress and Deficits in Justice and Home Affairs', in Lynch, P., Neuwahl, N. and Rees, W. (eds) *Reforming the European Union: From Maastricht to Amsterdam*, Longman, Essex.

Monar, J. (2004) 'The EU as an International Actor in the Domain of Justice and Home Affairs', *European Foreign Affairs Review*, 9, 3, Autumn, pp. 395–416.

Moravcsik, A. (2003) 'Striking a New Transatlantic Bargain', *Foreign Affairs*, 82, 4, July–August, pp. 74–89.

Muller, H. (2003) 'Terrorism, Proliferation: A European Threat Assessment', *Chaillot Paper No. 58*, European Union Institute for Security Studies, Paris, March.

Muller-Wille, B. (2004) 'For Our Eyes Only? Shaping an Intelligence Community within the EU', *Occasional Paper 50*, EU Institute for Security Studies, January, *www.iss-eu.org* (Accessed 30/6/2005)

Naylor, R. (1995), 'From Cold War to Crime War: The Search for a New "National Security" Threat', *Transnational Organized Crime*, 1, 4, Winter, pp. 37–56.

Nelson, D. (2002) 'Transatlantic Transmutations', *The Washington Quarterly*, 25, 4, Autumn, pp. 51–66.

Nelson, M. (1993) 'Transatlantic travails', *Foreign Policy*, 92, Fall, pp. 75–91.

Neuwahl, N. (ed.) (2003) 'The Atlantic Alliance: For better or for wars', *European Foreign Affairs Review*, 8, 4, Winter, pp. 427–434.

Nye, J. (2000) 'The US and Europe: Continental drift?' *International Affairs*, 76, 1, January, pp. 51–61.

Nye, J. (2003) 'US Power and Strategy after Iraq', *Foreign Affairs*, 82, 4, July–August, pp. 60–73.

Nye, J. (2003) 'The decline of America's soft power: Why Washington should worry', *Foreign Affairs*, 83, 3, May–June, pp. 16–21.

Odom, W. (2004) 'Understanding America's Empire (If It Really Has One)', *The Brown Journal of World Affairs*, 11, 1, Summer / Fall.

Oswald, F. (2004) 'German security after 9/11', in Shearman, P. and Sussex, M. (eds) *European Security after 9/11*, Ashgate, Aldershot.

Oudraat, C. de Jonge (2003) 'Combating Terrorism', *The Washington Quarterly*, 26, 4, Autumn, pp. 163–176.

Palmer, D. R. (2003) 'The road to Kabul', *NATO Review*, 2, Summer, http://www.nato.int/docu/review/2003/issue2/english/art3.html.

Penttila, R. (2003) 'The Role of the G8 in International Peace and Security', *Adelphi Paper 355*, International Institute for Strategic Studies, London.

Peterson, J. (2004) 'America as a European Power: The End of Empire by Integration?' *International Affairs*, 80, 4, July, pp. 613–629.

Politi, A. (1997) 'European Security: The New Transnational Risks', *Chaillot Papers 29*, Institute for Security Studies Western European Union, Paris, October.

Pollack, K. (2002) 'Next stop Baghdad', *Foreign Affairs*, 81, 2, March–April, pp. 32–46.

Pollack, K. and Takeyh, R. (2005) 'Taking on Tehran', *Foreign Affairs*, March–April, pp. 20–34.

Puchala, D. (2005) 'The Atlantic Community in the Age of Terrorism', *Journal of Transatlantic Studies*, 3, 1, Spring, pp. 89–104.

Rees, W. (2003) 'Transatlantic relations and the War on Terror', *Journal of Transatlantic Studies*, 1, 1, Spring, Supplement, pp. 76–90.

Rees, W. and Aldrich, R. (2005) 'Contending Cultures of Counterterrorism: Transatlantic Divergence or Convergence?' *International Affairs*, 81, 5, October, pp. 905–923.

Rice, C. (2000) 'Promoting the National Interest', *Foreign Affairs*, 79, 1, January–February, pp. 45–62.

Rose, G. (1999) 'The United States and Libya', in Haass, R. (ed.) *Transatlantic Tensions: The US, Europe, and Problem Countries*, The Brookings Institution, Washington DC.

Roy, O. (2003) 'EuroIslam: The Jihad Within', *The National Interest*, 71, Spring, pp. 63–73.

Roy, O., Hoffman, B., Paz, R., Simon, S. and Benjamin, D. (2000) 'America and the New Terrorism: An Exchange', *Survival*, 42, 2, Summer, pp. 156–172.

Ruhle, M. (2003) 'NATO after Prague: Learning the lessons of 9/11', *Parameters*, 33, 2, Summer, pp. 89–97.

Rynning, S. (2005) 'A new military ethos. NATO's Response Force', *Journal of Transatlantic Studies*, 3, 1, Spring, pp. 5–21.

Samore, G. (2003) 'The Korean Nuclear Crisis', *Survival*, 45, 1, Spring, pp. 7–24.

Schmitt, M. (2002) 'Counter-Terrorism and the Use of Force in International Law', *The Marshall Center Papers, No. 5*, Garmisch-Partenkirchen, November.

Segell, G. (2004) 'Intelligence Agency Relations between the European Union and the US', *International Journal of Intelligence and Counter Intelligence*, 17, 1, Spring, pp. 81–96.

Shapiro, J. and Suzan, B. (2003) 'The French Experience of Counter-terrorism', *Survival*, 45, 1, Spring, pp. 67–98.

Simon, S. and Benjamin, D. (2000) 'America and the New Terrorism', *Survival*, 42, 1, Spring, pp. 59–75.

Spear, J. (2003) 'The Emergence of a European "Strategic Personality" and the Implications for the Transatlantic Relationship', *Arms Control Today*, 33, 9, November, pp. 13–18.

Sprinzak, E. (1998) 'The great super-terrorism scare', *Foreign Policy*, 112, Fall, pp. 110–124.

Steinberg, J. (2003) 'An Elective Partnership: Salvaging Transatlantic Relations', *Survival*, 45, 2, Summer, pp. 113–146.

Stevenson, J. (2003) 'How Europe and America Defend Themselves', *Foreign Affairs*, 82, 2, March–April, pp. 75–90.

Stevenson, J. (2004) 'Counter-terrorism: Containment and Beyond', *Adelphi Paper 367*, International Institute for Strategic Studies, London.

Strauss, M. (2002) 'Attacking Iraq', *Foreign Policy*, March–April, pp. 14–19.

Takeyh, R. (2002) 'Re-imagining US-Iranian Relations', *Survival*, 44, 3, Autumn, pp. 23–36.

Talbott, S. (2002) 'From Prague to Baghdad', *Foreign Affairs*, 81, 6, November–December, pp. 46–58.

Thieux, L. (2004) 'European Security and Global Terrorism: The Strategic Aftermath of the Madrid Bombings', *Perspectives: The Central European Review of International Affairs*, 22, Institute of International Relations, Prague, pp. 59–73.

Toje, A. (2005) 'The 2003 European Union Security Strategy: A Critical Appraisal', *European Foreign Affairs Review*, 10, 1, pp. 117–133.

Tucker, D. (1998) 'Responding to Terrorism', *The Washington Quarterly*, 21, 1, Winter, pp. 103–117.

Walker, J. (1991) 'Keeping America in Europe', *Foreign Policy*, 83, Summer, pp. 128–142.

Wallace, W. (2001) 'Europe, the necessary partner', *Foreign Affairs*, 80, 3, May–June, pp. 16–32.

Walt, S. (1997) 'Why alliances endure or collapse', *Survival*, 39, 1, Spring, pp. 156–179.

Walt, S. (1998-99) 'The ties that fray: Why Europe and America are drifting apart', *The National Interest*, 54, Winter, pp. 3–11.

Walt, S. (2001-2) 'Beyond Bin Laden. Reshaping US Foreign Policy', *International Security*, 26, 3, Winter, pp. 56–78.

Weidenfeld, W. (1997) 'America and Europe: Is the Break Inevitable?' *The Washington Quarterly*, 20, 3, Summer, pp. 37–53.

Winer, J. and Roule, T. (2002) 'Fighting Terrorist Finance', *Survival*, 44, 3, Autumn, pp. 87–104.

Yaphe, J. (2001) 'Iraq: The exception to the rule', *The Washington Quarterly*, 24, 1, Winter, pp. 125–137.

Young, O. (1980) 'International Regimes: Problems of Concept Foundation', *World Politics*, 32, April, pp. 331–356.

Young, O. (1982) 'Regime Dynamics: The Rise and Fall of International Regimes', *International Organization*, 36, 2, Spring, pp. 277–297.

Zelikow, P. (2003) 'The Transformation of National Security', *The National Interest*, 71, Spring, pp. 17–28.

Reports and Documents

Aaron, D., Beauchesne, A., Burwell, F., Nelson, C. R., Riley, K. J. and Zimmer, B. (2004) 'The Post 9/11 Partnership. Transatlantic Cooperation Against Terrorism', Policy Paper, The Atlantic Council, Washington DC, December, *http://www.acus.org/docs/0412-Post_9-11_Partnership_Transatlantic_Cooperation_Against-Terrorism.pdf* (Accessed 28/2/2005)

Abshire, D., Czerwinski, J., Cross, W. and Angerholzer, M. (2005) 'Maximising NATO for the War on Terror. Presidential Leadership can Strengthen the Transatlantic Relationship by Defining and Pursuing Shared Homeland Security Interests', Washington DC, May, *www.Thepresidency.org* (Accessed 5/9/2005)

Akerboom, E. (2004) 'Counter-Terrorism in the Netherlands', General Intelligence and Security Service of the Netherlands, http://wwwaivd.nl/ (Accessed 11/10/2004)

Archik, K. (2004) 'Europe and Counterterrorism: Strengthening Police and Judicial Cooperation', *Congressional Research Service Report for Congress*, Washington DC, 23 August.

Ashcroft, J. (2004) 'Attorney General Ashcroft speaks at EU Justice and Home Affairs meeting', *US Federal News*, 30 September.

Baker, J. (1989) 'A New Europe and a New Atlanticism', Address by James Baker, Secretary of State, before the Berlin Press Club, Berlin, 12 December, American Foreign Policy, *Current Documents*, 1989, Department of State, Washington DC, 1990.

Bensahel, N. (2003) 'The Counterterror Coalitions: Cooperation with Europe, NATO, and the European Union', *RAND Project Air Force*, Arlington, VA.

Best, R. (2001) 'Intelligence and Law Enforcement: Countering Transnational Threats to the US', *Congressional Research Service Report for Congress*, Washington DC, 16 January.

Best, R. (2003) 'Intelligence to Counter Terrorism: Issues for Congress', *Congressional Research Service Report for Congress*, Washington DC, 27 May.

Bildt, C. (2003) 'We have crossed the Rubicon – but where are we heading next?' Speech at the Centre for European Reform, 17 November, http:/www.cer. org.uk/articles (Accessed March 2004)

'Blair Terror Speech in Full' (2004) BBC News, 5 March, *http://newsvote.bbc.co.uk?mpapps/pagetools/print/news.bbc.co.uk/1/hi/uk-poliitics/35* (Accessed 8/3/2004)

Blix, H. (2003) 'An Update on Inspection', Report by Hans Blix, Executive Chairman of UNMOVIC to the Security Council of the UN, 27 January, http://www.un.org/Depts/unmovic/Bx27.htm (Accessed 11/8/2003)

Bort, E. (2000) 'Illegal Migration and Cross-Border Crime: Challenges at the Eastern Frontier of the European Union', European University Institute, *Working Paper 2000/9*, Florence.

Burns, N. (2004) 'NATO and the Transatlantic Relationship', Remarks by Nicholas Burns, US Permanent Representative to NATO to the Bundeswehr Forum, 8 November, Berlin, *http://nato.usmission.gov/ambassador/2004/2004 Nov08_Burns_Berlin.htm* (Accessed 13/01/2005)

Bush, G. (2001) 'Presidential Address to the Nation Announcing Strikes against Al Qaeda Training Camps and Taliban Military Installations', The Whitehouse, 7 October, Washington DC.

Bush, G. (2001) 'Radio Address of the President to the Nation', *http://www.whitehouse.gov/news/releases/2001*

'Bush, Putin pledge a united front against terrorism' (2002) Press conference at G-8 June 27, Kananaskis, Canada, US Department of State Information Programs, *http://usinfo.state.gov/topical/econ/group8/02062702.htm* (Accessed 19/8/2002)

Bush, G. (2001) President George W. Bush, 'State of the Union Speech' to Joint Session of Congress, January, Washington DC. *Washington File*, Office of International Information Programs, US Department of State, *http://usinfo.state.gov*.

Bush, G. (2002) President George W. Bush, 'State of the Union Address', to both Houses of Congress, January, Washington DC. *Washington File*, Office of International Information Programs, US Department of State, *http://usinfo.state.gov*. (Accessed 17/3/2002)

Bush, G. (2002) President George W. Bush delivers graduation speech at West Point, The White House, 1 June, http:www.whitehouse.gov/news/releases/2002/06 (Accessed 21/8/2002)

Cabinet Office (2002) 'The United Kingdom and the Campaign Against International Terrorism. Progress Report', London, 9 September, *http://www.cabinetoffice.gov.uk/publications/reports/sept11/coi-0809.pdf* (Accessed 8/12/2004)

Center for Strategic and International Studies (2004) 'Transatlantic Dialogue on Terrorism', Washington DC, August, http://www.csis.org/index.php?option = com_csisproj&task = view&id = 368.

Chalk, P. and Rosenau, W. (2004) 'Confronting the Enemy Within: Security Intelligence, the Police and Counterterrorism in Four Democracies', *Research Brief, RAND, www.rand.org*. (Accessed 12/11/2004)

Cheney, R. (2003) 'Cheney says ending the links between terrorists and rogue states is vital', Remarks by the Vice-President to the Heritage Foundation, *Washington File*, 2 May, US Embassy to the UK, London, http://www.usembassy.org.uk/ (Accessed 9/7/2004)

Chertoff, M. (2005) 'Statement of Secretary Michael Chertoff, US Department of Homeland Security, before the US Senate Committee on Commerce, Science and Transportation, 19 July, Washington DC.

Christopher, W. (1995) 'Charting a Transatlantic Agenda for the 21st Century', Address at Casa de America by the US Secretary of State, Spain, 2 June.

Clarke, R., McCaffrey, B. and Nelson, R. (2004) 'NATO's Role in Confronting International Terrorism', *Policy Paper*, The Atlantic Council, Washington DC, June.

Clinton, W. (1996) Speech of US President William Clinton to the United Nations General Assembly, 24 September.

Cofer Black, J. (2004) Testimony by Ambassador Cofer Black, Coordinator for Counter Terrorism, Department of State, before the Senate Foreign Relations Subcommittee on Europe, US Senate, Washington DC, 31 March.

Cohen, W. (1999) 'Preparing for a Grave New World', Statement of the US Defense Secretary, *US Information Service*, 27 July.

Dam, K. (2002) 'The Financial Front of the War on Terrorism – The Next Phase', Speech by Kenneth Dam, Deputy Secretary of the Treasury to the Council on Foreign Relations, 6 June, New York, *Washington File*, US Embassy to the UK, London, *http://www.usembassy.org.uk/* (Accessed 26/7/2002)

Davis, Z. (1994) 'US Counterproliferation Doctrine: Issues for Congress', *Congressional Research Service Report for Congress*, The Library of Congress, Washington DC, 21 September.

Doyle, C. (2002) 'The USA PATRIOT Act: A Sketch', *Congressional Research Service Report for Congress*, The Library of Congress, Washington DC, 18 April.

Elsea, J. (2001) 'Terrorism and the Law of War: Trying Terrorists as War Criminals before Military Commissions', *Congressional Research Service Report for Congress*, Washington DC, 11 December.

European Commission (2004) 'EU Counter terrorism efforts in JHA field', Press Release, Mem0/04/59, 12 March, Brussels, *http://europaleu.intlrapidl startlcgilguesten.ksh?p-action.gettxt = gt&doc = MEMO/04/5* (Accessed 22/3/2004)

European Commission (2005) Review of the Framework for Relations between the European Union and the United States, Independent Study Commissioned by Directorate General External Relations C1, European Commission, Final Report.

European Communities (2001) 'Decision on a European Arrest Warrant from the Commission', COM 522.

European Communities (2002) Official Journal, L 22 June.

European Communities (2002) Official Journal, L 190 18 July.

European Communities (2003) Official Journal, 'Agreement on mutual legal assistance between the European Union and the United States of America, 181/34.

European Community Directive (1995) 95/46/EC 'On the protection of individuals with regard to the processing of personal data and the free movement of such data', 24 October, Official Journal N L281.

European Council (2001) 'Conclusions and Plan of Action of the Extraordinary European Council meeting on 21 September 2001', 21 September, Brussels.

European Council (2001) 'Informal European Council of Ghent', 19 October, Ghent.

European Council (2001) Justice and Home Affairs, 'Conclusions adopted by the Council', SN 3926, Brussels, 20 September.

European Council (2002) 'Decision on setting up Eurojust with a view to reinforcing the fight against serious crime', 28 February, Brussels.

European Council (2002) Presidency Conclusions, 21-22 June, Seville.

European Council (2002) 'Council Framework Decision of 13 June 2002 on Combating Terrorism', Brussels.

European Council (2003) 'Basic Principles for an EU Strategy Against Proliferation of Weapons of Mass Destruction', December, Brussels.

European Council (2004) 'EU-US Declaration on Combating Terrorism', Dromoland Castle, Ireland, 26 June, in Press Release, 10760/04, Brussels.

European Council (2004) 'The Hague Programme: Strengthening Freedom, Security and Justice in the European Union', 4-5 November.

European Council (2004) Presidency Conclusions, 17-18 June, Brussels.

European Parliament (2001) 'Report on the Role of the EU in Combating Terrorism', Committee on Citizens Freedoms and Rights, Justice and Home Affairs (2001 / 2016 INI), A5 0273 / 2001 Final, Rapporteur Graham Watson, 12 July.

European Parliament (2002) 'Report on the Commission Communication to the Council on Reinforcing the Transatlantic Relationship' Committee on Foreign Affairs, Human Rights, Common Security and Defence Policy, Focusing on Strategy and Delivering Results, Rapporteur J. Elles, A5-0148 / 2002, 25 April.

'European Union and United States Joint Program of Work on the Nonproliferation of Weapons of Mass Destruction' (2005) EU-US Summit, June.

Everts, S. (2001) 'Unilateral America, Lightweight Europe? Managing Divergence in Transatlantic Foreign Policy', Centre for European Reform, February.

Everts, S., Freedman, L., Grant, C., Heisbourg, F., Keohane, D. and O'Hanlon, M. (2004) *A European Way of War*, Centre for European Reform, London, May.

Fact Sheet: American Leadership in Combating Terrorism (1996) *European Wireless File*, 31 July.

Faull, J. (2004) 'Challenges and Accomplishments as the EU and the US Promote Trade and Tourism in a Terrorism Environment', Remarks by the Director General of Justice and Home Affairs, European Commission, to the Senate Committee on Foreign Relations, Sub-Committee on European Relations, 13 May, Washington DC.

Financial Action Task Force (2001) 'Financial Action Task Force on Money Laundering. Special Recommendations on Terrorist Financing', 31 October, Washington DC.

Foreign and Commonwealth Office (2003) 'UK International Priorities', http.//www.fco.gov.uk. (Accessed 23/11/2004)

Frattini, F. (2005) 'The Hague Programme: A Partnership for the European Renewal in the Field of Freedom, Security and Justice', Speech/05/441 to the Centre for European Policy Studies, 14 July, Brussels.

Frattini, F. (2005) 'The Fight Against Terrorism', Speech/05/474 to Mykolas Romeris University, 2 September, Vilnius.

Freeh, L. (1996) 'Statement of Louis Freeh, Director, FBI', Hearing before the Select Committee on Intelligence of the US Senate, 104th Congress, Second Session, 1 August, US Government Printing Office, Washington DC.

Freeh, L. (1998) 'Statement of Louis Freeh, Director, FBI', Hearing before the Committee on the Judiciary, US Senate, 105th Congress, Second Session, 3 September, US Government Printing Office, Washington DC.

Fukuyama, F. (2004) speaking at 'Troubled Partnership: What's Next for the US and Europe?' Brookings and Hoover Institutions briefing, Brookings Institution, Washington DC, 10 November, www. Brookings.edu/dybdocroot/comm./events/20041110.pdf. (Accessed 8/12/2004)

Garcia, M. (2005) Renditions: Constraints Imposed by Laws on Torture, *Congressional Research Service Report for Congress*, The Library of Congress, Washington DC, 28 April.

Gelbard, R. (1995) Testimony of Robert Gelbard, Assistant Secretary of State for International Narcotics and Law Enforcement, before the House of Representatives Committee on International Relations, 7 December, *Atlantic Outlook*, 91, 15 December, pp. 1–4.

Gelbard, R. (1995) 'US says drugs now threaten national governments', Testimony of US Assistant Secretary of State for International Narcotics and Law Enforcement Affairs, before the US Senate, US Department of State Information Service, Washington DC, 8 August.

Gennaro, G. de (1997) Testimony of Giovanni de Gennaro, Italian National Police, to Hearing before the Committee on International Relations, US House of Representatives, October, 105th Congress, US Government Printing Office, Washington DC.

'G-8 leaders announce Action Plan to fight Global Terrorism' (2003) *Washington File*, 2 June, US Embassy to the UK, London, http://www.usembassy.org.uk/ (Accessed 11/8/2004)

Goldman, S., Katzman, K. and Shuey, R. (1998) 'Russian Missile Technology and Nuclear Reactor Transfers to Iran', *Congressional Research Service Report for Congress*, Washington DC, 14 December.

Gregory, F. and Wilkinson, P. (2005) 'Riding Pillion for Tackling Terrorism is a High-risk Security Policy', Security, Terrorism and the UK, Report for Chatham House, *http://www.riia.org/pdf/research/niis/Bpsecurity.pdf* (Accessed 7/7/2005)

Haass, R. (2002) 'Charting a new course in the transatlantic relationship', Speech to the Centre for European Reform, London, 10 June, http:www.state.gov/s/p/rem/10968.htm (Accessed 10/7/2002)

Hart-Rudman Commission (2001) 'Road Map for National Security: Imperative for Change', Phase III of Report, Council on Foreign Relations, Washington DC, January, http://www.cfr.org/content/publications/attachment/Hart-Rudman3.pdf.

House of Lords (2005) 'After Madrid: the EU's Response to Terrorism', EU Committee, 5th Report of Session 2004-5, Paper 53, HMSO, London.

International Institute for Strategic Studies (2002) 'Iraq's Weapons of Mass Destruction. A Net Assessment', London, 9 September, *http://www.iiss.org/conferencepage.php?confID=3&PHPSESSID=b6029ee3ac61b86acab407fd9cc69d10* (Accessed 18/1/2003)

Katzman, K. (2000) 'Iraq: Compliance, Sanctions and US Policy', *Congressional Research Service Report for Congress*, Washington DC, 3 July.

Lesser, I., Hoffman, B., Arquilla, J., Ronfeldt, D. and Zanini, M. (1999) 'Countering the New Terrorism', *MR-989-AF, RAND*, Santa Monica.

Levey, S. (2004) 'Funding terror becoming costlier, riskier, US official says', Testimony of Stuart Levey, Under Secretary for Terrorism and Financial Intelligence, US Department of the Treasury, before the Senate Committee on Banking and Urban Affairs, 29 September, *Washington File*, 13 July, US Embassy to the UK, London, http://www.usembassy.org.uk/ (Accessed 4/9/2004)

Linde, E. van de (2002) 'Quick Scan of Post-9/11 National Counter-Terrorism Policy-making in Selected European Countries', Research Project for the Netherlands Ministry of Justice, MR-1590, RAND Europe, May, *www.rand.org/publications/MR/MR1590/MR1590.pdf.* (Accessed 10/11/2003)

Manningham-Buller, E. (2003) 'Global Terrorism: Are We Meeting the Challenge?' James Smart Memorial Lecture 2003, City of London Police Headquarters, 16 October, http://www.homeoffice.gov.uk/docs2/james_smart_lecture2003.html. (Accessed 12/8/2004)

McDonald, W. (2002) 'International Law Enforcement Cooperation and Conflict: McDonaldization and Implosion Before and After September 11th', unpublished paper, Georgetown University, Washington DC.

Miko, F. (2004), Removing Terrorist Sanctuaries: The 9/11 Commission Recommendations and US Policy, *Congressional Research Service Report for Congress*, Washington DC, 10 August.

Mueller, R. (2004) Testimony of the Director of the FBI to the Select Committee on Intelligence, US Senate, Washington DC, 24 February.

National Commission on Terrorism (2000) 'Countering the Changing Threat of International Terrorism', Report, 105th Congress, 2nd Session, Document 106– 250, US Government Printing Office, Washington DC.

NATO International Military Staff (2003) 'NATO's Military Concept for Defence Against Terrorism', NATO Headquarters, 15 December, Brussels, *http://www.nato.int/ims/docu/terrorism.htm* (Accessed 13/12/2004)

North Atlantic Council (1991) The NATO Strategic Concept, November, Rome, NATO Integrated Data Service, *natodoc<\\>@>HQ.NATO.INT* (Accessed 14/9/2004).

North Atlantic Council (1999) The NATO Strategic Concept, April, Washington, NATO Integrated Data Service, *natodoc<\\>@>HQ.NATO.INT* (Accessed 14/9/2004).

North Atlantic Council (2004) Istanbul Summit Communiqué issued by Heads of State, Istanbul, 28 June, NATO Integrated Data Service, *natodocHQ.NATO.INT* (Accessed 14/9/2004)

NATO–Russia Council (2004) Action Plan on Terrorism, 9 December, NATO Integrated Data Service, *natodoc<\\>@>HQ.NATO.INT*

Perl, R. (1995) 'Terrorism and US Foreign Policy', *Congressional Research Service Report for Congress*, Washington DC, 14 August.

Perl, R. (2002) 'Terrorism and United States Foreign Policy', Remarks by Raphael Perl, Congressional Research Service to the German Council on Foreign Relations, 2 July, Berlin, in *Washington File*, US Embassy in London, *http://www.usembassy.org.uk/terror428.html* (Accessed 26/7/2002).

Perl, R. (2003) 'US Anti-Terrorism Strategy', Speech to Konrad Adenauer Foundation, Berlin, 30 June, *http://www.usembassy.org.uk/terror512.html*. (Accessed 13/9/2004).

Perl, R. (2004) 'Terrorism and National Security: Issues and Trends', *Congressional Research Service Report for Congress*, Washington DC, 23 September.

Perl, R. (2004) Statement by Raphael Perl, Congressional Research Service, to the Subcommittee on National Security, Emerging Threats and International Relations, US House of Representatives, Washington DC, 22 September.

Pope, W. (2004) Principal Deputy Coordinator for Counter terrorism, US Department of State, Statement before the Sub Committee on Europe and on International Terrorism, Non-Proliferation and Human Rights, US House of Representatives, Washington DC, 14 September.

Prados, A. and Katzman, K. (2001) 'Iraq-US Confrontation', *Congressional Research Service Report for Congress*, Washington DC, 4 April.

President's Summary (2003) Justice and Home Affairs Ministerial Meeting, Group of Eight, Paris, 5 May.

Probst, P. (1996) ' Remarks of Peter Probst, Assistant Secretary for Terrorism Intelligence, Office of the Secretary of Defense', Report prepared for the Permanent Select Committee on Intelligence, US House of Representatives, by the Congressional Research Service, July, US Government Printing Office, Washington DC.

Pullinger, S. and Quille, G. (2003) The EU: Tackling the Threat from Weapons of Mass Destruction, Saferworld and the International Security Information Service, *Policy Paper*, Brussels.

Record, J. (2003) 'Bounding the Global War on Terrorism', Strategic Studies Institute, Carlisle Barracks, Pa, December, *http://www.carlisle.army.mil/ssi/pdffiles/PUB207.pdf*. (Accessed 21/2/2005).

Rice, C. (2002) 'Discussions of the President's National Security Strategy', Manhattan Institute, New York, 1 October, http:www.whitehouse.gov/news/releases/2002/10/20021001-6.html (Accessed 16/2/2003).

Robertson, G. Lord, NATO Secretary General (2001) 'International Security and Law Enforcement – A Look Ahead', Law Enforcement and National Security Global Forum, Edinburgh International Conference Centre, UK, 19 June.

Savona, E. (1998) 'The Organisational Framework of European Crime in the Globalisation Process', *Transcrime Working Paper No. 20*, Trento, February.

Schnabel, R. (2001) 'US Ambassador to the EU on Terrorism, Transatlantic Cooperation', *Washington File*, 13 December, US Embassy to the UK, London, http://www.usembassy.org.uk/ (Accessed 4/4/2003).

Serfaty, S. (1997) 'Stay the Course: European Unity and Atlantic Solidarity', *Washington Papers*, Center for Strategic and International Studies, Praeger.

Sheehan, M. (1999) 'Extremist Movements and their Threat to the US', Statement of Ambassador Sheehan, Coordinator for Counter-Terrorism, Department of State, to Hearing Subcommittee on Near Eastern and South Asian Affairs, 106th Congress, 1st Session, 2 November.

Sheehan, M (2000) 'Counter Terrorism Chief Seeks more International Cooperation', Text of speech by Ambassador Sheehan, State Department Coordinator for Counter-Terrorism, 10 February, *Washington File*, US Embassy to the UK, London, http://www.usembassy.org.uk/ (Accessed 2/10/2003).

Solana, J. (2003) 'A Secure Europe in a Better World', European Council, Thessaloniki, 20 June.

Solana, J. (2003) 'Europe and America: Partners of Choice', Speech to the Annual Dinner of the Foreign Policy Association, New York, 7 May, *http://ue.eu.int/newsroom* (Accessed 17/8/2003)

Snyder, J. (1977) 'The Soviet Strategic Culture: Implications for Nuclear Options', *RAND*, Santa Monica.

Steinberg, J., Graham, M. and Eggers, A. (2003) 'Building Intelligence to Fight Terrorism', *Policy Brief 125*, Brookings Institution, September, www.brookings.org/. (Accessed 1/11/2004).

Strengthening US–European Relations (2003) 'Group Calls for Fixing Transatlantic Rift', *News Release*, Center for Strategic and International Studies, May, Washington DC, http://www.csis.org/media/csis/press/pro3_34[1].pdf.

Taylor, F. (2002) 'Press roundtable with Ambassador Francis Taylor, US Department of State Coordinator for Counter-Terrorism', *Washington File*, 29 January, US Embassy to the UK, London, http://www.usembassy.org.uk/ (Accessed 18/4/2004).

Tellis, A. (2004) 'Assessing America's War on Terrorism: Confronting Insurgency, Cementing Primacy', National Bureau of Asian Research Analysis in cooperation with Carnegie Endowment for International Peace, 15, 4, December, http://www.carnegieendowment.org/files/NBRAnalysis-Tellis_December2004.pdf. (Accessed 21/2/2005).

Tenet, G, (2001) 'Worldwide Threat 2001: National Security in a Changing World', Statement by the Director of the Central Intelligence Agency, before the Senate Select Committee on Intelligence, 7 February, Washington File, US Embassy in London, *http://www.usembassy.org.uk/euro232.html* (Accessed 12/2/2001).

Ties, T. and Sipla, J. (eds) (2002) 'Drifting Apart? European Views of the Atlantic Relationship', *Research Report 17*, Series 2, National Defence College, Finland.

The 9/11 Commission Report, *Final Report of the National Commission on Terrorist Attacks upon the United States* (2004) W. W. Norton, New York.

UK Home Office, 'Terrorism Legislation', *http://www.homeoffice.gov.uk/terrorism/govprotect/legislation/index.html*. (Accessed 12/12/2004)

US Department of Justice (1999) 'Terrorism in the United States 1998', Counter-Terrorism Assessment and Warning Unit, National Security Division, US Government Printing Office, Washington DC.

US Department of Justice (1999) 'Terrorism 2000/2001' Counter-Terrorism Division FBI, US Department of Justice, US Government Printing Office, Washington DC.

US Department of Justice (2004) 'Fundamental Principles Governing Extraterritorial Prosecutions, Jurisdiction, Venue and Procedural Rights', Criminal Division, March.

US Department of Justice (2004) 'Report from the Field: The USA PATRIOT Act at Work', Washington DC, July.

United States Department of State (1999) *Patterns of Global Terrorism 1999*, US Government Printing Office, Washington DC.

US Department of State (2004) 'US, EU Discuss Transportation, Border Security', Press Release, 26 April, http://usinfo.state.gov/gi/Archive/ 2004/April/28-58541.html. (Accessed 8/10/2004)

US Department of State (2004) 'US, EU Discuss Transportation, Border Security', 28 April, USInfo.state.gov (Accessed 19/5/2004)

US Embassy (2002) 'Terrorist Groups Increasingly Linked to Drugs', *US Information Service*, London, 16 April.

US International Crime Control Strategy (1998) The Whitehouse, Washington DC.

US National Security Strategy (2003) The Whitehouse, Washington DC.

US National Strategy for Combating Terrorism (2003) The Whitehouse, Washington DC, February.

US National Strategy to Combat Weapons of Mass Destruction (2003) The Whitehouse, Washington DC.

US National Strategy for Homeland Security (2002) The Whitehouse, Washington DC, July.

US Strategy for Homeland Defense and Civil Support (2005) Department of Defense, Washington DC, June.

'US Officials Brief on June 25 US-EU Summit' (2004) Washington File, US Embassy in London, *http://www.usembassy.org.uk/euro232.html*. (Accessed 26/5/2004).

United States vs Bin Laden (2004) Southern District of New York for Conspiracy to Bomb US Embassies in Africa, US Department of Justice, March.

Vries, G. de (2004) EU Counter-Terrorism Coordinator Statement before the Committee on International Relations, US House of Representatives, Washington DC, 14 September.

Vries, G. de (2004) Introductory speech by Gijs de Vries to the seminar hosted by the EU presidency on the Prevention of the Financing of Terrorism, 22 September, Brussels.

Vries, G. de (2005) 'Gijs de Vries on Terrorism, Islam and Democracy', Interview to EurActiv.com, 4 March, *www.euractiv.com/Article* (Accessed 5/9/2005)

Wall, S. (2004) 'The UK, the EU and the United States: Bridge, or Just Troubled Water?' Speech at Chatham House, 8 November, www.riia.org/. (Accessed 5/12/2004).

Wayne, E. (2005) 'Evidence of E. Anthony Wayne, Assistant Secretary of State for Economic and Business Affairs' to the Senate Committee on Banking, Housing and Urban Affairs, Washington, *Washington File*, 13 July, US Embassy to the UK, London, http://www.usembassy.org.uk/ (Accessed 2/9/2005).

Wechsler, W. and Wolosky, L. (2004) 'Update on the Global Campaign against Terrorist Financing', Second Report of an Independent Task Force on Terrorist Financing Sponsored by the Council on Foreign Relations, 15 June, New York, *www.cfr.or* (Accessed 13/1/2005).

White House Fact Sheet (1996) 'Comprehensive Strategy to Fight Terrorism', 5 August, *Official Text*, US Information Service, US Embassy to the UK, London, http://www.usembassy.org.uk/ (Accessed 19/11/1997).

Wrench, P. (1998) 'The G8 and Transnational Organised Crime', in Cullen, P. and Gilmore, W. (eds) Crime Sans Frontières: International and European Legal Approaches, *Hume Papers on Public Policy*, 6, 1 and 2, Edinburgh University Press.

Zoellick, R. (1990) 'The New Europe in a New Age: Insular, Itinerant or International? Prospects for an Alliance of Values', Address by Robert Zoellick, Counselor of the State Department, before the American-European Community Association International's Conference on 'US/EC Relations and Europe's New Architecture', Annapolis, Maryland, 21 September, US Department of State Despatch.

Newspapers

Aldrich, R. (2005) 'A global battlefield', *The Independent on Sunday*, 10 July, p .28.

Bremner, C. (2004) 'Stoned to death . . . why Europe is starting to lose its faith in Islam', *The Times*, 4 December.

BBC News (2005) 'Profile: Islam Karimov', 17 May, *http://news.bbc.co.uk/1/hi/world/asia-pacific/4554997.stm*

Bernstein, R. (2005) 'German High Court blocks Qaeda suspect's extradition', *New York Times*, 19 July.

Bulletin Quotidien Europe (29/6/1996) 'The Lyon Summit decides to hold a meeting on the fight against terrorism in July', No. 6760, *Agence Presse.*

Bulletin Quotidien Europe (21/9/2001) 'Terrorism', No. 8052, *Agence Presse.*

Bulletin Quotidien Europe (12/10/2001) 'EU Money Laundering', No. 8068, *Agence Presse.*

Bulletin Quotidien Europe (22/9/2001) 'Finance Ministers put forward concrete initiatives for combating financial crimes committed by terrorists', No. 8054, *Agence Presse*, Special Edition.

Bulletin Quotidien Europe (24 & 25 /6/2002) 'Money laundering/terrorism', No.8240, *Agence Presse.*

Bulletin Quotidien Europe (5/5/2004) No. 8699, *Agence Presse.*

Bulletin Quotidien Europe (7/7/2004) 'ECOFIN Council recognises it is urgent to step up fight against terrorist funding', No.8742, *Agence Presse.*

Bulletin Quotidien Europe (19/3/2004) No. 8669, *Agence Presse.*

Bulletin Quotidien Europe (2/12/2004) 'Counterterrorist strategies at Thursday's council', No. 8839, *Agence Presse.*

Bulletin Quotidien Europe (2/6/2004) 'Presidency Conclusions, European Council, Brussels, 17–18 June 2004, I: paragraph 7', No. 8716, *Agence Presse.*

Bulletin Quotidien Europe (17/12/2004) 'EU/European Council /Terrorism', No. 8850, *Agence Presse.*

Bulletin Quotidien Europe (13/11/2004) 'NATO Secretary General urges EU to take the same attitude to terrorism and Iraq as the US', No.8826, *Agence Presse.*

Bulletin Quotidien Europe (24/7/2004) No. 8754, *Agence Presse.*

Bulletin Quotidien Europe (21/9/2004) 'EU/Terrorism: Europeans and Americans want to work together', No. 8789, *Agence Presse.*

Bulletin Quotidien Europe (20/3/2004) No. 8670, *Agence Presse.*

Bulletin Quotidien Europe (27/3/2004) No. 8675, *Agence Presse.*

Bulletin Quotidien Europe (17/3/2004) No. 8667, *Agence Presse.*

Bulletin Quotidien Europe (16/3/2004) No. 8666, *Agence Presse.*

Bulletin Quotidien Europe (22/9/2004) 'EU/Terrorism: Interview with Gijs de Vries', No.8790, *Agence Presse.*

Bulletin Quotidien Europe (1/10/2004) 'Debate on information exchange between member states', No. 8797, *Agence Presse.*

Bulletin Quotidien Europe (3/12/2004) 'Progress on information exchange on police records', No. 8840, *Agence Presse.*

Bulletin Quotidien Europe (16/10/2004) 'EU/Justice/Police', No. 8808, *Agence Presse.*

Bulletin Quotidien Europe (20/3/2004) No. 8670, *Agence Presse.*

Bulletin Quotidien Europe (23/4/2004) No. 8691, *Agence Presse.*

Bulletin Quotidien Europe (17/9/2004) 'EU-US Troika focuses on protection of biometric data', No. 8787, *Agence Presse.*

Bulletin Quotidien Europe (27/10/2004) 'Political agreement on biometric passports', No, 8815, *Agence Presse.*

Bulletin Quotidien Europe (24/7/2004) No. 8754, *Agence Presse.*

Bulletin Quotidien Europe (8/6/2004) No. 8720, *Agence Presse.*
Bulletin Quotidien Europe (13/3/2004) No. 8665, *Agence Presse.*
Bulletin Quotidien Europe (2004) 'European Council, "Declaration on Combating Terrorism", 25 March 2004', Europe Documents, No. 2366, Brussels, *Agence Presse.*
Bulletin Quotidien Europe (1/10/2004) 'EU/JHA/US: Highly consensual meeting Thursday between Europeans and Americans', No. 8797, *Agence Presse.*
Bulletin Quotidien Europe (11/5/2005) 'Commission's detailed programme for freedom, security and justice programme over next five years, No.8944, *Agence Presse.*
Bulletin Quotidien Europe (20/5/2005) 'EU steps up pressure to extend "visa waiver programme" to all member states', No.8950, *Agence Presse.*
Bulletin Quotidien Europe (11/5/2005) 'Counter Terrorism must be the key element in political dialogue with third countries, Council says', No.8993, *Agence Presse.*
Bulletin Quotidien Europe (19/8/2005) 'EU calls on Iran to change its mind about its unilateral rejection of EU-3 proposals', No.9008, *Agence Presse.*
Dinmore, G. (2005) 'US shifts anti-terror policy', *The Financial Times*, 31 July.
Economist, The (2001) 'Can sanctions be smarter?' Special Report: America, Iraq and Iran, 26 May, pp. 29–31.
Economist, The (2001) 'America the unready', 22 December, pp. 49–50.
Economist, The (2002) 'Special Report: The war on terror. Weapons of mass dislocation', 15 June.
Economist, The (2002) 'Inspecting, squeezing, threatening', 7 December, pp. 65–66.
Economist, The (2002) 'Washington's mega-merger', 23 November, pp. 51–53.
Economist, The (2002) 'Special Report: Civil liberties. For whom the Liberty Bell tolls', 31 August, pp. 19–21.
Economist, The (2003) 'Casus or casuistry? Special Report: Weapons of Mass Destruction', 31 May, pp. 22–23.
Economist, The (2003) 'Loose nukes', by special invitation Allison, G, 29 November, pp. 23–25.
Economist, The (2003) 'When bluff turns deadly', Special Report: North Korea, 3 May, pp. 29–31
Economist, The (2004) 'A world wide web of nuclear danger', Special Report: Proliferation', 28 February, pp. 25–27.
Economist, The (2004) 'Charlemagne: A Civil War on Terrorism', 27 November, p.50.
Economist, The (2004) 'After Van Gogh', 13 November, pp. 43–44.
Economist, The (2004) 'The nuclear route', 13 November.
Economist, The (2004) 'A long stretch', 5 June.
Economist, The (2004) 'Islamic Terrorism in Europe', 13 November.
Economist, The (2004) 'Big Dominique and his struggle against the Islamists', 18 December, pp. 57–58.
Economist, The (2005) 'Mr Bush goes to Belgium', 19 February, pp. 9–10.
Economist, The (2005) 'Into the lion's den', 26 February, pp. 39–40.
Economist, The (2005) 'Practice what you preach', 29 January, p.12.

Economist, The (2005) 'When the party has to stop', 12 February.

Economist, The (2005) 'The fight within', 23 July, pp. 35–36.

Economist, The (2005) 'The enemy within', Special Report: Muslim extremism in Europe, 16 July, pp. 24–26.

Economist, The (2005) 'Imagining something much worse than London', 16 July, pp. 40–41.

Economist, The (2005) 'The insidious wiles of foreign influence', 11 June.

Economist, The (2005) 'Just a few bad apples?' 22 January, pp. 47–48.

Economist, The (2005) 'Can its credibility be repaired? Special Report: The United Nations', 10–16 September, pp. 28–30.

Economist, The (2005) 'Can spies be made better? Special Report: Intelligence Reform', 19 March, pp. 29–31.

Evans, M. (2004) 'Iran bows to UN threat over nuclear programme', *The Times*, 23 November.

Green, A. (2003) 'Why Syria is America's next target', *Guardian Unlimited*, 17 April, *http://www.guardian.co.uk/comment/story/0,3604,938326,00.html*, (Accessed 16/8/2003)

Green, J. (2001) 'Weapons of Mass Confusion', *The Washington Monthly*, May, pp. 15–21.

Hussain, Z. (2004) 'Scientist pardoned for selling nuclear secrets', *The Times*, 6 February, p.18.

Linzer, D. (2005) 'Review finds Iran far from nuclear bomb: Estimate of progress contrasts with Administration statements', *The Washington Post*, 2 August.

Maddox, B. (2004) 'On the trail of nuclear supply and demand', *The Times*, 13 February, p.23.

Maddox, B. (2005) 'UN faces its biggest challenge in wars against poverty and terror', *The Times*, 15 September, pp. 40–41.

Maddox, B. (2005) 'Brinkmanship in Iran's nuclear potboiler', *The Times*, 13 May, p.36.

Maddox, B. (2005) 'Europe loses bargaining chip in negotiations', *The Times*, 27 June, p.28.

Naval, R. (2005) 'Hardliner turns back on US but will pursue nuclear aim', *The Times*, 27 June, p.28.

Priest, D. (2005) 'Alliance Base: US-sponsored, French-led Counter-Terrorism Centre in Europe', *The Washington Post*, 3 July

Robinson, L. (2005) 'Plan of attack. The Pentagon has a secret new strategy for taking on terrorists – and taking them down', *US News and World Report*, 1 August.

Times, The (2004) 'Law Lords Leave Terror Laws in Tatters', 17 December.

Timmerman, K, (1995) 'Trading with Iran: Clinton needs to club Europe', *The Wall Street Journal*, 5 April.

Watt, N. and Diver, K. (2005) 'Germany blocks extradition of al-Qaida suspect', *The Guardian*, 19 July.

Webster, P. (2004) 'Blunkett takes aim at crime to outflank the Tories', *The Times*, 22 November.

Interviews

Interview conducted by the author (2000) US Mission to the EU, September, Brussels.

Interview conducted by the author (2000) European Commission, Brussels, November.

Interview conducted by the author (2001) Office for European Union Affairs, US Department of State, May, Washington DC.

Interview conducted by the author (2001) US Department of Justice, May, Washington DC.

Interview conducted by the author (2001) Counter-Money Laundering Section, US Department of Justice, May, Washington DC.

Interview conducted by the author (2001) Office for International Affairs, US Department of Justice, May, Washington DC.

Interview conducted by the author (2001) Office for European Union Affairs, US Department of State, May, Washington DC.

Interview conducted by the author (2001) International Narcotics and Law Enforcement, US Department of State, May, Washington DC.

Interview conducted by the author (2001) US Embassy to the UK, June, London.

Interview conducted by the author (2001) European Commission offices, May, Washington DC.

Interview conducted by the author (2004) Office for International Narcotics and Law Enforcement, US Department of State, September, Washington DC.

Interview conducted by the author (2004), RAND, September, Washington DC.

Interview conducted by the author (2004), Europol Liaison Unit, Offices of the European Commission, September, Washington DC.

Interview conducted by the author (2004) Counter Terrorism Section, Criminal Division, US Department of Justice, September, Washington DC.

Interview conducted by the author (2004) Office of Counter Terrorism, US Department of State, September, Washington DC.

Interview conducted by the author (2004) European Commission offices, September, Washington DC.

Interview conducted by the author (2004) Department of Justice, September, Washington DC.

Interview conducted by the author (2004) Department of Homeland Security, October, Washington DC.

Interview conducted by the author (2005) US Mission to the EU, February, Brussels.

Interview conducted by the author (2005) Criminal Division, European Council, February, Brussels.

Interview conducted by the author (2005) Relex C1, European Commission, February, Brussels.

Index

5029 110